Joint Operating Agreements

Risk Control for the Non-Operator, Second Edition

Professor Eduardo G Pereira

Author
Professor Eduardo G Pereira

Managing director
Sian O'Neill

Joint Operating Agreements: Risk Control for the Non-Operator, Second Edition
is published by

Globe Law and Business Ltd
3 Mylor Close
Horsell
Woking
Surrey GU21 4DD
United Kingdom
Tel: +44 20 3745 4770
www.globelawandbusiness.com

Joint Operating Agreements: Risk Control for the Non-Operator, Second Edition

ISBN 9781787421240
EPUB ISBN 9781787421257
Adobe PDF ISBN 9781787421265
Mobi ISBN 9781787421272

Table of contents

Acknowledgements

I am extremely grateful for the support and advice given by Peter Roberts, Marc Hammerson, Andrew Derman, Julia Derrick, Keith Hall, Rachael Johnstone, Adrianne O'Reilly and Erik Arnold.

Introduction to the first edition

Peter Roberts

This book opens with a recognition that the joint operating agreement (JOA) is one of the most important documents in oil and gas transactions, and then makes the alarming assertion that most JOAs are unbalanced as between the interests of operators and non-operators. The position is then recovered, as the book goes on to suggest a foundation for a more balanced, 'future-proofed' JOA.

This book will probably dismay the upstream operator community, because it conceives of too much democracy for non-operators; traditional non-operators might also be dismayed simply because it does not go far enough. To borrow from Lydgate and Lincoln, "You can't please all of the people all of the time."

Despite the inevitable howls of protest, Dr Pereira is to be commended for tackling this thorniest of upstream topics in a pithy, well-informed manner. This book is an invaluable addition to the body of jurisprudence in the JOA world, and I am very pleased to have been asked to introduce it.

Glossary

The following terms are used in this book:

AAPL	American Association of Professional Landmen
ACPA	Agreement Concerning Petroleum Activities
ADR	Alternative dispute resolution
AFE	Authorisation for expenditures
AIPN	Association of International Petroleum Negotiators
AMPLA	Australian Mineral Petroleum Law Association
AP	Accounting procedures
API	American Petroleum Institute
APPEA	Australian Petroleum Production & Exploration Association
BNOC	British National Oil Corporation
CAPL	Canadian Association of Petroleum Landmen
DECC	Department of Energy and Climate Change UK
EU	European Union
E&P	Exploration and production
FD	Fiduciary duty
FOA	Farmout agreement
HG	Host government
IOC	International oil company
JBA	Joint bidding agreement
JOA	Joint operating agreement
JV	Joint venture
MWO	Minimum work obligation
NCS	Norwegian Continental Shelf
NOC	National oil company
NPD	Norwegian Petroleum Directorate
OP	Operating procedure
Oil & Gas UK/OGUK	Oil and Gas United Kingdom
Opcom	Operating committee
PI	Participating interest
PSA	Production sharing agreement
RMMLF	Rocky Mountain Mineral Law Foundation
UK	United Kingdom
UKCS	United Kingdom Continental Shelf

UKOOA	United Kingdom Offshore Operators Association
US	United States of America
WP&B	Work programme and budget

Chapter 1: Introduction

1.1 Scope

(a) *Objective*

The joint operating agreement (JOA) is one of the most important documents in oil and gas transactions and projects.[1] JOAs regulate the rights and duties of the parties to an unincorporated joint venture (JV) aimed at the exploration and exploitation of oil and gas.[2] Most of the duties under a JOA rest with the operator – that is, the party responsible for the administration of the day-to-day activities of the JV. Consequently, JOA models and studies commonly focus on the operator's perspective. However, such ventures are not the exclusive preserve of the operator: non-operators also make a vital contribution to the success of joint operations.

Non-operators might retain, individually, a smaller participating interest in the JV, as they might have fewer financial and technical resources than the operator, though this is not always the case.[3] This creates an environment where little attention is given to the perspective of the non-operators. Their situation is akin to that of minority shareholders, who similarly have less say than majority shareholders in the conduct of a company's operations. However, they still have shares in the company, along with their own views on how the company should be run.[4] Thus, it is necessary to understand the needs and perspectives of non-operators in order to establish an efficient, reasonable and fair agreement.[5] If the perspectives of non-operators are ignored, it is extremely difficult to create a balanced instrument.

1 "Probably the most significant contract used in the upstream business is the JOA. It sets out the fundamental and overarching relationship among joint venture parties from the initial exploration to the ultimate production of hydrocarbons." A Timothy Martin, "Model Contracts: a Survey of the Global Petroleum Industry" (2004) 22 *J Energy & Nat Resources L* p291.

2 For the purposes of this book, 'consortium' and 'JV' will have the same meaning.

3 This is not a hard and fast rule. There are a number of instances where the operator will not hold the largest participating interest, but this is more likely to happen in a major transaction and/or project with several large oil companies in the same consortium.

4 Because of such similarities, commentary on the situation of minority shareholders is provided where appropriate (although it is beyond the scope of this book to provide a comprehensive analysis of this position). For further information, see Victor Joffe QC *et al*, *Minority Shareholders: Law, Practice, and Procedure* (3rd ed, OUP, Oxford 2008), AIJA Law Library, *Protection of Minority Shareholders* (Wolters Kluwer, London 1997), AJ Boyle, *Minority Shareholder's Remedies* (CUP, Cambridge 2002), Robin Hollington QC, *Minority Shareholders' Rights* (3rd ed, Sweet & Maxwell, London 1999).

5 It is common to analyse a JOA from the operator's perspective, but it is important to note that some authors also recognise the importance of non-operators, such as John BB Bullough, "The Norwegian Experience – The Role of a Non-Operator" (1996) 11 *Oil and Gas Finance & Accounting* and Peter Roberts, *Joint Operating Agreements: A Practical Guide* (Globe Law and Business, London 2010) pp244–245.

Consequently, critical problems may arise and potentially jeopardise the existence of the consortium, as the cooperation of all its participants is crucial to success. Moreover, the JOA is usually in force for the whole duration of the petroleum title, which can last for 30 years or more.[6] A provision which appears to be favourable to one party in the early stages might, later in the life of the JOA, turn out to be less so. The JOA should thus offer reasonable terms for all contracting parties, from the beginning until the end of the agreement.

This book may be of particular value to mature provinces such as the UK and Norway,[7] as the major oil companies tend to withdraw their investments (especially in smaller projects) from such areas and reinvest in jurisdictions where larger projects promise greater rewards. These companies are in turn being replaced by small or medium-sized independent companies, commonly with less experience and lacking the robust financial resources required to operate in exploration and production (E&P) projects.[8] In other words, the traditional context, in which a JOA is based on a strong, dominant operator, is radically changing. Some JVs are composed of several parties in a more equal position. Many oil and gas regions have already reached maturity, so this trend is set to continue – even if new technology extends the life of current fields.[9] This new scenario requires better-balanced agreements to govern joint operations. It is thus more crucial than ever to understand the perspectives and views of non-operators, as these will assume even greater significance in future JOAs, where the parties are in a more equal position.[10]

The aim of this book is to analyse the most widely used JOA standard model forms from various jurisdictions, in particular the following:[11]

- The Association of International Petroleum Negotiators (AIPN) model (the International model);
- The Oil & Gas UK (OGUK) model (the British model);
- The American Association of Professional Landmen (AAPL) model (the American model);
- The Canadian Association of Petroleum Landmen (CAPL) model (the Canadian model);
- The Rocky Mountain Mineral Law Foundation (RMMLF) model (the old American model);

6 "Joint operating agreements are designed to last for the life of the field, during exploration, appraisal and development. Amendments, though not rare, are less common than might be expected for a document with a 30-year lifespan." Charez Golvala, "Upstream joint ventures – bidding and operating agreements" in Geoffrey Picton-Turbervill (ed), *Oil and Gas: A practical handbook* (Globe Law and Business, London 2009) pp45–46.

7 "The UK government has for some time recognised that the maturing provinces of the North Sea, coupled with more recent smaller developments, have created a need for a change in its approach to licensing and taxation." Stephen Dow, "The 20th Round Standard Form Joint Operating Agreement" (2003) 1 *OGEL*.

8 Daniel Johnston, "Contract Terms Worldwide: A Case for New Frameworks" (2004) 2 (3) *OGEL*.

9 "The basins of this planet have matured perhaps more quickly than many of us anticipated." *Ibid*.

10 Such scenarios might exist where operators are not the dominant party in the enterprise. For example, independent companies are more commonly found in onshore operations, but this scenario is unusual in offshore operations as the risks and costs are much more significant. However, this is generally not an ordinary situation, as the operator is in a better position to control the joint operations. Consequently, major companies prefer to secure their assets in an efficient operation conducted by them. Nevertheless, some major developments will require the participation of several major companies together, where the parties are in a position of equals.

11 See Chapter I, section 1.2.

- The Greenlandic model (issued by the Greenlandic government);
- The Norwegian model (issued by the Norwegian government); and
- The Australian Mineral and Petroleum Law Association (AMPLA) model (the Australian model).

The aim is to arrive at an understanding of how each of these models treats and positions non-operators and their major concerns.

Finally, it is crucial to establish a distinction between these different perspectives and views as outlined and any misalignment of interests[12] that might occur in a JOA. While the different views often relate to the roles of the parties, they do not signify a misalignment of interests. Misalignment of interests is a potential scenario that is likely to lead to an exclusive operation (ie, sole risk or non-consent clauses) as the parties might disagree on the potential value of certain areas, one party might lack the funds to proceed with a given project or there might be other corporate reasons for a difference of views as to whether to proceed. Thus, different views and perspectives of non-operators will always exist, from the moment a JV is established until it ends.[13] It is these different views that are fully analysed in the following chapters.

(b) Unbalanced provisions, imbalance of power

Ideally, a JOA should contain balanced provisions which reflect the concerns of all parties involved – operator and non-operators. It should also allow for the participation of all parties, as they all share ownership of the JV. However, this is not usually the case – current JOAs tend to be biased towards the wishes of the operator.[14] Further, the success of oil and gas operations clearly depends on the contribution of all parties (as such operations often involve extraordinarily high expenditure over lengthy timeframes).[15] The question is this: why are JOAs so often unbalanced? The answer lies in the context and history of oil and gas operations.

The operator's position of strength has its origins in the first JOA established back in 1956 (ie, AAPL JOA Form 1956), and still prevails today – it is considered the 'traditional' approach. This fact is recognised by the great majority of academics and professionals involved in oil and gas operations.[16] The oil and gas industry has always assumed a need for a dominant operator who could control the consortium and set the pace of operations.[17] The unbalanced relationships that resulted did not encourage a high degree of non-operator participation.

Why, then, was it thought necessary to give one party so much authority? Commentators offer three possible theories. The first is based on the fact that the

---

12 "The interests of the parties in their joint venture should be ostensibly the same – that is, to produce the greatest possible quantities of petroleum on the most cost-effective basis. This alignment of interests will be recognized in the JOA, but there could also from time to time be some misalignment between the interests of the parties which the JOA will also need to accommodate." Peter Roberts (n 5) p17.

13 See note 5.

14 "(T)raditionally the perception has been that the operator has *de facto* much more to say over the entire project and is best positioned to take the initiative; thus the operator is rewarded with greater power, rather than greater profits." Scott Styles, "Joint Operating Agreements" in John Paterson, Greg Gordon (eds), *Oil and Gas Law: Current Practice and Emerging Trends* (DUP, Dundee 2007) pp277–278.

15 See Chapter I, section 1.3(b).

operator has a number of performance and compliance responsibilities for which it should be compensated. The second is based on the formation of the consortium, the theory being that the leader requires a higher degree of benefit to encourage it to create the JV and take a leadership position. The third theory is the one most widely accepted by commentators, and is related to the level of commitment of the operator. Oil and gas operations involve significant risks and costs, which demand a high level of commitment from the operator if the JV is to succeed. At the same time, the operator's greater level of commitment reduces the risk that it will try to make more profit or recover any losses when negotiating the JOA, which it might seek to do if it were a smaller participant.

In addition, there is a general perception that the operator should have the largest participating interest in the consortium, which in turn demands a higher degree of control over the decision-making process.

The first and second theories are likely to be raised by the operator during the negotiation phase to support its arguments in favour of more control and a higher percentage interest from the JV, as Terence Daintith explains:

> *Usually, but by no means invariably, the operator will be the party holding the largest percentage interest or one of its affiliated companies. Reasons for this include a perception of the non-operators that the operator should hold a substantial interest as evidence of its commitment to the project and the fact that operators themselves are usually not keen to take on the burdens of operatorship if they have only a minor share of equity. Furthermore bidding groups are usually organized by an operator who makes it clear from the start that it requires a major interest.*[18]

However, the third reason for the operator's dominant position in terms of control and participating interest, which is founded on economic reasoning, is the most persuasive. Ernest Smith and Kenneth Mildwaters explain this theory as follows:

> *The operator under an international JOA is usually the party with the largest interest in the concession. A party with a less substantial interest may be hesitant to commit scarce personnel and technical resources to the management of the host government agreement, and the other participants may doubt that party's commitment to the project or fear that its motivation arises from a desire to profit from the position, rather than from the success of the operations.*[19]

---

16 See Terence Daintith, Geoffrey Willoughby, Adrian Hill (eds), *United Kingdom Oil & Gas Law* (3rd ed, Sweet & Maxwell, London 2009) p1140, Gerard MD Bean, *Fiduciary Obligations and Joint Ventures: The Collaborative Fiduciary Relationship* (OUP, Oxford 1995) pp14–15, Kenneth Charles Mildwaters, *Joint Operating Agreements, A Consideration of Legal Aspects Relevant to Joint Operating Agreements used in Great Britain and Australia by Participants thereto to Regulate the Joint Undertaking of Exploration for Petroleum in Offshore Areas with Particular Reference to their Rights and Duties* (PhD thesis presented to the University of Dundee, 1990) p427, John Wilkinson, *Introduction to Oil & Gas Joint Ventures: Volume One, United Kingdom Continental Shelf* (OPL, Ledbury 1997) p40, Ernest E Smith, John S Dzienkowski, Owen L Anderson, John S Lowe, Bruce M Kramer and Jacqueline L Weaver, *International Petroleum Transactions* (3rd ed, RMMLF, Westminster 2010) p542, Sandy Shaw, "Joint Operating Agreements" in Martyn R David, *Upstream Oil and Gas Agreements* (Sweet and Maxwell, London 1996) pp19–21, Antony Jennings, *Oil and Gas Exploration Contracts* (2nd ed, Sweet & Maxwell, London 2008) pp17–27, Hew Dundas, "Joint Operating Agreements: An Introduction" (1994 Summer Programme: UK Oil and Gas Law, CPMLP 09/09, 1994) pp5–11.

17 *Ibid.*

18 Terence Daintith *et al* (n 16) p1140.

19 Ernest E Smith *et al* (n 16) p542.

> *The operator is usually the participant with the largest interest. The rationale behind this is that the participant with the largest interest will incur the greatest expenditure and greater commitment will be generated in matters of co-ordination and conduct of the operations. It is hoped that a prudent and economic management and conduct will result.*[20]

The government might also play an important role in determining the higher participating interest of the operator, as in some cases the applicable legal regime will require that the operator retain a minimum percentage of interest for the whole duration of the JOA, subject to its removal if such obligation is not complied with.[21]

It can be seen that both non-operators and host governments sometimes fear that an operator with a smaller interest might not dedicate the necessary effort and commitment to the operations; the operator is therefore likely to be the party with the greatest interest and the strongest position in the JV.

It could also be argued that it is in the nature of business that the party in the better negotiating position gets the most benefits.[22] In general terms this may be true, but in an oil and gas context the scenario will be slightly different. Firstly, the operator will not wish to shoulder all the risks and costs of operations by itself, as they could be extremely high – it will want to have co-venturers to share the risks and costs. Secondly, the non-operators are not only part of the JV, but also jointly liable for the operations conducted by the operator in relation to third parties and the host government. Thirdly, oil and gas companies usually have their assets spread across different investments, so normally no party can realistically conduct all operations alone. Thus, it is extremely important that all parties, including the operator, maintain a certain equilibrium in terms of roles within the consortium, as in the end this will benefit all of them.

Failure to establish a balanced agreement may cause problems later on.[23] Firstly, there may be uncertainty, as any non-operator could seek court protection or relief against unfair provisions of the JOA (eg, under the Unfair Contract Terms Act 1977 in the UK), though such protection is not easy to obtain in practice. Secondly, it might lead to the withdrawal of non-operators on the grounds that they are unable to control the operations, yet remain liable for their consequences. If this happens, the operator has to find another co-venturer and negotiate another JOA, possibly while involved in litigation or arbitration with its previous co-venturers. Unbalanced JOAs, therefore, can cause serious damage to the consortium and indeed to the operator itself.

While the adoption of unbalanced JOAs within the traditional matrix may be understandable, albeit risky, it will become less appropriate for future operations as more oil and gas regions reach maturity. Mature regions are less attractive to major or large companies, as most of the reserves have already been produced, leaving only small or medium-sized fields to be explored. In this scenario, large companies tend to migrate towards new regions where reserves remain untapped. As they exit mature

20 Kenneth C Mildwaters (n 16) p427.
21 See Chapter 3, section 3.2(a).
22 Professor RW Bentham, "The Negotiation of Agreements" (1987) 5 *J Energy & Nat Resources L* p134.
23 *Ibid* p139.

provinces they are replaced by mainly small and medium-sized companies, and the whole paradigm of the JOA changes radically. The operator is no longer in a dominant but an equal position compared with the non-operators. An unbalanced JOA is no longer tenable, and a more equitable agreement is negotiated that reflects the views and concerns of all parties.

That said, the parties' respective bargaining power remains unequal in these non-mature areas, and the *de facto* dominant party is always likely to seek the best outcome for itself. This lack of equality can prove problematic when the smaller party seeks to include optional provisions in a model form. Optional provisions will not be implemented unless they are beneficial to the stronger party.[24] Therefore, the current standard forms do not provide truly balanced terms, as it is unlikely that under current operations the parties will achieve such balance by themselves.

The extent of such an imbalance is clearly seen in the roles of the parties in the consortium. Although the agreement refers to 'joint operations', the reality is that one party will conduct the operations, while the others will mainly contribute financially. However, all parties are jointly liable for the costs and liabilities of all operations performed under the petroleum title (except under limited circumstances related to gross negligence or wilful misconduct).[25] In other words, the costs and liabilities are shared, but the conduct of the operations is not. For non-operators, this can be a critical concern – they are in the same position as passengers in public transport, sharing the cost of the transport but unable to determine the route or the final destination (unless they can effectively control the operating committee). In an oil and gas operation, this lack of control might have severe consequences, as will be discussed in the following chapters.

(c) *Conclusion*

In the traditional framework of oil and gas operations, one party is granted extensive rights and powers in order to secure the performance of operations.[26] Historically, it was considered necessary to put the operator in such a strong position, but this view is changing. It is no longer desirable for the operator that the contract place a heavy burden on non-operators, as courts might provide reliefs for the smaller participating interest, for example by the establishment of fiduciary duties, modification of the restriction of liabilities or allowance of extra time to pay cash calls. However, such protection is not easy to obtain in practice and the extent of any interference will vary between jurisdictions, particularly in civil law countries.[27]

---

24 PR Weems, M Bolton, "Highlights of Key Revisions – 2002 AIPN Model Form International Operating Agreement", 1 *OGEL* 5 (2003) p32.

25 See Chapter 3, section 3.2(b).

26 Ernest E Smith *et al* (n 16) p835.

27 See EA Farnsworth, "Pre-contractual Liability and Preliminary Agreements: Fair Dealing and Failed Negotiations" (1987) 87 *Columbia Law Review* p217.

28 "The phrase 'good faith' is used in a variety of contexts and its meaning varies depending on the context. Good faith generally implies fidelity to an agreed common purpose and consistency with the justified and practical expectations of the other negotiating party. It excludes behaviour which could be characterised as "bad faith" in that it violates the standards of decency, fairness or reasonableness of the community." Mirian Kene Omalu, "Precontractual agreements in the energy and natural resources industries – legal implications and basis for liability (civil law, common law and Islamic law)" (2000) *J B L* 2000, pp303–331.

Clearly, good faith and balance are essential to maintain a consortium in good health in the longer term.[28] On the other hand, if an unfair agreement is established, the courts might modify the contract in order to resolve or adjust the imbalance.[29]

The inclusion of balanced terms helps to avoid uncertainties and can even be positive for the operator, which might enjoy greater cooperation from the non-operators. Best practice thus indicates that an efficient consortium should allow a high degree of participation by all parties, as experience and expertise can be shared towards a common goal.[30]

Another reason to provide balance is the marketability of the agreement. As previously mentioned, the JOA will be of long duration, in some cases over 30 years. During this period, the parties might change their priorities and are likely to assign a part or even their entire share of the consortium to a third party. Without a balanced agreement, third parties might be reluctant to engage with such a consortium, unless in the operator role.

The current operator-focused JOAs do not take into account the risks involved for non-operators. Elizabeth Pennington recognises this when she states that "some of the standard provisions would appear to favour the large incumbents rather than the smaller independent players and potential new entrants."[31] If the JOA does not establish a measure of balance, it is difficult to expect any significant participation by non-operators.

That said, the Canadian Association of Petroleum Landmen (CAPL) recognises at least the principle of balanced provisions in order to achieve a reasonable agreement for all parties: "We believe that the 2007 CAPL Operating Procedure offers significant benefits to operators, non-operators, large and small companies."[32] In another document, the CAPL mentions the drivers behind the latest revision of its model form:

- *Opportunities identified by Industry's experiences with the document.*
- *Evolving business needs.*
- *The challenge was to meet the needs of today and to anticipate the needs of tomorrow in a way in which industry uses the product.*[33]

The CAPL clearly refers to the need to "anticipate the needs of tomorrow" – it is important to secure an equitable agreement for mature province operations. The

29 "The courts adopting the classic view subordinated the equity of a particular situation to the overmastering need of certainty in the transaction of commercial life. If the negotiations succeeded and resulted in a final contract, a party that had acted inappropriately could be stripped of the bargain on the basis of misrepresentation, duress, undue influence or unconscionability. If the negotiations failed because of similar conduct, courts traditionally have been reluctant to impose precontractual liability." *Ibid* pp303–331.

30 Michael Jensen and Willian Meckling discussed an analogous situation in their publication about the theory of the firm as they asked "why his failure to maximize the value of the firm is perfectly consistent with efficiency." Michael C Jensen, William H Meckling, "Theory of the Firm: Managerial Behavior, Agency Costs and Ownership Structure" (1976) 3(4) *Journal of Financial Economics*, pp305–360.

31 Elizabeth Pennington, "Issues for new entrants to the UKCS – a legal analysis" (2002) *IELTR* p281.

32 www.landman.ca/pdf/operating_procedures/2007/final/Cover%20Letter%20for%20Web%20(letterhead)%20July%202007.pdf. Accessed 14 September 2017.

33 www.landman.ca/pdf/operating_procedures/2007/final/2007%20Overview%20of%20Changes-July%202007.pdf. Accessed 14 September 2017.

CAPL goes beyond that and expressly recognises the need for balanced terms as part of the "major document objectives" as follows:

(a) *Make required modifications, while maintaining the integrity and substance of the 1990 document.*
   - *Provide a new and improved "car manual" that provides users with clear and complete answers to their questions.*

(b) *Create a document that will be used widely shortly following completion.*

(c) *Ensure that the document is balanced.*
   - *Operators and non-operators.*
   - *Operator as the QB [quarterback] of the "team".*
   - *Generally win and lose as a team.*
   - *Operator's exposure generally limited to its WI [working interest].*
   - *Individual Parties and the Parties collectively.*
   - *How far can an individual Party go in pursuing its own interest?*

- *Inclusion of controls to limit what a Party can do to others.*
- *Large companies and small companies.*

(d) *Simplification.*

(e) *Structure document to exploit advances in systems technology.*[34]

In other words, in the CAPL operating procedure the parties should strive to create an agreement that balances the following:

- needs of operators with those of non-operators;
- needs of individual parties with those of the parties collectively; and
- needs of small companies and those of larger companies.[35]

The CAPL should be congratulated for its efforts to equalise the parties' positions – and indeed it does provide for some balances and corrections, as will be analysed in the following chapters (eg, in terms of the challenge of operatorship, the AFE mechanism and the title of the agreement); but in general terms it is not entirely successful, as the operator is still the dominant party in the consortium, the title of the agreement referring to 'Operating Procedures' rather than 'Joint Operating Procedures'.

These unbalanced standard agreements only fit one scenario, in which a single party dominates the consortium and smaller parties accept the terms in exchange for the opportunity to participate in a larger operation and to gain experience.[36] It is clear, however, that where an operation involves more than one major company, they will not accept a situation where one party is granted too many rights. Rather,

---

34 *Ibid.*

35 www.landman.ca/pdf/operating_procedures/2007/final/Introduction%20to%20the%202007%20CAPL%20Operating%20Procedure%20(Final).pdf. Accessed 14 September 2017.

36 "The outcome of a successful negotiation is, of course, an agreement, but not an agreement at any price. Negotiations which lead to a failure to agree are not necessarily a disaster, and to discover, through negotiation, that agreement is not possible has its own value, and in the process each party will have learned a good deal about its own position and the realities of the situation. Of course, it may be in certain instances that some agreement may be better than none at all, but that I think may be more true of political than commercial negotiations." RW Bentham (n 22) pp138–139.

they will modify the key provisions of the JOA so that everyone has *de facto* shared control of the operations.

For traditional (ie, non-mature) areas, the standard models should provide equilibrium between the parties, as they may not be able to achieve such equilibrium by themselves. On the other hand, for future operations in mature provinces, the parties should be able to achieve equilibrium through negotiation. As one of the purposes of a model form is to reduce the time spent on negotiation, it would thus be far more efficient to include balanced terms in the standard models. Equitable[37] provisions would also be useful so that contracts could be performed without further uncertainty:

> *The law of contract prioritises stability and certainty, and rightly so. Thus, legal advisers to negotiators ought to avoid all these legal conundrums and ensure that at each point in the negotiations, their clients are well aware of the legal consequences of their actions. Due to the threat of a finding of indefiniteness, the drafter of the precontractual agreement must tread a fine line between drafting to allow flexibility and drafting to assure that the agreement will be enforceable. Extra care has to be exercised since the shadow of the law certainly looms above.*[38]

Finally, it is important to note the fact that the consequences of imbalance might be painful for the operator – as was graphically demonstrated by the BP Deepwater Horizon accident. Briefly, the non-operators sought court relief from their obligations, as they claimed that they had no participation in the operations, which were poorly performed under BP's control. The result of the decision could cost BP several billion dollars. This type of claim creates uncertainties and problems for the consortium, but there are no easy answers, and of course this was not the first significant accident in the history of oil and gas exploration. The great risks involved and the human factor mean that the risk of accidents is always high, which might lead to court disputes as non-operators seek relief from the consequences.

1.2 Comparative analyses

(a) *Comparative JOA models*

The oil and gas industry operates globally. Each region has its own particular needs and requirements. However, these regions are not isolated from each other and most of the major companies have assets all over the world. As a consequence, all regions share certain similarities and they tend to learn from past experience in other regions in order to improve their own regimes.

The same holds true for JOAs. Most of the oil and gas regions have their own JOA model form to address their own needs. However, all of the JOAs are based on similar principles and assumptions, described by Catia Malaquias as follows:

> *The creation and use of internationally accepted model form joint operating agreements in the area of oil and gas exploration and development seems sensible given that,*

37 See Mark Gerus *et al*, "Equitable Interests in Mining Tenements – Resulting and Constructive Trusts – Rebuttable Presumption – s119 Mining Act 1978 (WA) and s34 Property Law Act 1969 (WA)" (2000) 19 *AMPLJ* pp115–118.

38 Mirian K Omalu (n 28) pp303–331.

broadly speaking, all joint operating agreements have certain basic elements in common. For example, all joint operating agreements will provide for:

(a) the pooling and co-ownership of project assets;

(b) the establishment of a method for the conduct of the joint operations by which certain parties are given the authority to make certain decisions in particular circumstances (eg the operator, all the joint venture parties or, in the case of sole-risk projects for example, some of the joint venture parties);

(c) the apportionment of risks among the parties (including the operator);

(d) the participation by each party in costs; and

(e) the participation by each party in production or revenues.[39]

On the other hand, it is impossible to deny the fact that there are some differences between different jurisdictions, as each region has adopted its own JOA model form. A. Martin describes this context as follows:

The North Sea environment still stands apart from the mingling of JOA concepts seen in some other jurisdictions. Companies operating in the United Kingdom have never really taken to the AIPN model JOA and have always rejected the North-American-style onshore JOAs.[40]

Regardless of the necessity of special model forms to address local or regional concerns, it is impossible to ignore the importance of standard agreements in this industry. As A. Martin describes in the following terms:

Model contracts have been developed and used in a wide variety of ways in different jurisdictions. They are extremely flexible tools that allow users to draft effective petroleum contracts quickly and efficiently. They have spread throughout the global petroleum industry because of the significant benefits and immense value they provide to the entire business cycle. As a result, model contracts in the international industry will undoubtedly expand in their development and application in the future.[41]

Although standard forms are valuable instruments to accelerate and conclude an oil and gas transaction, it cannot be a case of one size fits all – there must be some room for adjustment.[42] From a non-operator's perspective, it is desirable that the JOA provide as much detail as possible, so that sheer lack of bargaining power will not require it to adjust the model, which is supposed to represent standard practice in a particular region. Paradoxically, though, as the current models tend to be operator-biased, any additional detail is likely to support the operator role, making it difficult for the non-operator to achieve protection.

There are several standard JOA models available in the petroleum industry. However, for the purposes of this book, only the following models will be considered in detail:

---

39 Catia Malaquias Miles, "AIPN 2002 Model Form Joint Operating Agreement in Oil and Gas Joint Ventures" (2003) 22 *Australian Resources & Energy L J* pp153–160.

40 A Timothy Martin (n 1) p284.

41 *Ibid* p339.

42 *Ibid* p293.

43 Andrew Derman provides a valuable analysis of the evolution of the AAPL JOA model forms. See Andrew B Derman, *Joint Operating Agreement: Working Manual* (American Bar Association, Tulsa 1986), Andrew B Derman, *The New and Improved 1989 Joint Operating Agreement: A Working Manual* (American Bar Association, Tulsa 1991).

AAPL models:[43] The American Association of Professional Landmen (AAPL) was the first organisation to issue a standard form of JOA, in 1956, known as the 'Form 610'.[44] This historic form was the basis for others – for example, the British and Canadian models. The Form 610 JOA was subsequently revised, with minor changes, in 1977, 1982, 1989 and finally in 2015.[45] All these versions were focused on onshore operations; however, a major change came in 2002 with AAPL Form 710 (subsequently revised in 2007 as Form 810), which was aimed at deepwater operations in the Gulf of Mexico.[46] The American Petroleum Institute (API) also issued a JOA for offshore operations in 1984, which was revised in 1996; however, it was not well accepted by the industry and it is currently out of print.[47] For the purposes of this book, any reference to the AAPL model is based on the Form 610 (for onshore operations) as revised in 1989 and again in 2015; and/or the Form 810 issued in 2007 (for offshore operations).

RMMLF model: The Rocky Mountain Mineral Law Foundation (RMMLF) "is a collaborative educational non-profit organisation dedicated to the scholarly and practical study of the law and regulations relating to mining, oil and gas, water, public lands, land use."[48] The RMMLF JOA model form was published in 1968 and focused on US onshore operations.[49]

Exploration and production operations in the US started as early as the 19th century, and as a result companies have adopted several different JOA model forms, including those of the AAPL, AIPN, API and RMMLF. The most widely accepted models for US operations are those of the AAPL;[50] nevertheless, it is useful to compare the RMMLF and AAPL (Form 610) model forms, as both addressed onshore operations.

CAPL model:[51] The Canadian Association of Professional Landmen (CAPL) aims to represent all the parties engaged in the Canadian oil and gas industry. The first OP model form issued by the CAPL was in 1971. It was based on the AAPL's Form 610 and was subsequently revised in 1974, 1981, 1990, 2007 and again in 2015.[52] In 1988 a frontier OP model was issued, but that is now considered obsolete. For the purposes of this book, any reference to the CAPL model is based on the OP 2007 model form (with minor updates in 2015 focusing on technical procedures for horizontal wells).

---

44 Ernest E Smith *et al* (n 16) p538.

45 www.landman.org.

46 www.landman.org.

47 A Timothy Martin (n 1) p318.

48 www.rmmlf.org.

49 "The RMMLF developed this model JOA for joint venture operations in the US Rocky Mountain area where there is no field-wide federal unit involved. It incorporates similar concepts found in other model JOAs where there is a sharing of financial risk and benefits by the parties. It was issued in 1968 and never revised. It is referred to as Form 3 in the RMMLF catalogue." A Timothy Martin (n 1) pp293–294.

50 Ernest E Smith *et al* (n 16) p538.

51 For further information see Al Hudec, Joni Paulus, "Current Oil and Gas Issues in Canada and the 1990 CAPL Operating Agreement" (1992) 10 *J Energy & Nat Resources L* p194; Robert M Boyer, "The 1981 CAPL Operating Procedure" (1983) 21 *Alta L Rev* p82; James A Maclean, "The 1990 CAPL Operating Procedure, An Overview of the Revisions" (1992) 30 *Alta L Rev* p133; Michael D Josephson, "How Far Does the CAPL Travel? A Comparative Overview of the CAPL Model Form Operating Procedure and the AIPN Model Form International Operating Agreement" (2003) 41(1) *Alta L Rev* pp1–3.

52 www.landman.ca/store/capl_publication_list.php.

British model:[53] The British JOA model form was historically[54] based on the AAPL JOA model Form 610, until the fifth UK Continental Shelf Licensing Round, when the British National Oil Corporation (BNOC)[55] issued a pro-forma JOA version which was compulsory at the time. Later,[56] the pro-forma version was replaced by another version issued, by the United Kingdom Offshore Operators Association (UKOOA), and more recently, by the 2009 version issued by Oil & Gas United Kingdom (OGUK)[57] which aims to represent all parties involved in the offshore industry.[58] Minor updates to this version were made in 2013. All references in this book are to the latest JOA version issued in 2009 by OGUK, as updated in 2013.

Norwegian model: The Norwegian Petroleum Directorate (NPD) is an administrative body created in 1972 to provide assistance to the Norwegian Ministry of Petroleum and Energy.[59] If a single party or a consortium is awarded a licence to explore and produce oil on the Norwegian Continental Shelf (NCS), the licensee must cooperate with the national oil company (NOC) by signing an agreement in the format of a JOA,[60] but only to the extent that the government decides to take part in the enterprise.[61] The Norwegian JOA model is provided by the Ministry of Petroleum and Energy (MPE) with the support of the NPD, in the Norwegian language. However, the MPE website provides a different title ("Agreement Concerning Petroleum Activities") as an unofficial English version of the Norwegian JOA. The difficulty in finding such an agreement on the website and the different title of the agreement explains why it is so rare to find any reference to such a JOA model form, but it also increases the originality of this book.[62]

Australian model: There are several JOA model forms available in Australia. Historically, the form issued by the Australian Petroleum Production and Exploration Association (APPEA) used to be the most important, but it is out of date, out of print and unsuitable for recent operations.[63] The AIPN also issues guidance notes for Australian operations. If two or more parties desire to sign an AIPN JOA model form in Australia, they must use the traditional AIPN JOA model form but amend it

---

53 See Stephen Dow (n 7), Pia Mandler, "New Oil & Gas UK standard joint operating agreement (JOA)" (2008) 5 *IELR* 111, 112 and Hilary Worboys, "Boiler plate or boiler fuel? A critical analysis of a standard term of the North Sea joint operating agreement" (1986/87) 5(12) *OGLTR* pp299–302.

54 Michael PG Taylor, Sally M Tyne, *Taylor and Winsor on Joint Operating Agreements* (2nd ed, Longman, London 1992) p22.

55 For more information about the BNOC see: AW Baker, GH Daniel, "BNOC and Privatisation –The Past and the Future" (1983) 1 *J Energy & Nat Resources L* p149, Malcolm Foster, Donald N Zillman, "The British National Oil Corporation: The State Enterprise as Instrument of Energy Policy" (1982–1983) 3 *Journal of Energy Law and Policy* p57.

56 The department responsible for offshore operations on UKCS is the Department of Energy and Climate Change (DECC). According to the Petroleum Act 1998 and Petroleum Licensing (Production) (Seaward Areas) Regulations 2008, the creation of or amendment within a JOA has to be approved by the DECC: www.og.decc.gov.uk.

57 www.oilandgasuk.co.uk/aboutus/aboutus.cfm.

58 Scott Styles (n 14) pp266–267, Peter Roberts (n 5) p19.

59 www.npd.no/en/about-us/.

60 www.statoil.com/annualreport2009/en/ouroperations/regulation/pages/thenorwegianlicensingsystem.aspx.

61 Sections 3.4 and 3.6 of the Petroleum Activities Act 1996 (Norway).

62 www.regjeringen.no/en/dep/oed/Documents-and-publications/Laws-and-rules-2/Rules/2007/framework.html?id=455506.

63 Timothy Martin (n 1) pp293, 294.

according to the Australian guidance notes. In other words, the basis is the International model with certain regional adjustments.[64]

However, the most common model form in Australia is the JV version provided by the Australian Mining and Petroleum Law Association (AMPLA). AMPLA is a "not-for-profit association established in 1976 to advance the knowledge of law relating to mineral and petroleum resources".[65] In the past 30 years, the AMPLA has issued several mining agreements.[66] In 2009 its board approved a new model Mining Joint Venture Agreement. As the name suggests, this model is aimed at mining operations, but it is commonly adjusted for oil and gas operations. In 2011 AMPLA approved a JOA model form for oil and gas operations. The basis of this new model is similar to the Mining Joint Venture Agreement. For the purposes of this book the focus will be on the more well-known Mining Joint Venture Agreement but comments will be relevant to the new JOA model and specific reference is made to the JOA model where required.

AIPN model:[67] The Association of International Petroleum Negotiators (AIPN) is a non-profit organisation which aims to assist professionals in the field of energy negotiations.[68] The AIPN issued its first JOA standard model in 1990; this was subsequently revised in 1995, 2002 and finally 2012. The AIPN JOA model form is widely used in the international context,[69] as its flexible terms and provisions[70] allow for its application in different regions and jurisdictions. On the other hand, such flexibility is criticised for hindering the implementation of standard forms.[71] A significant number of existing JOAs are governed by the 2002 model form rather than the latest 2012 version.[72] Therefore, this book focuses on the traditional 2002 model form but includes updates from the 2012 model form where applicable. The

---

64 Catia Malaquias Miles (n 39) pp153–160.

65 www.ampla.org/scripts/cgiip.exe/WService=AMPLA/ccms.r?PageId=50.

66 www.ampla.org/scripts/cgiip.exe/WService=AMPLA/ccms.r?PageId=10016.

67 For further information about these model forms see Andrew B Derman, *International Oil and Gas Joint Ventures: A Discussion with Associated Form Agreements* (American Bar Association, Tulsa 1992), Andrew B Derman, *Model Form International Operating Agreement, An Analysis and Interpretation of the 1995 Form* (American Bar Association, Tulsa 1997), PR Weems, M Bolton (n 24), Geoff Hewitt, "The AIPN Model Form International Operating Agreement 2002" (2003) 11 *IELTR* pp309, 311, Catia Malaquias Miles (n 39) pp153–160.

68 www.aipn.org/about-aipn/.

69 "The Association of International Petroleum Negotiators' Model Form International Operating Agreement has become the seminal model form joint operating agreement for international petroleum development throughout the world." PR Weems, M Bolton (n 24) p5.

70 "The model [AIPN] aims to be a flexible one, to accommodate the preferences of individual parties and the different legal regimes that may govern the joint venture operations. It achieves this by providing text alternatives for many of its provisions as well as drafting and guidance notes which call attention to legal issues that may be relevant to the context in which the document is proposed to be used." Catia Malaquias Miles (n 39) pp153–160.

71 "The more flexible approach in international models has not pleased all commentators. The AIPN model JOA was criticised in an Oil and Gas Journal article as having a 'smorgasbord of options' which failed to establish or legitimise any one standard for the international petroleum industry. Those critics stated that '[b]y not providing an approved solution, the [1995 AIPN model JOA] misses the opportunity to impose tested standards on parties new to the industry.' These comments reflect an expectation for the narrow, standardised approach common in US domestic model JOAs rather than the more diverse and complex operating environment encountered in international JOAs. Most experienced international practitioners would maintain that those expectations are unrealistic and do not reflect the requirements of international operations." A Timothy Martin (n 1) p293.

72 The writer has been a member of AIPN since 2008 and was also a member of the revision committee of the 2002 model form.

reason for this approach is to illustrate the changes in the most relevant International JOA model form in the past 10 years. However, not all provisions have been amended – many were subjected to stylistic rather than substantive changes. References to the updated version are therefore included only where necessary.

Greenlandic model: Greenland is an autonomous region of the Kingdom of Denmark. Its government issued its first JOA model form in 2002; this was revised in 2004, 2006 and finally 2008. Minor updates have appeared in recent years but the focus of this book is the 2008 version.[73] However, each of these JOA model forms is significant, as they each require the participation of a state-owned company (Nunaoil) which is controlled by the Danish and Greenlandic governments. Consequently, an NOC is a party to the JOA, so this standard form reflects a different approach.

The aforementioned JOA models form the basis of this book, as they reveal the position of non-operators in different regions. This position will be compared with the ideal scenario for any non-operator, to illustrate the extent to which the current JOAs are unbalanced and how they could be improved. The JOA models will be analysed in chronological order; the American JOAs are the oldest models and the Greenlandic JOAs the most recent.

(b) Relevance

Although the oil and gas industry operates on a global scale, different regions have their own particular needs and demands. For example, the UK and Norway require an approach tailored for mature provinces (eg, decommissioning obligations). On the other hand, newer territories like Australia and Greenland require a different approach (eg, incentives for exploration). Additionally, each region has its own jurisdictional system which might treat common issues, such as representation and the relationship between parties, differently. Consequently, the JOA model forms should provide what the industry demands and establish standards for each region.

A. Timothy Martin refers to the essential ingredients in the creation of model forms,[74] but the most important elements are industry demands,[75] industry support[76] and drafting philosophy.[77] There is no doubt about the importance of industry demands and support; otherwise there would be no need for model forms. This is the main reason why so many JOA model forms are analysed in this book.

Industry support gives comfort to the parties, as they are going to sign an agreement based on common practice for the particular region. In this sense, it would be natural to expect some measure of balance and fairness in the terms of the standard model form. This is why the third element, the drafting philosophy, is so important to secure the industry's support and meet its demands.

73 www.bmp.gl/.
74 Such as Project Managing, Resources, Deliverables, Marketing, Education and Future Revisions. A Timothy Martin (n 1) pp331–339.
75 *Ibid* pp331–332.
76 *Ibid* pp332–333.
77 *Ibid* pp336–337.

As previously mentioned, the framework on which all JOAs are based dates from a time when costs were considerably lower, there was little or no environmental regulation, the conditions for exploration and exploitation of oil and gas were considerably easier to manage and expertise was concentrated in a few parties on a global scale. However, this scenario has changed: operations are more costly, highly regulated and complex, and performance benefits from the input of a greater number of parties to the JOA. The scenario is even more complex for mature provinces, as larger companies tend to exit the territory in search of bigger projects, leaving operations in the hands of smaller companies.

In order to improve the performance of operations, it is important to understand the way that each JOA analysed in this book positions non-operators, so as to identify best practice that might apply to particular issues worldwide. The oil and gas industry is globally connected and experience is passed from one region to another, so it is much easier to suggest modifications if the suggestions are founded in practice rather than theory.

It is important to remember that no model form can address every issue which might be relevant for every situation, as this is a highly complex industry and the structure of the project might change from jurisdiction to jurisdiction. For example, in Greenland, the NOC will be part of the JOA, whereas in North American jurisdictions there is no NOC in the system. The standard form should provide the basis for most transactions within a particular jurisdiction, but the parties should consider whether the standard form might require adjustment appropriate to a particular negotiation.[78]

However, if the JOA model form provides several options – like the AIPN model – then this flexibility might be problematic for non-operators to the extent that they are usually in a weaker position than the operator. In this case, any flexibility might enable the operator to secure better terms, so in an unbalanced scenario, non-operators may prefer to keep the JOA as close as possible to the standard form.

Finally, it would not be possible to understand the importance of the great variety in JOA model forms if every related jurisdiction were analysed: it simply would not be possible to accommodate all the information in one study. Consequently, the British jurisdiction will be the main focus of this book (in particular the laws of England & Wales), as the UK is a leading province in the oil and gas industry; however, reference is made to other jurisdictions where necessary.[79] The main reason for this is the fact that the oil and gas industry tends to accept more willingly best practices from other standard forms rather than from purely theoretical recommendation. Gary Conine describes this situation as follows:

As with oil and gas leases, there is not a "standard operating agreement." Specific provisions vary to allow for the peculiar needs of the parties to the instrument and

---

78 Stephen Dow (n 7).

79 The jurisprudence concerning JOAs is not as developed as other areas of the oil and gas industry. For this reason, this book may refer to cases in different jurisdictions. See Ernest E Smith, "Joint Operating Agreement Jurisprudence" (1994) 33 *Washburn Law Journal* pp834–835, Gary B Conine, "Property Provisions of the Operating Agreement, Interpretation, Validity, and Enforceability" (1988) 19 *Tex Tech L Rev* p1265.

special concerns inherent in the immediate transaction. Nevertheless, there is considerable similarity in the basic provisions of most operating agreements. This results in large part from the development of model forms of the instrument which have received widespread acceptance in the industry. Over time, these model forms have contributed greatly to the simplification of negotiations, the standardization of technical terms and, to a more limited degree, consistency in legal interpretations.[80]

Of course, every JOA should represent the industry's requirements in a particular region, consistent with local legislation. All jurisdictions, therefore, will be analysed.

(c) Conclusion

Any comparative analysis requires an in-depth examination of differences in structure between the systems under comparison. A more superficial comparison risks failing to explain how a mechanism that appears suitable for one jurisdiction might not fit another. The parties should be aware of the potential impact of any provision in the agreement on the jurisdiction where the operations will take place.[81, 82]

Ultimately, it is impossible to deny the importance of standard forms, as they provide a useful tool both to accelerate the negotiation process and to keep the parties apprised of the realities of the industry. These realities will vary from region to region according to the specific requirements and demands involved. In this sense, the great variety of JOAs provides insights into practices all around the world.

This book will compare the most important JOA models utilised in the petroleum industry, to facilitate an understanding of how each of these models positions and deals with non-operators' major concerns, so that best practices can be transferred to other regions.[83] In addition, the weaknesses of each model will be analysed so that a wider contribution can be made.

1.3 The oil and gas industry

(a) Upstream and downstream agreements

The oil and gas industry is a highly technical and specialised field. Traditionally, the industry has been divided into two sections: upstream and downstream.[84] The former

---

80 Gary B Conine (n 79).

81 For an in-depth analysis of the complexity in terms of comparative law, see Esin Örücü, *The Enigma of Comparative Law: Variations on a Theme for the Twenty-First Century* (Martinus Nijhoff, Leiden/Boston 2004), Esin Örücü, David Nelken (eds), *Comparative Law: A Handbook* (Hart, London, 2007) and Esin Örücü (ed), *Mixed Legal Systems at New Frontiers* (Wildy, Simmonds and Hill, 2010).

82 "However, like all model form agreements, the provisions contained in the 2002 Version should be carefully considered for their suitability to the particular circumstances and the legislative framework in respect of which they are intended to operate." Catia Malaquias Miles (n 39) pp153–160.

83 "Even though model operating agreements from various areas of the world deal with many similar issues, their approach in handling these issues can be quite different. For instance, there is a marked difference in various model JOAs on how the relationship between the operator and non-operator(s) is addressed." Bruce M Kramer, Gary B Conine, "Joint Development and Operations' vehicles to conduct exploration, development and production", in Ernest E Smith *et al* (n 16) p561.

84 This is the traditional classification. Nevertheless, it is worth noting that other classifications exist which mention a 'midstream' phase, which includes some of the activities of the traditional downstream classification, such as storing, transportation and marketing. See Charlotte J Wright and Rebbeca A Gallun, *Fundamentals of Oil & Gas Accounting* (5th edn, Penwell, Tulsa 2008) pp1, 2.

relates to the E&P phases, which include the following activities: exploration, appraisal, drilling, developing and, finally, producing oil and gas. The latter relates to the sequence of activities required to prepare oil and gas for final consumption, namely refining, distribution, transportation, storing, marketing and selling activities.[85]

Charlotte Wright summarises this classification as follows:

[U]pstream activities generally include all of the activities involved in finding and producing oil and gas up to the initial point that the oil and gas is capable of being sold or used ... Downstream activities generally include refining, processing, marketing, and distribution.[86]

It may be said that oil and gas activities are divided by phases according to the state of the natural resource. The nature of the contracts involved in each phase will also change to reflect each specific situation. However, all oil and gas arrangements take place against a common backdrop, as the industry has been establishing a set of common ground rules since Colonel Drake first struck oil in Pennsylvania in 1856.[87] During the long history of operations, the industry has come to realise that standard agreements can save a considerable amount of time and effort in discussion and negotiation of agreements.[88]

Each sector of the oil and gas industry has since implemented its own standard agreements for different phases of the process, such as joint bidding agreements (JBA), joint study agreements (JSA), joint operating agreements (JOA), farmout agreements (FOA), lifting agreements (LA) and distribution agreements (DA). For the purposes of this book, the focus will be on the JOA, which is the most important and relevant private contract for the E&P phases,[89] since it regulates operations to explore for and produce oil and gas.

(b) JOA background

The definition of the JOA is important, since this has several consequences, as will be analysed in the following section of this chapter. However, in order to understand the definition fully, it is necessary to explain briefly the context in which the JOA normally operates.

First, the JOA should be linked to a petroleum legal regime that allows the JOA parties to explore for and produce oil and gas.[90] As a general rule, any company wishing to explore for oil and gas must receive authorisation from the host government,[91] as the natural resources commonly belong to that government.[92] This

85 *Ibid.*
86 *Ibid.*
87 For further information see Daniel Yergin, *The Prize: The Epic Quest for Oil, Money & Power* (2nd ed, Free Press, New York 2008).
88 See note 16.
89 Terence Daintith *et al* (n 16) p1136, Charez Golvala (n 6) p45.
90 Bernard Taverne, *An introduction to the regulation of the petroleum industry: Law, Contracts and Conventions* (Graham & Trotman, London 1994) p133.
91 "The JOA does not operate in isolation: It has to be viewed on the background of the production licence (PL), to which it is made a formal condition. And further: The PL is based on the Petroleum Act, and has to be viewed in this context." Juris Knut Kaasen, "Scope of Joint Operating Agreements in Norway", Petroleum Law Seminar, St Raphael, 2000 p8.

authorisation could take the form of a petroleum licence, a production sharing agreement, a service agreement or a hybrid form.[93] All these instruments confer rights and duties on the contracting parties (or licensee) so they can explore for and produce oil and gas in a specific location; it is illegal to conduct operations without such an agreement.[94]

Second – and probably the key point of most oil and gas operations – is the fact that the oil and gas industry operates in a hostile environment and involves several risks,[95] geological,[96] technical,[97] environmental and political. In other words, a number of diverse factors affect exploration and production projects in a particular region, and for that reason the oil and gas industry is regularly forced to speculate on uncertainty.[98]

Third, financial expenditure is a critical issue for oil and gas operations, as the amount of capital required for exploration and production is usually extremely high, even for major companies like Exxon, BP, Shell, Chevron or Total.[99] Operations in the Brazilian pre-salt area are a good example, as the reservoir is over 7,000 metres below sea level and more than 300km from the shore.[100] The logistical and technical challenges increase the costs of oil and gas operations still further.

The hostile environment and the significant amount of expenditure involved are the key drivers that encourage companies to share the costs and risks with other companies by establishing a JV.[101] Instead of owning 100% of a single project, the contracting parties have a share in many different projects.[102] Consequently, if a

92 Most of the jurisdictions provide that natural resources located in the subsoil belong to the government and can only be explored if authorised by the respective government. However, there are exceptions to this rule, such as in US jurisdictions. See Bernard G Taverne, *Petroluem, Industry and Governments: A study of the Involvement of Industry and Government with the Production and use of Petroleum* (2nd ed, Kluwer Law International, Alphen aan den Rijn 2008) p380.

93 For the purposes of this book, 'Petroleum Licence', 'PSA' and 'Service Agreement' all refer to the petroleum title signed between the private party and the host government.

94 For further information about the petroleum title see Eugene V Rostow, *A National Policy for the Oil Industry* (YUP, London 1948) pp3–26, Danièle Barberis, *Negotiating Mining Agreements: Past, Present and Future Trends* (Klumer Law International, London 1998) pp4–60, Mike Bunter, "The Iranian Buy Back Agreement" (2003) 1 (2) *OGEL*.

95 See also George K Foster, "Managing Expropriation Risks in the Energy Sector: Steps for Foreign Investors to Minimise their Exposure and Maximise Prospects for Recovery when Takings Occur" (2005) 23 *J Energy & Nat Resources L* pp36–59, Andrew B Derman, A Melsheimer, "Changing the Rules of the Game: Issues that arise under the 2002 AIPN JOA when a host government mandates a 'replacement contract'" (2010) 8(4) *OGEL* pp1–7, V Lowe, "Recognition or Expropriation" (2004) 2 (3) *OGEL*.

96 http://geocompendium.grid.unep.

97 R Fabrikant, "Oil Discovery and Technical Change in Southeast Asia – Legal Aspects of Production Sharing Contracts in the Indonesian Petroleum Industry" (2005) 3 (1) *OGEL*.

98 See Bryan Cooper, TF Gaskell, *North Sea Oil, The Great Gamble* (Heinemann, London 1966).

99 For further information see David Johnston, Daniel Johnston, *Introduction to Oil Company Financial Analysis* (PenWell, Tulsa 2006), Daniel Johnston, *International Exploration Economics, Risk, and Contract Analysis* (PenWell, Tulsa 2003), Robert C Nicholls, "A Review of Some Aspects of the Organization and Financing of Mineral Resource Ventures" (1976) 1 *UNSW Law Journal* p271.

100 www.presalt.com/.

101 "Participants in the resource industry, while generally operating as competitors, will often form alliances to explore co-operatively in a particular area." John Tarrant, "Agreements to Co-Operate at Common Law" (2006) 25(3) *Australian Resources and Energy Law Journal* p281.

102 "There is nothing to prevent an interested party from applying on its own. In so doing, such a party will be assuming 100% of the risk. The joint venture, on the other hand, represents a form of risk sharing and consequently risk reduction between the interested parties. It also offers an effective mechanism for the pooling of resources and provides the added security of being part of a group." John Wilkinson (n 16) p11.

particular area is not successful, the remaining assets might compensate the company for any losses. The Deepwater Horizon accident in the Gulf of Mexico is a good example: if BP (the operator) and its co-venturers (the non-operators) had only had this one asset, they would have gone bankrupt, as costs and damages were likely to exceed $20 billion. In the event, there were other assets against which to offset and minimise the losses.

The diagram below summarises the context in which a JOA operates.

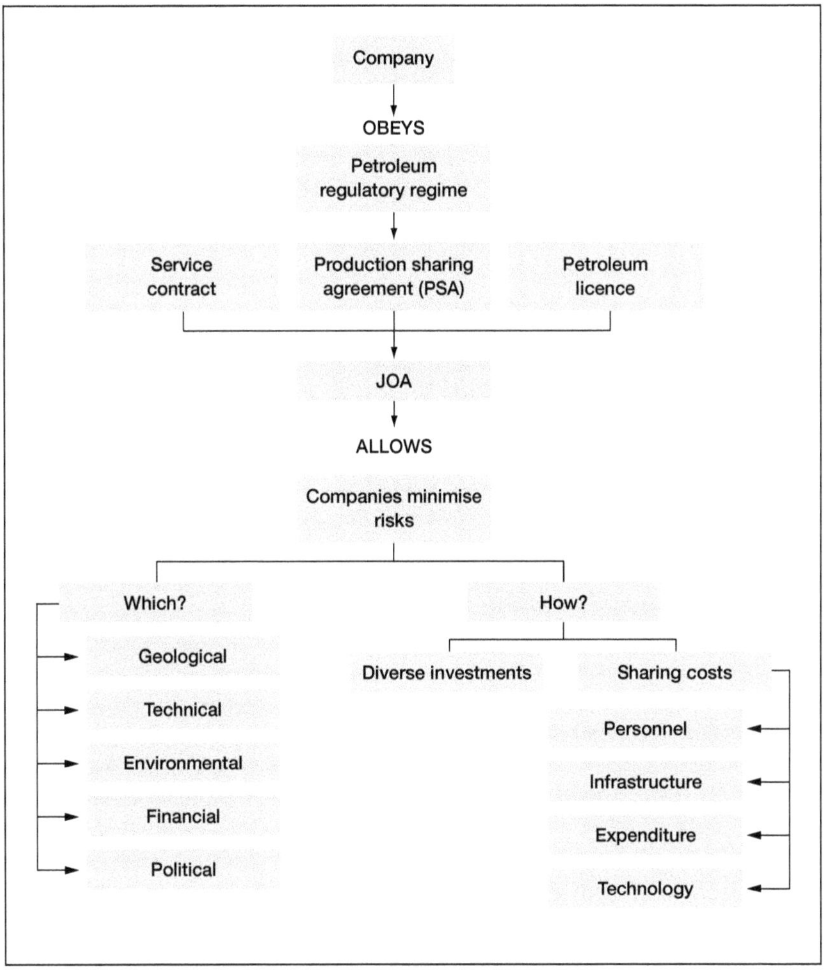

It can thus be said that minimising risks and sharing costs are at the heart of the JV.[103] In this sense, the JV is the key instrument through which to achieve the common goal of the host government and the private parties: that is, to maximise

103 See Chris Wilkinson, *Joint Ventures & Shareholder s Agreements* (3rd ed, Bloomsbury Professional, West Sussex 2009) pp3–5 and Gerard MD Bean (n 16) p19.

the economical recovery of petroleum in the licensed area. However, this traditional perspective might change in certain mature provinces, as the risk and cost assessments might not justify the establishment of a consortium. The parties may argue that the consortium will bring additional problems and that establishing a consortium for smaller and simpler operations is not justified. Nevertheless, it is undeniable that the vast majority of projects, even in mature provinces, benefit from the sharing of risks, costs, technology and expertise via consortium agreements.

(c) *Conclusion*

It can thus be seen that oil and gas companies prefer to join forces to spread the risks and costs of exploration and production operations, as these can be extremely high. They also prefer to spread their assets across a number of areas in order to maximise their chances of success. These tactics help to guard against the major problem of the oil and gas industry – that it is attended by uncertainty.

It is also clear there is some interaction between the petroleum title and the JOA, as the latter cannot exist without the former. The petroleum title is usually highly regulated, as it involves a vertical relationship between the government and the private parties; however, the JOA is only indirectly controlled by the government, as it concerns a horizontal relationship between the private parties.[104]

That said, in certain jurisdictions the government will have direct influence and control over the JOA, as is analysed with the Greenlandic JOA model form and later the Norwegian model form.[105]

Having explored the context in which the JOA operates, it becomes easier to understand the nature of the instrument.

1.4 JOA definition

(a) *Definition*

The term 'joint venture' did not originate in English or Scots law (although there are some influences from Scots law),[106] but rather in American law.[107] It commonly refers to different forms of association, such as unincorporated JVs, incorporated JVs, limited liability companies and others.[108] This book focuses on the unincorporated form, as it is the most common in the oil and gas industry for taxation and liability reasons.

As mentioned previously, the host government decides which legal regime will apply in its own jurisdiction. This regime commonly imposes joint and several liability on all the contracting parties of the JV throughout the life of the petroleum

---

104 "Whereas the Licence sets forth the rights and obligations of the parties vis-à-vis the Government, the JOA sets out the rights and obligations of the parties amongst themselves." Sandy Shaw (n 16) p13.

105 For further information about governmental participation in JVs: Rajendra Ramlogan, "State Participation in Joint Ventures: The Republic of Trinidad and Tobago Experience" (1992) 10 *J Energy & Nat Resources L* pp279–284, Mirian Kene Omalu, Armando Zamora, "Key Issue in Mining Policy, A Brief Comparative Survey as a Background Study on the Reform of Mining Law", CEPMLP Paper No CP 9/98.

106 DJ Gately, "The Unincorporated Joint Venture, A Fiduciary Relationship?" 5(1) *AMPLA Bulletin* p12.

107 See John D Carter *et al*, *The Handbook of Joint Venture* (Price Waterhouse, Homewood 1988).

108 See Scott Styles (n 14) p264, Peter Roberts (n 5) p251, Joseph T Sneed, "More About Associations in the Oil and Gas Industry (1954–1955)" *Tex L Rev* p168.

title.[109] The government's protection is thus strengthened, as all parties are liable for the obligations of the petroleum title, regardless of the size of their participation.[110] This is the public relationship between the JV and the host government (ie, the vertical relationship). On the other hand, the JOA will establish the private parties' relations and can specify different liabilities and responsibilities for each party (within the horizontal relationship).[111]

This book will focus on the horizontal relationship of the JV parties, as the JOA is predominantly a private document.[112] The JOA parties are free to determine the rules which will regulate their relationship, to the extent that these do not conflict with applicable law. This basic nature of the JOA is explained by Anthony Jennings as follows:

The joint venturers will commonly negotiate and execute a Joint Operating Agreement (JOA), or equivalent, which will govern the rights and liabilities of the parties as between themselves and their relationship with the group member responsible for conducting the joint operations, known as the operator.[113]

Therefore, it may be said that the JOA "sets out the rights and obligations of the parties among themselves. It is the bedrock of operations as it sets forth the framework and detailed rules upon which the Joint Venture will operate."[114] In other words, the JOA is the main instrument in determining the procedures and rules which will govern the joint operations of the contracting parties.[115] However, in some jurisdictions the host government might exercise greater control before any change is established in the JOA (as, for example, in Mozambique).[116]

It is important to analyse the definition of each word in the name of this type of agreement, as this will shed light on the content and spirit of the JOA. The first and most important word is 'joint' which is defined by the Oxford English Dictionary as:

[Adj.] (i) shared, held, or made by two or more people together: a joint statement, (ii) sharing in a position, achievement, or activity: a joint winner, (iii) Law applied or regarded together. Often contrasted with several.[117]

In other words, the term refers to something which will be made or shared by two or more parties.

The second word, 'operating', is defined as follows:

---

109 This situation is very similar to a tenancy, as the joint tenants have a "collective, unitary interest where each joint tenant is entitled to possession of the whole of an interest which is subject of co-ownership". Peter Roberts (n 5) p47.

110 "The link between the PL and the JOA also implies a modification to the general rule that parties to a joint venture agreement (such as the JOA) may change the agreement by unanimous vote: Any amendment or addition to the JOA has to be approved by the state in order to be valid. Apart from the formal reason for this (i.e. the acceptance of the JOA being a condition for being granted the PL), the rationale for the provision presumably lies in the state's general wish for standardisation and for controlling 'the rules of the game'." Juris Knut Kaasen (n 91) p3.

111 Any modification of the liabilities does not affect third parties, but applies exclusively to relations between the JV parties.

112 As previously mentioned, the impact of the NOC will be analysed in the Greenlandic and Norwegian JOA model forms.

113 Anthony Jennings (n 16) p23.

114 Sandy Shaw (n 16) p13.

115 Terence Daintith *et al* (n 16) p1136.

116 Juris K Kaasen (n 91) p3.

117 www.oxforddictionaries.com/.

[with object] (of a person) control the functioning of (a machine, process, or system): (...) manage (a business; [no object, with adverbial] (of an organization) be managed in a specified way or from a specified place.[118]

That is to say, the term refers to the conduct or performance of a specific activity. Finally, the word 'agreement':

[A] negotiated and typically legally binding arrangement between parties as to a course of action: a trade agreement, a verbal agreement to sell.[119]

Thus, a 'joint operating agreement' can reasonably be expected to involve the participation of the non-operators in the conduct and performance of the operations, either directly or indirectly. However, this is not the case: all standard JOA model forms clearly provide that the performance of the 'joint' operations is by only one party, namely the operator. This is less problematic for non-operators when there is an operating committee and sub-committees in place through which they can participate in, and make decisions on, the operations. However, it is more problematic for certain non-operators, as in several JOA model forms they will not participate in decisions about the performance of operations at all, due either to lack of control of the operating committees and sub-committees (eg, lack of veto powers) or the absence of these systems from the JOA altogether (eg, in North American JOAs). In this scenario, the name of the agreement is unlikely to reflect the reality, as the parties will not share the performance, just the consequences of the performance, including the risks, costs and liabilities.

The CAPL operating procedure is unique among model forms in that its definition recognises that the term 'joint' is inappropriate, given that operations are conducted solely by one party. The title is evidence enough of this argument, but the CAPL operating procedure committee also mentioned the modification in a paper entitled "Modification to 1990 CAPL Operating Procedure" by Jim MacLean:[120]

Provision	Modification	Rationale for change
Definition of joint-operator.	Deleted, with consequential impact.	Term wasn't needed.

To an extent, the Greenlandic JOA model form also recognises this concern, providing for a more active role by the NOC in the conduct of the operations by way of an attachment referring to a co-operatorship framework in which the NOC will acquire more knowledge and control.[121]

It is thus clear that the name 'JOA' is inaccurate, as it indicates a situation that does not match the reality of the agreement (as the CAPL recognised). However, this

118 www.oxforddictionaries.com/.
119 www.oxforddictionaries.com/.
120 www.landman.ca/pdf/operating_procedures/2007/final/Modifications%20to%201990%20Oper%20Proc%20(Aug%2016%202007).pdf.
121 www.govmin.gl/images/stories/petroleum/udbud/udbud_2018_2018/Davis_Strait_2018/Model%20Joint%20Operating%20Agreement_App%20B_Davis%20Strait%202018.pdf.

fact appears to have been overlooked in the oil and gas industry, most likely for the same reason that the imbalance in JOAs generally has not been explored in depth, the industry still positioning the operator at the centre of the consortium.

(b) Implications

The words 'joint', 'operating' and 'agreement', as usually defined, would imply a legal document regulating the conduct of a business by more than one person. The word 'joint' would in fact be the essence of such an agreement, as it implies a collaboration between all parties in the conduct of operations, either directly or indirectly, since all parties have an interest in the JV – that is to say, there is co-ownership.

Claude Duval expresses the difficulty for non-operators as follows:

> *[T]he operator may not look favourably on project subcommittees headed by non-operators which might infringe on the operator's 'exclusive charge' over joint operations.*[122]

In fact, the definitions of the parties to the JOA (ie, 'operator' and 'non-operators') are far more accurate than the name of the agreement itself. If these definitions are correct, it would be more accurate to call the agreement a 'joint costs agreement', as it focuses on the shared costs between the contracting parties, but not on shared performance and participation in operations. Juris Kaasen describes this situation as follows:

> *A defining mark of the joint venture established by the JOA is that it does not constitute an "income partnership", just an "expense partnership".*[123]

On the other hand, if the name of the agreement is correct, then different names for the parties should be used, in order to reflect the collaboration between them (eg, 'operator' and 'co-operator').

A similar situation could arise when the revenues from a PSA are not properly shared. For example, Ian Rutledge argues that an unusual PSA signed by the Russian government should really be called a 'production non-sharing agreement',[124] on the basis that the host government will only receive any revenue from production once the international oil company (IOC) has recovered all costs and a certain percentage of the return – a provision which is highly uncommon for this type of agreement. This is a practical example of a situation where the name of the agreement establishes an expectation of its content. The name should express the essence and spirit of the agreement; otherwise it is meaningless.

Finally, the name is clear evidence of the imbalance of current JOAs, where parties do not enjoy substantial participation, yet share the full burden. Of course, changing the name will not solve the problems: the Canadian model, from which the word 'joint' is absent, recognises the inaccuracy of the name of the agreement but does not address the lack of participation by non-operators in the performance

---

122 Claude Duval *et al*, *International Petroleum and Exploration Agreements: Legal, Economic & Policy Aspects* (2nd ed, Barrows, New York 2009) p293.

123 Juris K Kaasen (n 91) p15.

124 Ian Rutledge, "The Sakhalin II PSA – a Production 'Non-Sharing' Agreement, Analysis of Revenue Distribution" (2004) SERIS.

of the consortium's operations. It is not a matter simply of wording, but of content. Nevertheless, it is striking that recognition of the evident imbalance between the positions of the JOA parties is implicit in the name of the Canadian agreement.

(c) *Conclusion*

From a legal perspective, the name of an agreement is of fundamental importance, as it will inform any interpretation of its individual clauses. The name 'JOA' indicates a high degree of participation and collaboration between the parties. However, the reality is far from this: one party has sole control over the performance of operations (eg, in North American JOAs) and the remaining parties have no participation in – and may not even influence – such operations, lacking, for example, veto powers in the operating committee. On the other hand, the consequences of such sole performance are entirely shared, insofar as performance involves costs and liabilities. In other words, the word 'joint' refers to the burdens, and nothing else.

This book does not advocate the simple modification of the names of the agreements; this would not redress the imbalance, but would only remedy the disconnect between the name and the reality. Indeed, the current name has positive associations for non-operators, as it at least suggests they have a share in the decisions and performance of operations; and in case of litigation, the courts will focus not only on the wording of the agreement but also on actual industry practice, as this will help define the rights and duties involved.[125]

The issue with the name should be resolved once the provisions are balanced, as the definition of the agreement should match the reality of its content. But modification of the title alone will achieve nothing.[126] Revision of the content of the JOA to create a new and balanced agreement is the key to securing, not just the position of the non-operators, but ultimately the long-term survival of the consortium.

1.5 Conclusion

It is thus clear that the current JOAs are unbalanced. This imbalance creates uncertainty and reduces the efficiency of the consortium, preventing proper cooperation and the sharing of expertise and best practice. Under the traditional model, the participation of the non-operators is considered a burden for the consortium, and should thus be avoided. However, the real burden – the costs and liabilities – is fully shared. Consequently, these agreements present a biased notion of balance and fairness in relation to the commitments and participation of the parties.

As previously mentioned, many companies sign unbalanced agreements in order

---

125 Juris K Kaasen (n 91) p15.

126 "The combinations under review are generally called 'unincorporated joint ventures', 'joint operating agreements', or 'operating procedures.' The terminology varies from project to project and from country to country but the salient features are reasonably constant." James G Jackson, "Agency in Joint Operating Agreements and Joint Ventures", 1986 AMPLA Yearbook p239.

127 "Consequently, the standardised JOA defines to which extent an individual participant to the PL [Petroleum Licence] (and thus to the JOA) has sacrificed his autonomy on the altar of effective joint operations." Juris Knut Kaasen (n 91) p3.

to secure investments, even in the knowledge that they might have to deal with problems and uncertainty down the line.[127] However, the maturing of oil and gas regions could impose a radical change in the paradigm of the dominant operator. Smaller and medium-sized companies will be the new players in these regions, and they are likely to enjoy greater equality. If model forms are to fulfil their basic purpose – to meet the demands of the industry – balanced terms will be required to regulate these new relationships.

Furthermore, it is arguable that as long oil and gas exist there will be a necessity for JVs, as the industry must continue to manage uncertainty, notwithstanding that in certain cases some companies might prefer to proceed alone in specific projects from a cost, risk and benefit point of view.[128] It is not possible to eliminate all risks, but it is certainly possible to mitigate some of them. For example, in a mature province the geological risk might be reduced, but the fiscal risk will be even higher as the host government will be keen to maintain higher rates of revenue.

This book will analyse several JOAs in order to understand how each of them treats non-operators. Such a comparison will not only facilitate the exchange of best practices, but will also reveal the flaws in each model form. The ultimate aim is to suggest the key elements on which a new and balanced JOA might be founded – one which addresses the current uncertainties and offers a new paradigm for the future.

---

128 John R Reeves, J Matthem Thompson, "The Development of the Model Form Operating Agreement: An Interpretative Accounting" (2001) *Okla L Rev* p211, Alexander J Black, Hew R Dundas, "Joint Operating Agreement: an international comparison from petroleum Law" (1992) 8 *Journal of Natural Resources & Environmental Law* pp49–79.

Chapter 2: The relationship between the JOA parties

2.1 Parties

(a) *The operator and the non-operators*

There are two types of party to a JOA: the operator and non-operators. The operator is the leader of the JV, responsible for conducting daily operations on behalf of the consortium.[129] The operator is commonly the party with most rights and duties, and tends to hold the largest interest in the JV, as it is understood that the operator will require robust financial and technical resources to conduct such operations. Under the current JOAs, the operator is thus placed in a dominant position, as it is granted extensive rights and is subject to significant duties.

Non-operators conduct no operations themselves; their participation is restricted to financial contributions to enable the performance of such operations and eventually, if applicable, voting rights in relevant committees.[130] However, beyond this the role of non-operators is shrouded in uncertainty. Some JOA models strengthen their position by increasing their control of the joint operations,[131] while others arguably position the non-operators as mere observers of, or investors in, the same joint operations.[132] Nevertheless, no JOA affords the non-operators the degree of effective participation and collaboration in operations that the name of the models suggests; this discrepancy is analysed further in the following chapter.

The imbalance between the parties also affects their roles in the JOA, as the power resides exclusively on one side of the consortium, namely the sole operatorship of the operator. Peter Roberts recognises the fact that JOAs favour the operator's position:

> *One of the consequences to a party of being appointed as the operator is that the appointment as such gives that party the ability to better satisfy these desires, and so the real issue here relates to what provision can be made in favour of the other, non-operating parties.*[133]

129 See Chavez Golvala (n 6) p46, Claude Duval *et al* (n 122) pp289–291, Anthony Jennings (n 18) p24, Taylor and Tyne (n 54) pp1–5, Bernard Taverne (n 90) pp135–136.

130 See Terence Daintith *et al* (n 16), Peter Roberts (n 5) pp79–87, Scott Styles (n 14) p288.

131 "But non-operators are active investors in that they have an active say in the managing of the project through the JOC. The existence of the Opcom is one of the most significant differences between the typical UKCS JOA and US one based on AAPL Form 610." Scott Styles (n 14) p286.

132 "The role of non-operators in the alliance is one of non-operating, non-working, interest owners or, to put it more simply, the role of an investor." *Ibid.*

133 Peter Roberts (n 5) p95.

It is easy to understand the reasons for the different views and perspectives held by the operator and non-operator parties, as each one has a different role in the JV. The operator, as the manager of the JV,[134] desires more power to conduct the joint operations. On the other hand, the non-operators, as participants in the JV, desire more control over the joint operations.[135]

The disproportionality between these roles not only affects the balance of participation between the parties, but also segregates their positions in the JOA, ultimately increasing tension between them and providing ample grounds for dispute. In an ideal scenario, all parties would participate in the decision-making process and make an equitable – or at least proportionate – contribution in relation not only to the financial burden, but also to the performance of operations.

(b) Governmental participation

As previously mentioned, the JOA is usually between private parties, as this type of agreement relates to the horizontal relationship between the consortium parties. The state's participation is limited to certain approvals required in the host government contract, as the resources tend to belong to the host government. The terms of the JOA, as forming a private contractual arrangement, are not usually dictated by the host government, but may require approval to the extent that they affect certain strategic issues from the governmental perspective – for example, changes to the operatorship or a participating interest.

However, in certain jurisdictions (eg, Norway, Nigeria, Saudi Arabia, Iran and even the historical legislation in the UK relating to BNOC) state participation in oil and gas operations is required or allowed by law, and there may be an obligation to include the host government in the relevant JOA.[136] This participation can occur at an earlier or later stage. The former is likely to occur through a carried interest, and the latter once a commercial discovery has been made, as the NOC (except, perhaps, in the case of larger NOCs like Petrobras and Statoil) will be unwilling to share risk during the exploration phase.

In principle, when it decides to join the operations the NOC should be treated as a normal party to the JOA. The reality, however, is rather different: the NOC might seek a mechanism to avoid shouldering some or all of the massive costs involved (eg, by way of a carry), and the default provision might be far more difficult to enforce against a NOC, due to its relationship with the host government. On the other hand, having the NOC as co-venturer is arguably a positive thing, as the political risks might be reduced and it should be easier to obtain any additional permits or licences related to operations – for example, environmental consents and access to land and infrastructure.[137]

From this perspective, the Greenlandic JOA model will be analysed, which

134 Gerard MD Bean (n 16) pp161–175.
135 Sandy Shaw (n 16) pp21–22.
136 See Rajendra Ramlogan (n 105) pp279–284, Mirian Kene Omalu, Armando Zamora, "Key Issue in Mining Policy, A Brief Comparative Survey as a Background Study on the Reform of Mining Law", CEPMLP Paper No CP 9/98.
137 Peter Roberts (n 5) pp49–51.

expressly provides for the participation of the NOC as a party to the JOA; also, the Norwegian model form, where the NOC may or may not be a party to the JOA at the host government's discretion. However, although state participation adds an interesting perspective in that it produces an agreement with more than one strong party, the major focus of this book is the relationship between the private parties within the consortium.

(c) Conclusion

The JOA is primarily a commercial arrangement between private parties. Therefore, the parties are free to negotiate their agreement in accordance with their views and wishes. However, the parties are in an unequal position during the negotiating process. The standard model forms should thus strive to provide balance so as to mitigate the effects of these unequal bargaining positions and secure a high degree of participation by all parties.

Although it would seem only fair to expect a balanced standard form, this is not the case in practice. The roles of the parties are a natural consequence of the wider structural imbalance that characterises the industry. The operator, on one side of the consortium, has far too much to say and do and the non-operators, on the other side, too little.[138] This militates against the kind of cooperation and collaboration one might expect in any joint venture, and may ultimately lead to uncertainty, conflict and even litigation.[139] The current role of the operator should be distributed among the parties, so that a greater degree of consensus and participation is achieved across all the activities of the consortium. For that reason it is important to analyse JOAs which provide for direct state participation, as the state will naturally balance the terms of the agreement. The simplest example of this scenario is the Greenlandic JOA model form, as under this model the NOC will be the co-operator of the consortium and the host government will wish to ensure that extensive powers do not vest in one party alone.[140]

2.2 Relationship

The relationship between the parties is key in any JOA, as it will affect the rights and duties carefully negotiated and drafted in the agreement. It is thus vital to establish the relationship in clear terms and to understand the impact of the governing law on specific issues.[141] Lee Jones recognises this:

> *The parties to operating agreements usually desire a relation other than mining partnership or general partnership, and operating agreements frequently expressly*

---

138 See Chapter I, section 1.1(b).

139 Bernard Taverne refers to JOAs as 'co-operation agreements' and the JOA parties as 'co-operating parties'. Juris Knut Kaasen has a similar view: "The Production Licence (PL) constitutes the licence that is needed to carry out 'petroleum activities'. In practice, the PL is always granted to a group of companies, not to one single company. Obviously, these companies have to cooperate in order to pursue the rights granted by the licence. The legal framework for the cooperation is the JOA." Such references describe the ideal situation within the consortium; however, the reality is that 'cooperation' currently refers to the share of the burdens of the consortium rather than the performance of the operations. Bernard Taverne (n 90) p133, Juris K Kaasen (n 91) pp2–3.

140 Greenlandic JOA §3.1.2.

141 For the purposes of this analysis, the United Kingdom's legislation and jurisprudence will be considered.

provide that the parties do not intend to form a partnership of any type. Such a provision, while of value as indicating intention, is not legally controlling. If the relationship established by agreement essentially conforms to the partnership pattern, partnership law will govern, at least as to strangers, whatever may be the expressed intention of the parties. *It is of extreme importance, therefore, that the operating agreement contain terms and provisions which establish rights and duties between the parties inconsistent with the partnership relation.*[142] (emphasis added)

The most important issues which may be affected by national laws are highlighted in the following diagram:

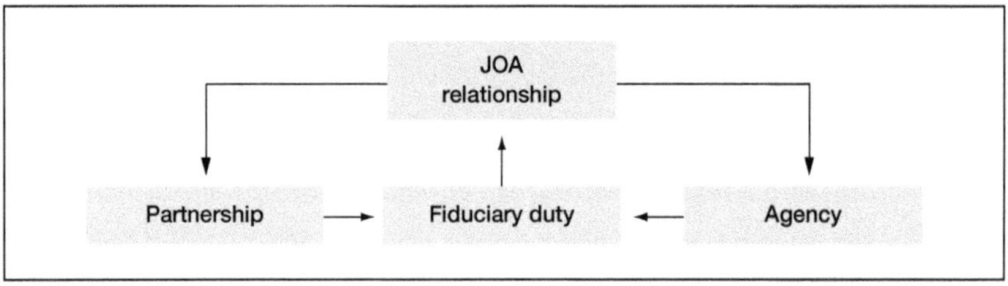

Any of the above arrangements could subject the parties to supplementary rights and duties, since they are governed not by the JOA, but rather by general legal provisions. Most of these obligations will principally fall on the operator, as it is responsible for conducting the joint operations.[143] In such cases, the definition of the relationship between the parties is likely to strengthen the protection of the non-operators. This book therefore analyses each of the issues that might affect the relationship of the parties, in order to determine their implications with regard to the rights and duties of non-operators. An in-depth analysis of these issues, however, is beyond the scope of this book; therefore, the focus will be on the key issues and the potential consequences for non-operators.

(a) *Partnership*

From a legal standpoint, the possibility that the JOA might be treated as a partnership is potentially troublesome for the contracting parties, as it might increase the costs and responsibilities of the parties by imposing additional tax and other liabilities, while at the same time reducing allowances.[144]

Anita Himebaugh describes the 'real' impact that tax applications can have on certain oil and gas operations as follows:

In 1981 the oil and gas industry paid in excess of $17 billion in federal income taxes and an additional $8 billion in windfall profits taxes. Obviously any energy company's great concern

---

142 Lee Jones, "Problems Presented by Joint Ownership of Oil, Gas and Other Minerals" (1953–1954) 32 *Tex L Rev* p717.

143 See Chapter 2, section 2.2(b).

144 For further information see Thomas P Briggs, Bruce N Lemons, "Basic principles of tax partnerships for oil and gas operations" (1991) 39 *Oil & Gas Tax Quarterly* pp428–484, David H Glusman, Gabriel Daniel Martin Ciociola, *Fiduciary Duties and Liabilities, Tax and Trust Accountant s Guide* (CCH, Chicago 2006), James M Boyle, Gary C Karch, Adam J Narot, "Alliances Not in Partnership or Corporate Form, Will you be my Partner? No Thanks" (1994) 72 *Taxes* p812.

is the specific tax treatment accorded its exploration and development arrangements.[145]

It is therefore crucial that all parties give careful thought to the structure of their arrangements; otherwise, the economics of the operation might be very different from what was initially expected. Tax, however, is not the only concern for the JOA parties: the way the agreement is structured might subject them to additional duties beyond those set out in the JOA.

A partnership structure might not benefit oil and gas operations. As a consequence, on one hand it is common for the JOA parties to avoid the kind of links that characterise a partnership, either directly or by implication.[146] On the other hand, there are undeniable similarities between a JOA and a partnership agreement. Peter Roberts illustrates the point as follows:

The JOA performs the same role between the parties as a partnership agreement performs between partners (although the JOA could go to some lengths to make it clear that it is not intended to be a partnership).[147]

Because this is a grey area, it is worth analysing the extent of these similarities.

As explained, the JOA does not exclusively regulate the relationship of the parties. The cases of *Adam v Newbigging*[148] and *Weiner v Harris*[149] demonstrated that the English courts will not always adhere strictly to the letter of the agreement, but will sometimes seek the spirit behind its scope and terms.[150]

An express exclusion cannot always forestall this issue. It is therefore important to analyse what the law requires for the creation of a partnership, so as to decide whether a JOA might be regarded as such.

Definition: Partnerships in the UK are regulated by the Partnership Act 1890.[151] Section 1(1) states that: "Partnership is the relation which subsists between persons carrying on a business in common with a view of profit."[152] Section 2 provides examples of what does not constitute a partnership:

(1) Joint property does not of itself create a partnership;

(2) Sharing gross returns does not of itself create a partnership;

(3) Sharing profits is prima facie evidence of a partnership, but does not of itself create a partnership.

Therefore, according to the act, the most important element in defining a partnership is the sharing of profits between two or more parties who work together

---

145 Anita Gefreh Himebaugh, "An Overview of Oil and Gas Contracts in the Williston Basin" (1983) 59 *North Dakota Law Review* p49.

146 AAPL JOA Form 810 §22.1; AAPL JOA Form 610 article IX; RMMLF JOA §16.2; AIPN JOA § 14.1; CAPL OP §1.05A; OGUK JOA §22.2; AMPLA JV §3.4 (c); AMPLA JOA §3.3 (f); Greenlandic JOA §12.2.1; Norwegian JOA definition 16.

147 Peter Roberts (n 5) p14.

148 *Adam v Newbigging* (1888) 13 App Cas 308 at 315.

149 *Weiner v Harris* [1910] 1 KB 285, per Cozens-Hardy MR at 290.

150 Lewis G Mosburg, "The joint operating agreement: partnership or not?" (1986) 4(2) *J Energy & Natural Resources*, p80.

151 See Frederick Pollock, *A Digest of the Law of Partnership: Incorporating the Partnership Act, 1980* (Law Publishers and Booksellers, London 1890).

152 The Canadian jurisdiction has a similar provision as it states in section 1(g) of the Partnership Act 2000 (Government of Alberta) that "'partnership' means the relationship that subsists between persons carrying on a business in common with a view to profit."

to develop a business. Importantly, neither cooperation *per se* nor the existence of joint property is conclusive evidence of a partnership. This definition will benefit the JOA parties, as they clearly have joint property but do not necessarily share in the profits, as is explained below.

Application to a JOA: A key factor in determining if a JOA is a partnership is the distinction between sharing profit and sharing gross revenues.[153] The JOA parties might argue that the JV is based on the sharing of gross revenues, as each party takes its own share of the production in kind and will deal with its own disposal in order to avoid any link with a share in the profits. In other words, the JOA parties will share not profits, but mainly gross revenues – which section 2 of the Partnership Act 1890 does not recognise as conclusive evidence of a partnership.

Mark Blackett-Ord mentions this particularity of oil and gas agreements when he says:

Their venture may not be intended to yield profit 'in common' as in the case of share farming (further discussed below) or some mining ventures or the profit-sharing may be of gross rather than net receipts.[154]

The JOA parties do not share profits as the product is not jointly marketed; rather, each party takes its share of the production independently. Peter Roberts also recognises the distinction:

In the JOA each party will from time to time contribute its PI-based share of the costs which are necessary to allow performance of the joint operations through the cash call or the invoice request provision, rather than there being an upfront pooling of capital contributions. The distribution which each party receives is one of its net petroleum entitlements in kind at the defined delivery point, rather than a share of profits of the business as a whole.[155]

Therefore, it is important to provide for the right to take in kind, and for the separate disposal of the natural resources produced, in order to avoid any connection to a share of the profits.[156]

However, if the JOA allows the operator to sell all of the shares of the production jointly, and then to distribute revenue among the parties, there is a greater chance that the enterprise will be considered a partnership – the parties would share profits rather than gross revenues.[157]

Other factors distinguish a JOA from a partnership:

- Carrying on a separate business in common – it can be argued that the JOA constitutes an agreement whereby each party has its own separate business with its own profits;[158] that is, the parties only carry out jointly certain phases of the project.[159] In other words, each participant will have a percentage of an undivided interest in the consortium, and as a consequence they will have separate rather than joint and several liability.[160]

153 Lewis Mosburg (n 150) pp80–84.
154 Mark Blackett-Ord, *Partnership Law* (3rd ed, TP, London 2007) p43.
155 Peter Roberts (n 5) p254.
156 Lewis Mosburg (n 150) p82.
157 See Peter Roberts (n 5) p252, Scott Styles (n 14) pp274–275, Taylor and Tyne (n 54) p25.
158 Lewis Mosburg (n 150) p81.
159 *Ibid.*

- Employees – as a partnership has legal capacity,[161] it can hire individuals directly in the name of the partnership. By contrast, the JV resulting from a JOA does not normally have legal capacity – only the operator can hire individuals to work directly in own its name (as operator personnel); or, these individuals can be seconded from the non-operators, but not in the name of the JV.
- Accounting – a partnership requires that the accounts show profits and losses; however, this is not normally the case within a JOA, albeit the operator will have kept accounts for the benefit of the parties. Australian case law specifically requires partnership accounting in order to establish a partnership.[162]
- Independent operations – this is probably the most significant distinction between a JOA and a partnership. The JOA allows operations by fewer than all the parties.[163] By contrast, independent operations are not permitted in a partnership.

The situation on the UK continental shelf is particularly awkward. Despite the fact that companies have been operating in offshore waters since 1964 (even earlier in the case of onshore operations – 1934),[164] no definitive decision has been taken by the English or Scottish courts as to the legal status of unincorporated joint ventures that would directly address the partnership issue.[165] However, several cases do recognise the existence of unincorporated joint ventures, which might give comfort to oil and gas operations – *Spree Engineering & Testing Ltd v O'Rourke Civil & Structural Engineering Ltd* in the High Court, and *Venture North Sea Gas Ltd v Nuon Exploration & Production UK Ltd* in the Commercial Court, among others.[166]

So what happens if a partnership is found to exist? It has been argued that the effects can be minimised, as partners are able to regulate their own liabilities by internal contractual arrangements. However, this will not affect third parties,[167] and the establishment of a partnership could raise other issues whose effects might be hard to mitigate, such as taxation,[168] agency[169] and fiduciary duties.

Scott Styles argues that the main impact of the judicial establishment of a partnership would be on taxation, and that other concerns could be fully mitigated

160 John F Curran, "American Tax Considerations in the Drafting of Canadian Joint Operating Agreements" (1970) 8 *Alberta Law Review* p204.

161 English law does not recognise a partnership as a legal entity, as Scottish law does. See Law Commission, Scottish Law Commission, *Partnership Law, A Joint Consultation Paper* (The Stationery Office, London 2000) pp6–7.

162 *Beckenham v Port Jackson and Manly Steamship Co* (1957) 57 SR (NSW) 403.

163 AAPL JOA Form 810 §18; AAPL JOA Form 610 article VI (B) (2); RMMLF JOA §9.3; AIPN JOA §7; CAPL OP §10; OGUK JOA §15; Greenlandic JOA §7; Norwegian JOA §18; AMPLA JOA §13.

164 Terence Daintith *et al* (n 16) pp1120–1123.

165 Lewis Mosburg (n 150) p80.

166 See *Spree Engineering & Testing Ltd v O'Rourke Civil & Structural Engineering Ltd*, unreported, 1999 WL 33453546 (High Court of Justice, Queen's Bench Division) in Scott Styles (n 14) p274, *Venture North Sea Gas Ltd v Nuon Exploration & Production UK Ltd* [2010] EWHC 204 (Comm) and *Shell Egypt West Manzala GMBH v Dana Gas Egypt Ltd (formerly Centurion Petroleum Corp)* [2010] EWHC 465 (Comm).

167 Taylor and Tyne (n 54) p15.

168 See Peter Roberts (n 5) p252, Scott Styles (n 14) pp273–277, Taylor and Tyne (n 54) p27.

169 See chapter 2, section 2.2(b).

by contractual arrangements.[170] This is certainly true as regards the parties' liabilities, but it is far less certain as regards fiduciary duty, as Mr Justice McWilliam observed in *Williams v Harris*: "The mere existence of a partnership creates a fiduciary relationship between the partners."[171] If a fiduciary relationship exists, then the rights and duties of the JOA parties might also change because additional duties might be imposed by general law, such as trust and loyalty: "Being in this position of trust, the partners are required not to abuse this trust and this duty between fiduciaries is the primary control of the partners' behaviour inter se."[172] The establishment of a partnership may strengthen the protection of the non-operators, since fiduciary duties will mainly be imposed on the operator.[173]

Conclusion: There are reasonably strong similarities between a partnership and a JOA.[174] The JOA parties are likely to exclude the existence of a partnership in their agreement, but to be effective, such exclusion must be consistent with the implementation of the agreement, and not just the wording.

The most effective way to achieve such an exclusion is to avoid any provision for, or reference to, the sharing of profits, so that the criteria of the Partnership Act 1890 are not satisfied.[175] If a partnership is found to exist, the parties can seek to reduce the impact by contractual arrangements, but it will be difficult to mitigate fully the implications relating to taxation, agency and fiduciary duties. Tax considerations are the most important implications of such a finding, as they might place an additional burden on the consortium;[176] but the addition of agency and fiduciary duties is also significant, as these might change the rights and duties carefully established in the JOA.

(b) Agency

Another important issue in the relationship between the JOA parties relates to the agency[177] status of the operator.[178] Without such status, the non-operators would

---

170 Scott Styles (n 14) p277. Scott Styles' perspective is followed by several authors, such as Sandy Shaw (n 16) p15 and Lewis Mosburg (n 150) pp80–84.

171 *Williams v Harris*, High Court, unreported, 15 January 1980 at p12 of the transcript. See also *Herlmore v Smith* (1886) 35 Ch D 436 at 444, *Meinhard v Salmon* (1928) 164 NE 545 at 546, Michael Twomey, *Partnership Law* (TP, London 2000) pp343–369.

172 Michael Twomey, *Partnership Law* (TP, London, 2000) p344.

173 "I therefore think that it is strongly arguable that a typical joint operating agreement does not constitute a partnership." Lewis Mosburg (n 150) p83.

174 "Partnership has been defined as a 'relation founded upon a contract between two or more persons to do business as individuals on joint, undivided account'. The similarity between this definition and the ordinary oil operating agreement is striking, to say the least." Thomas E Jenks, Lawence E Cohn, "The Taxation of Oil and Gas Partnerships" (1958) 27 *The George Washington Law Review* p34.

175 "So long as there is a division of the production in kind or for sale for the account of each individual co-owner in the organization (as opposed to a division or sale for the organization's joint account) the test of a joint profit is not met." John F Curran (n 160) p194.

176 For further information see John F Curran (n 160) p194, J E Gaughan, "Tax Warning to Oil and Gas operators" (1948–1949) 3 *Ark L Rev* p303, Kenneth E Barnhill Jr, "Taxation of Oil and Gas Operating Agreements, The Scope and Application of IT 3930" (1953–1954) 26 *Rocky Mountain Law Review* p133.

177 For further information about agency see Floyd Russell Mechem, *A treatise on the Law of Agency V2, Parts 1 and 2* (Callaghan and Company, Chicago 1914), FMB Reynolds, *Bowstead on Agency* (15th ed, Sweet & Maxwell, London 1985) and Roger Gresley Woodyatt, *The Law of Agency* (BiblioLife, London 2009).

178 See Gerard Bean (n 16) pp111–114, Taylor and Tyne (n 54) p10, Sandy Shaw (n 16) pp16–17, Peter Roberts (n 5).

retain too many rights of participation with regard to the conduct of operations. However, recognition of agency status can change the relationship of the parties, as further obligations may be imposed on the operator in its performance of operations. Such additional obligations would be a disadvantage for the operator in its dominant position in the JOA; indeed, some JOAs seek to provide for the express exclusion of agency.[179] The question then is, will the courts recognise such a provision? The answer lies in the legal definition of agency and the wider context of the JOA, as explained below.

Definition: The legal definition of 'agency' was established in English jurisprudence in the 18th century.[180] Its essence is described by F Bowstead as follows:

> *[T]he relationship which exists between two persons, one of whom expressly or impliedly consents that the other should represent him or act on his behalf, and the other of whom similarly consents to represent the former or so to act.*[181]

Thus, an agent is "A person duly authorised to act on behalf of another; or one whose unauthorised act has been duly ratified".[182]

Application to JOA: There is no doubt that a JOA includes two or more parties and one party acts on the behalf of others. But it might be argued that the consent of the principal is required to create the agency relationship, and that some JOAs expressly deny the existence of agency.[183] So, can it be said that some JOAs will not satisfy the basic criteria for establishing an agency relationship? The answer is that consent will always exist, either expressly[184] or implicitly, as the terms of the JOA models clearly stipulate that the operator will act on behalf of the other parties in order to perform the joint operations.[185] For example, the operator's powers to award contracts, to represent the consortium in dealings with government authorities and to market another party's production in the event of default, expressly demonstrate the authority given to the operator to conduct the joint operations on behalf of the non-operators.

The recognition of an agency relationship between the operator and non-operator was clearly noted in the most important oil and gas case decided in the Canadian courts – *Midcon Oil and Gas Ltd v New British Dominion Oil Co Ltd.*[186] As George Pellat observes:

179 "Joint operating agreements might deny that an agency relationship exists between the operator and non-operators, or attempt to provide for a limited agency in the operator, or they might simply be silent on this issue." James Jackson (n 126) p292.

180 For example, *Nicholson v Chapman* (1793) 2 H Bl 254 & 3 RR 374; *Pickering v Busk* (1812) 15 East 38, *Markwick v Hardingham* (1880) 15 Ch D 339, CA, *Sagal (t/a Bunz UK) v Atelier Bunz GmbH* [2008] EWHC 789 (Comm); *Temple Legal Protection Ltd v QBE Insurance (Europe) Ltd* [2008] EWHC 843 (Comm).

181 FMB Reynolds (n 177) p1.

182 "Evans on Agency" in Roger Gresley Woodyatt (n 177) p1.

183 "In *Markwick v Hardingham* (1880), 15 Ch D 339 CA, we find it laid down, that the relation of principal and agent requires the 'consensus' of both parties; and that such relation must be assented to either expressly, impliedly, or by subsequent ratification." Roger Gresley Woodyatt, *ibid* p1.

184 OGUK JOA § 6.5.8.

185 AAPL JOA Form 810 §5.1; AAPL JOA Form 610 article V (A); RMMLF JOA §4.1; CAPL OP §3.01; OGUK JOA §6.1 and 6.2; Norwegian JOA §3.1, 3.2 and 3.3; AMPLA JV & JOA § 3.3, 6.1, 7.1 and 7.2; AIPN JOA §4.2; Greenlandic JOA §3.2 and 3.3.

186 *Midcon Oil and Gas Ltd v New British Dominion Oil Co* [1958] SCR 314.

The Appellate Division admitted that the motive for promoting the new company was to enable New British to fulfil its agency responsibility under the agreement, that being to sell the gas as agent for Midcon.[187]

It can therefore be said that an agency relationship between the JOA parties will always exist, either expressly or implicitly, even if there is an express provision to the contrary (eg, a clause stating that "nothing in this agreement shall create an agency relationship between the parties,"[188] or describing the operator as an independent contractor[189]). In other words, the powers given to the operator are nothing more than ostensible authority to conduct the operations under any JOA.[190] Admittedly, JOAs provide for a different version of agency, as the operator will be agent and principal at the same time, but this will not affect the agency relationship between operator and non-operators.[191]

There is compelling evidence that the operator acts as an agent of the JOA parties. On the other hand, it is arguable that one essential right of an agent – remuneration – is absent from a JOA, since it is a general principle of JOAs that the operator shall not make profits, nor suffer losses, from its operations.[192] However, in practice the operator does enjoy benefits[193] from its position (including receiving overhead charges) and does not suffer losses[194] from conducting the joint operations; and this also indicates the existence of an agency relationship.[195]

If an agency does exist, this might raise issues regarding third-party liability and fiduciary duties owed by the operator to the non-operators.[196] The former will vary considerably depending on whether or not the agency status is disclosed, that is, whether the operator expressly acts in its own name or on the consortium's behalf.[197] This becomes important if a non-operator sues or is sued in relation to a contract signed by the operator on behalf of the consortium. However, such distinctions will be covered in a specific clause relating to the liabilities of the parties. The latter issue – fiduciary duties – will be examined in the next section.

If the operator expressly contracts with a third party as the agent of all the parties

---

187 George R Pellatt, "The Fiduciary Duty in Oil and Gas Joint Operating Agreements, Midcon Re-Examined" (1967–1969) 3 *U Brit Colum L Rev* p199.

188 AAPL JOA Form 810; CAPL OP § 1.5 (A); AMPLA JV § 3.4 (c); AMPLA JOA § 3.3 (f); Greenlandic JV § 12.2.1, § 5.1; AIPN JOA § 14.1.

189 CAPL OP §3.03.

190 James G Jackson (n 126) pp255–263.

191 See Scott Styles (n 14) p281, Taylor and Tyne (n 54) p10, Sandy Shaw (n 16) p16, Terence Daintith *et al* (n 16) pp1137–1139.

192 See AIPN JOA § 4.2; CAPL JOA §5.01; OGUK JOA § 6.2.2 (d); Greenlandic JOA § 3.2; Norwegian JOA§ 3.1. For further information see Peter Roberts (n 5) p79, Scott Styles (n 14) pp277–278.

193 When the operator accepts this role, he must not make profit nor suffer loss from it. Why, then, does the operator accepts this role? The main reason is that by acting as the operator of the JV, the operator is in the best position to determine the overall operations of the JV. There are other advantages such as: a) a better reputation within the government which can help in a future licence round, b) asset value if it is possible to transfer this role whenever a transfer of its interest might occur, and c) the operator might have more access to data and information regarding the joint operations, unless it is provided that all parties have full access. For further information see Peter Roberts (n 5) pp79–80, Scott Styles (n 14) pp277–278.

194 See Chapter 3, section 3.2(b).

195 *Adamson v Jarvis* (1827), 4 Bing. 6; *Whitehead v Izod* (1867), LR 2 CP 228 and *Campbell v Larkworhty* (1893), 9 TLR, 528.

196 Taylor and Tyne (n 54) pp10–11.

197 James G Jackson (n 126 pp246–254.

to the JOA – irrespective of whether the JOA says anything about agency capacity – this will put the matter beyond doubt.

There is no consistency among the JOA models with regard to recognition of the existence of agency status as between operator and non-operators. The British model recognises agency,[198] while others, such as the Australian, American, Canadian, Greenlandic, and International models, deny its existence altogether (although they might empower the operator to represent the other parties).[199] Still others, like the Norwegian model, fail to address the issue.[200]

The English courts will likely recognise the operator as an agent of the JV. First, the British JOA model is clear in establishing the operator as an agent of the contracting parties. Second, even if there were a provision denying the existence of an agency relationship, the English courts would look beyond the wording of the contract to focus on the nature of the relationship itself.[201]

The Court of Appeal recognised this situation in *Commissioners of Customs and Excise v Pools Finance (1937) Ltd*:

> *Take now R. II. It purports to make the collector the agent of the investors and not the agent of the promoters. It says that "the collector acts solely for his clients". This rule again goes too far. The true relationship of the parties is to be discovered from the facts, not from this clause ... The rule contradicts the facts and is to that extent invalid. This is no new doctrine. In life, actions speak louder than words. So they do in law ... So, here, these conditions cannot under the cloak of contract, be allowed to speak that which is false. They cannot assert that black is white and expect the courts to believe it. The courts do not willingly go behind the conditions of a contract in this way. They would far rather reconcile the conditions with the transaction as a whole than reject them altogether. But there does sometimes come a point when they must be overridden.*[202]

Thus, the fact that the operator will perform operations on behalf of the consortium is sufficient to establish the operator as an agent for the consortium,[203] regardless of any provisions to the contrary. An exclusion clause in the agreement will not be upheld in court as reality will prevail over wording.[204] The operator's agency is inevitable; without it, performance of the operations on behalf of another party would be impossible. Indeed, the party so performing could not legitimately be called the operator.

Conclusion: The JOA parties might avoid the establishment of a partnership if they draft their agreement in such a way as to exclude the possibility of a share of profits. Agency, however, is another matter: the JOA parties cannot avoid the establishment

---

198 OGUK JOA § 6.5.8.

199 For example, CAPL OP § 1.5 (A); Greenlandic JV § 12.2.1, § 5.1; AMPLA JOA § 6.1; AAPL Form 610 (2015) article V (A).

200 AMPLA JV § 3.4 (c); AMPLA JOA § 3.3 (f); AAPL JOA Form 810; CAPL OP § 1.5 (A); Greenlandic JV § 12.2.1, § 5.1; AIPN JOA § 14.1.

201 See note 165.

202 *Commissioners of Customs and Excise v Pools Finance (1937) Ltd* [1952] I All ER 775.

203 *Halsbury's Laws of England* (4th ed) Vol 1 para 701.

204 See *Garnac Grain Co, Inc v HMF Faure and Fairclough Ltd & Bunge Corporation* [1967] 2 All ER 353, *Commissioners of Customs and Excise v Pools Finance (1937) Ltd* [1952] I All ER 775, *Weiner v Harris* [1910] 1 KB 285, *Pickering v Busk* (1812) 15 East 38.

of an agency arrangement unless they change the structure of the current model forms. The current JOAs are so structured as to enable one party to act on behalf of the others, which is the basic requirement for agency to exist.[205] Exceptionally, the JOA parties might avoid an agency between themselves by delegating the operatorship to a third party, or by sharing it with a company partly composed of the JOA parties. This kind of balanced agreement might circumvent the agency issue, as all parties would conduct the joint operations rather than just one. However, all of the JOAs analysed in this book provide for a single party to be the operator. The Greenlandic JOA does refer to a co-operator (ie, the NOC), but only for the development phase.

Once agency is established, it will affect the non-operators in two ways. The first relates to the possibility that a third party might seek to enforce a contract not just against the operator but also against the non-operators. When this arises, the non-operator will seek to rely on the distinction between disclosed and undisclosed agency – more on this in Chapter 3.[206] The second, more positive effect of agency status is that any agent must act diligently and in a safe and prudent manner on behalf of the other parties.[207] That is to say, the operator has a number of fiduciary duties towards the non-operators, including:[208]

- not to allow its interests to conflict with those of its principal;
- to make full disclosure;
- not to take advantage of its position;
- not to take bribes or secret commissions;
- to act in good faith;
- to keep accounts;
- to maintain confidentiality; and
- not to delegate its position.[209]

In short, the operator has to conduct the joint operations in a safe, diligent and prudent manner in accordance with good oilfield practice so as to maintain the high standards of the operations.[210]

It can be argued, then, that an agency arrangement will exist in all JOAs so long as the main party, the operator, performs the operations on behalf of the other

205 See Roger G Woodyatt (n 177) p4.

206 For further information regarding disclosed or undisclosed agency, see Floyd Russel Mechem, *A Treatise On the Law of Agency V2, Part 1* (2nd ed, Callagham Company, Chicago 1914) pp1706–1772, Gerard M D Bean, "Duties of disclosure and confidentiality in JOAs" (1993) 11 *Journal Energy & Natural Resources Law* pp75–89.

207 See also Roger G Woodyatt (n 177), pp38–50, Deborah A DeMott, *Fiduciary Obligation, Agency and Partnership, Duties in Ongoing Business Relationships* (West Group, St. Paul 1991) pp67–346.

208 "The distinguishing obligation of a fiduciary is the obligation of loyalty. The principal is entitled to the single-minded loyalty of the fiduciary. This core liability has several facets. A fiduciary must act in good faith; he must not make profit out of his trust; he must not place himself in a position where his duty and his interest may conflict; he may not act for his own benefit or for the benefit of a third person without the informed consent of his principal. This is not intended to be an exhaustive list... They are the defining characteristics of the fiduciary." *Bristol & West BS v Mathew* [1998] Ch1, 18.

209 See FMB Reynolds (n 177) pp137–204, Roderick Munday, *Agency, Law and Principles* (OUP, Oxford 2010) pp149–185.

210 AIPN JOA § 4.2 (A) (B) (2); AMPLA JV § 1.1 (Good Australian Mining Practice); OGUK JOA § 6.2.2(a) (b); AAPL JOA 810 § 5.1., 5.2; Greenlandic JOA §3.3.2; CAPL OP § 3.04; Norwegian JOA§ 11.1.

parties; and that therefore a fiduciary duty will exist.[211] Indeed, the existence of fiduciary duty is a natural consequence of both partnership and agency, as will be explained below.[212]

(c) *Fiduciary duty*

Fiduciary duty is common to several types of association, as described by Peter Graham:

> *Fiduciary relationships and the duties which they impose are of many kinds. In the commercial world it is well established that fiduciary relationships exist between partners, between an agent and his principal and between directors of a company and the company itself.*[213]

The JOA is no exception. In fact, fiduciary duty is one of the most important concerns (after taxation) for the operator because of the additional burden placed upon it in the conduct of its function in the JOA.[214] As explained, the parties might avoid characterisation of the arrangement as a partnership – which would imply fiduciary duties from one partner to another. However, the agency relationship that necessarily exists within the current structure of the JOA, as between operator and non-operators, will certainly lead to a fiduciary relationship. This is logical – an agent cannot enjoy unfettered performance of its activities, as it is representing someone else's interests. The agent must comply with certain rules and procedures to maintain a satisfactory level of performance.

So if a fiduciary duties always exist under current JOAs, what is the ultimate consequence? How will it affect the relationship of the parties? In order to answer these questions, it is necessary first to analyse the definition of fiduciary duty and then to consider the possible implications for the JOA.

Definition: 'Fiduciary duty' was defined by Chief Justice Gibbs in *Hospital Products Ltd v United States Surgical Corp,*[215] as follows:

> *A fiduciary relationship exists where the facts of the case in hand establish that in a particular matter a person has undertaken to act in the interests of another and not one's own.*[216]

It is a fairly broad definition as it deals not only with the action performed on behalf of someone else, but the ability to affect the interests of the other party. In other words, fiduciary duty "contemplates a duality of 'interests', one being the interest of the person on whose behalf the fiduciary is acting and the other being the personal interest of the fiduciary himself."[217]

---

211 Deborah A DeMott (n 207) pp67–346.

212 *Ibid.*

213 Peter L Graham (Rev) *"Fiduciary obligations and joint ventures: the collaborative fiduciary relationship" ICCLR* p397.

214 For further information on fiduciary duties, see Christian D Rahaim, *The Fiduciary, An In-depth Guide to Fiduciary Duties – From Studebaker from Enron* (iUniverse, New York 2005) pp52–61, David H Glusman, Gabriel Daniel Martin Ciociola, *Fiduciary Duties and Liabilities, Tax and Trust Accountant s Guide* (CCH, Chicago 2006).

215 *American Hospital Supply Corp v Hospital Products Ltd,* 780 F 2d 589 (7th Cir 1986).

216 *Ibid.*

217 George R Pellatt (n 187) p190.

Once a fiduciary duty is established, it will raise a duty of care and loyalty between the parties, as described by Mr Justice Rand in *Midcon Oil & Gas Ltd v New British Dominion Oil*:

> *The fiduciary relationship is that of a trust in one who is to act in relation to the beneficial interest of another. It creates a standard of loyalty that calls for a refined sensibility to duty, the exclusion of all personal advantage and the total avoidance of any personal involvement in the interest being served or protected, a sense of obligation not always appreciated by those who enter upon it.*[218]

It is important to analyse the application of the concept within the JOA, as it will create duties for operator and non-operators alike.

Application to a JOA: The relationship between the JOA parties, especially the operator to the others, may fit within the legal definition of fiduciary duty.[219] D MacWilliam describes this aspect of the relationship between operator and non-operators as follows: "Where in a joint venture in the petroleum industry one person undertakes to act in the interests of another a fiduciary duty may arise."[220]

However, this issue remains controversial, both in academia and in legal practice, and there is no clear consensus on the matter. Peter Roberts warns that the parties should take special care when drafting the JOA,[221] as if fiduciary duties are established it will certainly affect the rights and duties carefully negotiated in the JOA.

It is thus helpful to analyse the standard JOA provisions in order to understand the extent to which fiduciary duties might apply and how this might affect non-operators. The following table provides some examples of JOA terms to illustrate whether or not fiduciary duty might apply in individual cases.[222]

It can be seen from the table below that the terms chosen by the parties to regulate their relationship can strengthen or weaken the connection between a JOA and a fiduciary duty.[223] DJ Gately made the point in referring to the decision in *United Dominions Corporation Ltd v Brian Pty Ltd*, as follows:

> *The most that can be said is that whether or not the relationship between joint venturers is fiduciary will depend upon the form which the particular joint venture takes and upon the content of the obligations which the parties to it have undertaken.*[224]

---

218 *Midcon Oil & Gas Ltd v New British Dominion Oil* [1958] SCR 335.

219 For further information about the relationship between fiduciary duty and the JOA see Bryan Clark, "Fiduciary relationships under the Joint Operating Agreement" (1999) 20 (6) *BLR* pp150–153, Ernest E Smith, "Duties and Obligations Owed by an operator to Nonoperators' Investors, and Other Interest Owners" (1986) 32 RMMLF 12, Z Gounari, "Duties and Liabilities of the operator under UK Oil and Gas Joint Operating Agreements: Is the operator a Fiduciary?" [2003] *OGEL*, Peter Roberts, "Fault lines in the joint operating agreement: fiduciary duties" (2008) 6 *IELR* pp218, 222, 362–363, Gerard MD Bean, "The operator as a Manager: a new fiduciary duty" (1993) JBL pp24–35.

220 DA McWilliam, "Fiduciary Relationships in Oil and Gas Joint Ventures" (1970) 8 *Alberta Law Review* p233.

221 Peter Roberts (n 5) Appendix F.

222 Peter Roberts (n 5) Appendix F.

223 See also *Kelly v Cooper* [1993] AC 205, per Lord Browne-Wilkinson at 215.

224 DJ Gately, "The Unincorporated Joint Venture, A Fiduciary Relationship?" 5(1) *AMPLA Bulletin* 11, referring to the decision in *United Dominions Corporation Ltd v Brian Pty Ltd* (1985) 59 ALJR 679.

Standard JOA provision/issue	Supporting existence of fiduciary duty	Negating existence of a fiduciary duty
Conduct of operations	If the operator can act freely, with no – or with only minor – control by the other parties, this will favour the existence of a fiduciary duty. The North American JOA models are great examples, as they treat non-operators as mere investors, with few opportunities to participate in decisions of the consortium.	If non-operators can effectively participate in the conduct of operations, such as through an operating committee (eg, as in the International, Australian, Norwegian, Greenlandic and British JOA models), this may not favour the existence of a fiduciary duty.
Mutual interest	The fact that the parties are jointly engaged in the JV might constitute a basis for the existence of a fiduciary duty.	On the other hand, it could be argued that each party has its own business inside the JV (including the power to dispose of its own share of production, if applicable).
Limitation of operator's liability to other parties	This provision favours the existence of a fiduciary duty, as commonly the operator shall not be 100% liable for its actions. This clause indicates an agency relationship between the parties, which could lead to a fiduciary duty (see below).	
Operator cannot make a profit	This principle confirms the operator's agency status, as an agent cannot make secret profits. It could thus lead to a fiduciary duty.	

continued on next page

Standard JOA provision/issue	Supporting existence of fiduciary duty	Negating existence of a fiduciary duty
Operator acts on behalf of all JOA parties	This provision favours the establishment of a fiduciary duty, as the operator is acting as an agent of the JV.	There is no mutual agency, as is required in a partnership. It could thus be argued that this provision denies the existence of a partnership, which could lead to a fiduciary duty (see below).
Partnership	If a partnership is established, this also leads to a fiduciary duty.	
Sole risk	A fiduciary duty might be established between co-venturers with regard to the disclosure of information and the costs of exercising the buy-back provision.	As this provision does not exist in a partnership relationship, it arguably does not favour the existence of a partnership and consequently a fiduciary duty.

The stronger the operator's position, the more likely it is that a fiduciary duty exists. Peter Graham recognises this situation as follows:

Mr Bean analyses the nature of joint ventures, with particular reference to joint operating agreements, with great clarity. He argues that a joint operating agreement gives rise to a vertical fiduciary relationship between the operator and the joint venturers and a horizontal fiduciary relationship between the joint venturers themselves. He goes on to argue that although it is possible to contract out of a fiduciary relationship by including appropriate wording in the contract, a generally worded exclusion clause is unlikely to be effective in the light of the contra proferentem rule. However, it may be that the trend, at least in some jurisdictions, is not to recognise a fiduciary relationship where the parties are of equal bargaining strength.[225]

The approach adopted by the various the JOAs differs from one to another. There is a clear exclusion of fiduciary duty in the majority of the JOA models (eg, the International, American, Australian, and British models).[226] The question is, to what extent such an approach will affect the existence of a fiduciary duty. Exclusion clauses

225 Peter L Graham (n 213) p397.
226 AAPL JOA Form 810 §5.1; AIPN JOA §14.1; AMPLA JV §3.5 (d); AMPLA JOA § 3.4 (d); CAPL JOA §1.05A.
227 See Chapter 1.

are likely to have different effects in North American jurisdictions[227] compared to, for example, the UK, Norway, and Greenland, because the operator in North American models can act more freely, with no effective control by the non-operators.[228] The remaining models provide rather more control to the non-operators, for example by the creation of operating committees (Opcoms), sub-committees, work plans and budgets, and procurement systems. In other words, while the American and Canadian models position the non-operators as mere investors, which raises concerns with regard to fiduciary duty, this is less true of the other models.

The American,[229] Australian[230] and Canadian[231] courts have already recognised the existence of a fiduciary duty for mining and oil and gas operations in their own jurisdictions, but there is no jurisprudence on the issue in the English courts. Nevertheless, the English courts are arguably less likely to recognise such a duty, due to the combination of a clear exclusion in the British model and the fact that the non-operators can more easily control the joint operations. The North American courts are thus more likely to recognise fiduciary duty than the British courts.[232] That said, it is impossible to discount completely the possibility of a fiduciary duty arising from the operator's agency status, which exists in all JOAs.

As George Pellat observes, "Having then defined a 'fiduciary' it is necessary to define his duty to complete the identity of the concept."[233] Once a fiduciary duty has been established, all parties must act in good faith and shall follow the 'prudent man' rule.[234] Most JOAs already provide for performance of operations in a diligent and prudent manner, and in accordance with good oilfield practice. The distinction lies in the legal basis for each obligation; the latter is derived from the contract (the JOA) while the former is derived from the legal system. The fiduciary duty thus increases the degree of diligence required. However, the key distinction of the fiduciary duty is the obligation of loyalty between the parties, as observed in *Bristol & West Building Society v Mathew*.[235] The Norwegian and Greenlandic models are less concerned with this issue as good faith principles are recognised in their civil law codes.

Given the manager status of the operator, a fiduciary duty would normally exist between the operator and the non-operators. However, the non-operators might owe some fiduciary duty to the operator. This duty is less certain, but arguably when the JOA establishes an Opcom, the non-operators owe a fiduciary duty when voting.[236] Do the parties in the Opcom vote for their own direct benefit or for that of the

---

228 See also Richard James, "Kansas Oil and Gas Law: Defining the Duty between Participants in a Joint Operating Agreement" (1999–2000) 39 *Washburn LJ* pp128–142, Alastair R Lucas, "Canada – Alberta – oil and gas – fiduciary duties – joint operating agreements" (1994) 12(3) *JERL* pp362–363.

229 *Amoco Production Co v Wilson,* 976 P2d 941, *Frankfort Oil Company v Snakard* 279 F 2d at 443 (10th Cir 1960), *Andrau v Michigan Wisconsin Pipe Line Co* 712 P 2d 372 at 376 (Wyo 1986), *Norman v Apache,* 19 F 3d 1017 at 1024 (10th Cir 1994), *Oklahoma Co v O'Neil,* 333 P 2d 534 (Okla 1958).

230 *Pacific Coal p/l v Idemitsu Queensland p/l and ors* BC9202590, *Noranda Australia Ltd v Lachlan Resources NL* [1988] 12 NSWLR 1 at 17.

231 *Midcon Oil and Gas Ltd v New British Dominion Oil Co* [1958] SCR 314. See other Canadian cases: *Bank of Nova Scotia v Société Générale* (Canada) (1988) 87 AR 133; 58 Alta LR (2d) 193 (Alberta, CA); *Luscar Ltd v Pembia Resources Ltd* (1995) 24 Alta LR (3d) 305; [1995] 2 WW153 (Alberta, CA).

232 Scott Styles (n 14) pp287–288.

233 George R Pellatt (n 187) p190.

234 See Christian D Rahaim (n 214) pp52–61 , Gary B Conine, "Prudent operator standard: applications beyond the oil and gas lease" (2001) 41 *Natural Resources Journal* pp23–76.

235 *Bristol & West BS v Mathew* [1998] Ch1, 18.

consortium? There is no straightforward answer. Sometimes, a party's private interest might also be to the overall benefit of the consortium (eg, greater efficiency); at other times these interests may conflict (eg, financial problems, strategic priorities).[237] It is thus possible to suggest that fiduciary duties in the Opcom might exist to the extent that the petroleum title is not at risk; otherwise, the parties will have the right to express their own views on the success of the consortium. This issue goes back to the nature of the JOA, which is commonly an unincorporated JV in which each participant remains separate and distinct – while they have joined forces, they are not a single unit. Nevertheless, the fiduciary duty will primarily rest with the operator as it clearly acts on behalf of the non-operators.

Conclusion: The connection between the JOA structure and fiduciary duty is evident, even if some models do not acknowledge the fact. Once a fiduciary duty is recognised, the operator may become subject to higher performance standards and its duties will increase; ultimately, this might even affect the voting procedures in the Opcom. If a fiduciary duty is breached,[238] the party in breach must compensate the other parties for their losses,[239] and might even lose its position as the operator of the JV (where applicable).[240] D MacWilliam recognises this situation as follows:

> *If a person who undertakes to act in the interests of another person breaches his duty of undivided loyalty to that person by failing to disregard his own interests in exercising his fiduciary duty, he must account to the beneficiary for any benefit gained by him from such a breach. He must give to the beneficiary any profit resulting from this breach of duty.*[241]

The majority of courts will likely follow the principle described by Lord Russell of Killowen in *Regal (Hastings) Ltd v Gulliver*:

> *The rule of equity which insists on those, who by the use of a fiduciary position make a profit, being liable to account for that profit, in no way depends upon fraud or absence of bona fides; or upon such questions or considerations as whether the profit would or should otherwise have gone to the plaintiff, or whether the profiteer was under a duty to obtain the source of the profit for the plaintiff... or whether the plaintiff has, in fact, been damaged or benefited by his action. The liability arises from the mere fact of a profit having in the stated circumstances, been made.*[242]

This situation favours non-operators, as the operator's status as manager of the JV attracts the majority of the obligations. The role of the non-operators is similar in some ways to that of minority shareholders, with the operator playing a similar role

---

236 "The role of the non-operator is largely passive with the result that there is both less need and less scope for the imposition of fiduciary obligations upon a non-operator than upon the operator. One important issue which may however arise in practice is whether or not a non-operator is subject to any fiduciary duties when voting at the operating committee." Taylor and Tyne (n 54) p29.

237 For further information about this issue see Gerard MD Bean (n 16) pp176–208.

238 DA MacWilliam, "Fiduciary Relationships in Oil and Gas Joint Ventures" (1970) 8 *Alberta Law Review* p249.

239 *Ibid.*

240 For further information see Matthew Conaglen, *Fiduciary Loyalty, Protecting the Due Performance of Non-Fiduciary Duties* (Hart, Portland 2010) pp76–104, Andrew Stafford QC, Stuart Ritchie, *Fiduciary Duties, Directors and Employees* (Jordan, Bristol 2008) pp5–79.

241 DA MacWilliam (n 238) p235.

242 *Regal (Hastings) Ltd v Gulliver* [1942] 1 ALL ER 379 at 386.

to a company director. There is little doubt that a director owes a fiduciary duty to a company. Likewise, the operator to a JOA, albeit some model forms reduce the likelihood of the existence of fiduciary duties by increasing the participation of non-operators.

The potential existence of a fiduciary duty is a serious concern for the operator as it is likeliest in the current JOA model forms. Some jurisdictions might be more reluctant than others to recognise fiduciary duties, but to the extent that the operator acts as an agent of the consortium, it is difficult to eliminate fiduciary duties altogether. If the parties wish to minimise their impact, they must frame the JOA so as to ensure that operations are not conducted by a single party.

2.3 Conclusion

The relationship between the parties is crucial, as it can affect the rights and duties carefully drafted in the JOA.

From the factors analysed above (which are commonly external to the JOA) it can be said that partnership is of least concern, followed by agency and fiduciary duty, which are the more pressing issues. The JVs established under the current JOAs are unlikely to be considered partnerships under the Partnership Act 1890, as they commonly provide for separate disposition of production – the parties can avoid the presumption in favour of partnership which arises from sharing profits. The agency concern is directly connected to fiduciary duty, one effectively leading to the other. The current JOAs cannot avoid the existence of an agency relationship as they are structured so that that the stronger party – the operator – will conduct operations on behalf of the remaining parties to the consortium. So long as the operator retains this authority, there is a strong presumption that it will owe a fiduciary duty to the non-operators. As a result, the standard of performance required will necessarily be increased, as any agency relationship will require a higher degree of diligence and prudence than normal. Ultimately, this has implications for all parties in the Opcom, but it is unlikely to affect non-operators as much as the operator.

The stronger position of the operator in the JOA is likely to increase its duties, as the non-operators will have a lesser degree of participation in the conduct of the joint operations. This is the view of Scott Styles, as quoted by George Pellat:

> *What are the usual fiduciary resolutions? They include the relation of trustee and beneficiary, guardian and ward, agent and principal, attorney and client, executor and administrator, legatees and next of kin of the decedent. The directors and officers of a corporation are in a fiduciary relation to the corporation, and to some extent at least to the shareholders. In a partnership each partner is in a fiduciary relation to the others, since, although he has his own interests to look after, he also has the power and the duty to look after the interest of others. Some fiduciary relationships are undoubtedly more intense than others. The greater the independent authority to be exercised by the fiduciary, the greater the scope (application) of his fiduciary duty.*[243]

That said, the delegation of the operatorship to a third party or to a joint authority would remove, or at least minimise, the implications of fiduciary duties.

243 George R Pellatt (n 187) p190.

There are ways in which the JOA parties can reduce the possible impact of the law on partnership, agency and fiduciary duty, but the current structures do not make this easy. A new approach to the structure of the JOA would be required, where all parties can actively participate in the conduct of the joint operations. This would mitigate not only these concerns, but also the uncertainties inherent in the unbalanced allocation of participation in the conduct of operations, and the sharing of costs and liabilities.

To sum up, an analysis of the issues behind the relationship between the parties is crucial to an understanding of the problems within the relationship itself. The next chapter will analyse in detail the difficulties that arise from the position that each party occupies within the JOA.

Chapter 3: Non-operators' concerns

Debate about the different roles of the JOA parties started with the early editions of JOA model forms and continues today. The operator conducts the joint operations and the non-operators contribute to the costs, so it is natural to expect different perspectives within the consortium.[244] The operator will want greater authority to perform the joint operations, while the non-operators will want more control over the conduct of operations and a greater degree of participation overall.

When the operator's dominance precludes any real participation by the non-operators, several concerns emerge from this unbalanced relationship. The most critical of these for non-operators are in two areas: control of operations and remedies. This chapter examines the means by which each of the standard JOA models addresses these concerns.

3.1 Control of operations[245]

The non-operators will inevitably have concerns about the control of operations, since this is the exclusive preserve of the operator, which conducts the joint operations on behalf of all the JOA parties. Sandy Shaw describes the position as follows:

> *Having determined the relationship of the parties, their relative interests and the appointment of the Operator to act on their behalf, the next major JOA concern is administrative provisions for the handling of operations.*[246]

All non-operators, therefore – whether passive or proactive – will be keen to control the joint operations to ensure that they are being carried out diligently, efficiently and in the best interests of the JV.

Peter Roberts explains the importance of the control of operations for non-operators as follows:

> *The non-operating parties will wish to secure a fair measure of control over the operator's conduct of the joint operations, in order to ensure that such conduct is exercised in a prudent manner. This could be achieved through a package of provisions relating, for example, to: the operator's obligation to obtain the non-operating parties' consensus at the time of setting any relevant WP&B, the securing of ongoing AFE approvals, control of the award of all forms of contract for the conduct of the joint*

244 "The differences in expectation between the operator and the non-operating parties, and how those expectations must be reconciled in order to produce a workable JOA." Peter Roberts (n 5) p95.

245 Michael PG Taylor, Sally M Tyne (n 54) chapter 2.

246 Sandy Shaw (n 16) p18.

operations, a voting mechanism at the OpCom which gives the non-operating parties the ability to influence the execution of the joint operations.[247]

The control of operations has its foundations in the principle that the operator should act as a prudent, diligent and reasonable operator.[248]

As discussed, non-operators have limited, if any, opportunities to participate in the conduct of the joint operations.[249] The non-operators have much less to say[250] because the operator commonly has the largest interest[251] and the strongest position in the JV, and can therefore secure better terms (including overall control of the joint operations) during the negotiation process.[252]

Control of operations might be the sole route through which non-operators can achieve a degree of participation in the performance of the joint operations, and mitigate the dominance of the operator. Arguably, control of operations is at once a basic duty for the operator and a fundamental right for the non-operators so that they can verify that the operator is conducting joint operations as diligently, reasonably and prudently as it ought to be.

Several mechanisms are available to the non-operators for control of the joint operations. For the purposes of this book, however, the focus is on information, the Opcom and costs and expenditures.[253] Exclusive operations (ie, sole risk and non-consent clauses) are also available, but their complexity puts them beyond the scope of this book.[254]

(a) Information

It is not possible for the non-operators to address the issue of control of operations if they do not first have access to the information and data produced by or originating from the JV.[255]

As the operator acts on the behalf of all JOA parties, its duties include reporting to the non-operators on the overall conduct of the joint operations. Scott Styles refers to the importance of this duty as follows:

As the operator is very much in control of day-to-day operations, one of his major duties

---

247 Peter Roberts (n 5) pp244–245.

248 This principle is well established in the oil and gas industry. See Bernard Taverne (n 90) p136, Sandy Shaw (n 16) p16, Scott Styles (n 14) pp278–279, Peter Roberts (n 5) pp82–86.

249 See Chapter I, section 1.1(b).

250 *Ibid.*

251 *Ibid.*

252 Kenneth Mildwaters reminds us that exceptions do exist: "It is not always the case that the operator has the largest interest. The operator of the Ninian field development in the East Shetland basin of the United Kingdom Continental Shelf, for example, has a smaller Interest than a number of the other Participants." Kenneth C Mildwaters (n 16) p427.

253 Peter Roberts (n 5) p244.

254 For further information see Taylor and Tyne (n 54), Sandy Shaw (n 16) p21, Terence Daintith *et al* (n 16) p1140, Kenneth C Mildwaters (n 16) p427, Ernest E Smith *et al* (n 16) p542, Peter Roberts (n 5) p80 and Scott Styles (n 14).

255 Chavez Golvala (n 6) p48.

256 Scott Styles (n 14) p288.

257 "[I]t might be said that the party-operator will enjoy a greater level of access to data and information which has been generated in consequence of the performance of the joint operations than might be enjoyed by any non-operating party. However, this advantage will be less apparent if the JOA provides for all of the parties to have equal access to the data associated with the joint operations." Peter Roberts (n 5) p80.

to the members is to keep them informed of developments and this will be done by providing the Opcom representatives with reports and data.[256]

Reports and information are potential areas of conflict, as the operator will prefer to keep the burden as light as possible, while the non-operators will emphasise its importance.[257]

Further, any non-operator has the right to inspect all information retained by the operator about the joint operations,[258] and to audit the joint operations records.[259]

Non-operators should thus seek to include the following protections in the JOA:

- an efficient method of receiving information as it is produced;
- a right to receive government reports;
- a right to request further information from the operator;
- a right to request clarification of information provided;
- a right to reject any information provided and request further diligence, where reasonable and justified; and
- a right to inspect and audit the records of the joint operations.[260]

The ideal, balanced JOA should include these provisions, but do the current JOA models provide such protection?

AAPL models: AAPL Form 810 (for deepwater operations) includes the non-operators' right to compel the operator to supply data acquired from the conduct of joint operations, as it becomes available.[261] It also requires the operator to provide all non-confidential reports exchanged with regulatory agencies, rather than placing the onus in this respect on the non-operators to request further documentation, or information which may have been retained by the operator.[262] Form 810 places a general obligation on the operator to keep records of the joint operations,[263] and gives the non-operator the right to have the relevant records audited.

By contrast, the majority of the operator's duties with regard to supplying information to the non-operators are absent from AAPL Form 610, which provides for the non-operators' right to demand information – at their own expense – rather than the operator's duty to supply it. Consequently, the non-operators cannot enjoy the benefit of receiving information as it is produced or obtained. This approach puts the non-operators in a very weak position, as it is extremely difficult to follow the operator's performance without regular reports in this regard.

However, even this historic model form secures the right of non-operators to obtain the most important information regarding the joint operations (including

258 "The operator must keep books of account (referred to as the joint account) with respect to the joint operations, ie, with respect to the operations carried out on behalf and for the benefit of all parties, and separate books of account for each sole risk operation, ie, for any operation carried out on behalf and for the benefit of one or more but not all of the parties." Bernard Taverne (n 90) p136.

259 Claude Duval *et al* (n 122) p302 and Terence Daintith *et al* (n 16) p1146.

260 This issue will not be part of a full analysis as it is mainly part of the AP which is outside the scope of this book. Consequently, this book will only refer briefly to the application of this provision with regard to the right to information.

261 AAPL JOA Form 810 § 5.7, 5.8 and 5.9.

262 AAPL JOA Form 810 §5.6 and 5.9.

263 AAPL JOA Form 810 §5.5.

government reports); places an obligation on the operator to keep records of the joint operations; and affords the non-operators the right to carry out an audit of the respective records.[264]

The approach adopted in AAPL Form 810 is very similar to that of the AIPN model. The main difference is in disclosure of government reports, an obligation on the operator in AAPL Form 810 which is absent from the AIPN model, where a specific request must be made by the non-operators. However, the same cannot be said of AAPL forms 810 and 610. With Form 810, non-operators were in a stronger position, as the operator had a duty to provide information on the conduct of operations, and at the same time the non-operators had a right to request it. Form 610 reduced as far as possible the burden on the operator to provide information and placed the onus entirely on the non-operators to request it – at their own expense and risk.

Finally, both models fail to provide additional rights to request clarification or amendment of the information provided, unless an audit of the joint account gives reasonable grounds to do so. This is an important omission, as such a right would facilitate the full participation of non-operators in achieving best practice and results for the JV.

RMMLF: This model eliminates the burden on the operator to provide information to the non-operators. However, it does not eliminate the obligation to maintain records of the joint operations so that the non-operators can have access to these records at their own expense.[265]

In addition, if the non-operators request further information about drilling operations, the operator must provide it as soon as possible.[266] It is not clear, however, whether the non-operators can request further information about other activities, and in particular government reports.

It can thus be said that the RMMLF model adopts a soft approach which favours the operator, as its obligations are as light as possible. This soft approach is prejudicial for any non-operator (especially a dormant non-operator) as it is far more difficult to follow the conduct of the joint operations if the operator has no obligation to provide information on them. Nevertheless, there are provisions to ensure access to information for non-operators, if they wish to proceed at their own expense.

The lack of obligations on the operator, of clarity about government reports, and of a right to request clarification and/or modifications, clearly put non-operators in a weak position to control and participate in the JV.

Canadian model: This model obliges the operator to "keep [the non-operator] informed in a timely manner about the Joint Operations planned or conducted by it (the operator)".[267] However, precisely what kind of information the operator must provide is less clear than in the models above.

264 AAPL JOA Form 610 clauses 5, 6 and 7.
265 RMMLF JOA §5.1 (F).
266 RMMLF JOA §5.1 (F).
267 CAPL OP model §3.01.

On the other hand, the Canadian model is very precise about other duties of the operator. It must keep records and accounts of the joint operations in order to "minimize the possibility of materially inaccurate recording".[268] This provision gives some comfort to non-operators, as there will be a designated place where any relevant information is available for consultation and inspection. If the non-operators wish, they can request the audit of such records or accounts.

This JOA model places fewer duties on the operator and consequently provides fewer rights for non-operators. Although the operator has the obligation to keep the non-operators informed about the joint operations, it seems that if any non-operator desires to obtain precise information about the joint operation, it must do so at its own expense.

British model: The British model compels the operator to provide the non-operators with all the information and data acquired in connection with the joint operations.[269] The model also contains a very interesting provision regarding correspondence with government. The operator must send to non-operators, in advance, a copy of all non-routine correspondence and material the operator intends to send to the relevant government agency; and must obtain the non-operators' consent.[270]

Like others, the model places an obligation on the operator to keep records of the joint operations, and at the same time allows the non-operators' to verify such records by means of inspections and audits.[271]

The British JOA model thus adopts a similar approach to the AIPN and AAPL Form 810, as it imposes duties on the operator and at the same time ensures there are additional rights granted to the non-operators which can be exercised at their own expense. In other words, it affords the non-operators a good level of awareness regarding information about the JV (especially information provided by the operator itself), but it fails to provide clear provision for requests for clarification or amendment of information on reasonable grounds.

Norwegian model: As under any other JOA, the operator must "carry out and administer the day to day management of the joint venture activities".[272] One of the administrative duties, and probably the most important for the non-operators, is the duty to provide information.

The Norwegian JOA model form establishes a bureaucratic procedure for the exchange of information, expressly referring to the Opcom. However, any party can request information regardless of the procedural means – that is, through the Opcom or directly.[273]

The most important provision is a detailed obligation requiring the operator to provide certain information to the Opcom.[274] The operator has to keep records of the

268 CAPL OP model §3.07.
269 OGUK JOA §6.8 and 6.9.
270 OGUK JOA §6.6.
271 OGUK JOA §6.7.
272 Norwegian JOA model §3.1.
273 Norwegian JOA model §3.4.
274 Norwegian JOA model §3.4.

joint operations and also allow the non-operators to audit such information on request.[275] Furthermore, even though the operator is required to provide detailed information to the non-operators (including government reports), any party can request supplementary information, which the operator must provide.[276] This is a valuable protection for the non-operators as further explanation or information might be required on certain occasions.

The Norwegian JOA model thus affords non-operators a significant degree of information, both by imposing detailed obligations on the operator and by allowing non-operators to request further information. One flaw in the agreement is that the obligation to provide the information is specifically through the Opcom, which may not be the most effective method if the Opcom does not meet regularly. However, this could be addressed by setting up sub-committees to facilitate the exchange of information. A further issue is that the model does not clearly provide a right for non-operators to reject the information provided by the operator.

Australian model:[277] This model also places the obligation on the operator to provide relevant information to the non-operators. However, the model is unique in providing an elaborate system prescribing the frequency of reports.[278] Under this system, there are four different categories of report frequency:

- as soon as possible;
- monthly;
- quarterly; and
- annually.

While this might appear welcome at first glance, there are some problems with such a system. First, the category 'as soon as possible' applies only to two situations:

- whenever the operator feels it is necessary; and
- whenever this information will be disclosed to the market (as a public announcement).

The first situation gives the operator far too much discretion, while the second is a basic requirement, as the non-operator is also a member of the JV. Moreover, the reference to 'monthly' means one month from completion of the material, so the operator can retain the information for 30 days before the non-operators have access to it. It can thus be argued that such an elaborate process does not adequately safeguard the non-operators' position. To do so it should exclude, or at least reduce, the operator's discretion in providing the information. The provision for monthly disclosure of the information to the non-operators, rather than as soon as it is produced, makes this all the more apparent.

The Australian model places an obligation on the operator to keep records of the

---

275 Norwegian JOA model §1.4.1.
276 Norwegian JOA model §3.4.
277 AMPLA JOA model §10 – The new model retains the same provision as the JV model. The only relevant difference is the additional obligation on the operator to provide wells and reservoir information to the non-operators.

joint operations, and allows the non-operators to request an audit to verify the precision and diligence of the operator in this regard.[279]

Although the non-operators can have access to the reports and records of the joint operations at their own expense, it is unclear whether the non-operators can request further information, or even clarification of any information provided.[280] This might be a problem for the efficiency of the JV as, if any non-operator has doubts about a report provided by the operator, it will be forced to start an audit procedure in order to clarify any misunderstanding. If a provision allowing a request for further information or clarification was included, this might avoid unnecessary audit procedures and give more comfort to the non-operators in the JV.

The Australian model recognises the importance of information for all parties to the JV. However, it fails to ensure full collaboration of the non-operators towards the success of the JV, as it allows less than complete access to the information produced by the operator on behalf of the JV. In addition, the model prescribes bureaucratic procedures which are unfavourable to the non-operators and the JV as a whole. Finally, the model is unclear on the non-operators' right of access to government reports.

AIPN model:[281] The AIPN model gives the non-operators the right to receive most of the information and reports concerning the joint operations as soon as they are produced or compiled.[282] It also provides a right of access to any additional information, including government reports, retained by the operator which is related to the joint operations, on request by the non-operators and at their own expense.[283] However, this model is not clear as to whether the non-operators can request clarification of the information provided, or reject – partially or totally – the results of the data on reasonable grounds.

The operator must keep records of the joint operations so that the non-operators can exercise their right to audit the performance of the operator.[284]

The AIPN model thus clearly imposes a duty on the operator to provide relevant information to the non-operators, and at the same time secures the non-operators' right of access to additional information at their own expense. Given that the right of non-operators to request clarification or reject the information provided by the operator is unclear, the non-operators are likely to deal with such requests or rejections by exercising their right to audit the records of the joint operations – which might not be the most efficient procedure for the JV as a whole.

278 AMPLA JV model §9.2.
279 AMPLA JV model §9.3.
280 AMPLA JV model §9.5.
281 The AIPN 2012 model form is based on the old version, with a few minor changes. General information must be provided in a timely manner and in digital form. More importantly, there are new duties on the operator to provide more information about development operations, production reports, reservoir studies, seismic sections, HSE performance and reservoir estimates.
282 AIPN § 4.4 (A).
283 AIPN JOA § 4.4 (B).
284 AIPN § 4.2.(B) (7), 7.12 (C).

Greenlandic model: This model safeguards the position for the non-operators as there is an obligation on the operator to inform the non-operators of all relevant data and reports on the joint operation,[285] and the non-operator has an additional right to request further information from the operator.[286] This approach is similar to that of the AIPN, AAPL Form 810 and British models.

As with the British and Norwegian models, there is also an obligation on the operator to provide any government reports to the non-operators. However, the Greenlandic model goes even further: the operator must not only provide government reports, but also allow full participation by non-operators in discussions with government authorities.[287]

The operator has also an obligation to keep records of the joint operations so that the non-operators can verify and control their performance.[288] This is common among JOA models, but the Greenlandic model goes further, providing for a 'common database' to provide information for the parties "who are technically active to an equal footing from the start of the Joint Operations" to take decisions on the applicable Opcom.[289] In other words, this model makes an unusual distinction between proactive non-operators and dormant non-operators – the former have better access to information than the latter. However, the distinction aims to address the very first stage of the joint operations, when the parties retain information from the joint bidding agreement. In practice, there will be no difference between proactive and dormant non-operators.

This model is thus favourable for non-operators, as they have two layers of protection: the operator's duty to provide all the relevant information to the non-operators, and the right to request further information or to verify the records of the joint operations. The model can be classified alongside the AIPN, AAPL Form 810 and British models, which all adopt a similar approach. It is highly beneficial that the model requires the operator to provide government reports to non-operators. However, there is no clear procedure for requesting clarification or modification of the information provided by the operator, which would have increased the non-operators' participation and contributed to the efficiency of the JV.

Conclusion: In short, it can be said that all JOA model forms secure the non-operators' right to receive information and data about the joint operations; to request additional information retained by the operator about the joint operations; and finally to inspect and audit the records and accounts of the joint operations. The differences between the models are procedural, such as whether the information should be supplied as a matter of duty by the operator, or whether access to information is a right which the non-operators can exercise upon request. The former approach increases the burden on the operator but provides a second layer of protection to the non-operators. The latter approach reduces the burden on the

285 Greenlandic JOA model §3.3.1.(d).
286 Greenlandic JOA model §3.6.2, 3.9.2, 3.10, etc.
287 Greenlandic JOA model §3.7.
288 Greenlandic JOA model §3.8.
289 Greenlandic JOA model §3.9.1.

operator and makes control of the operations from a non-operator's perspective more difficult, as it might be difficult for the non-operators to request information if they are unaware of its existence.

The JOA models may be compared as follows:

JOA model/rights	AAPL	RRMLF	CAPL	OGUK	NOR	AMPLA	AIPN	GRE
Early exchange of information	Partial	No	No	Yes	Partial	Yes	Yes	Yes
Reference to government reports	Yes	No	No	Yes	Yes	No	Yes	Yes
Additional information	Yes	Yes	Yes	Yes	Yes	Yes	Yes	Yes
Rejection/ adjustments	No	No	No	No	No	No	No	No
Clarification	No	No	No	No	No	No	No	No
Inspect/audit	Yes	Yes	Yes	Yes	Yes	Yes	Yes	Yes

It is thus apparent that the AIPN, AAPL (Form 810), Australian, British and Greenlandic JOA models afford non-operators a greater degree of control over the information relating to the JV. On the other hand, the CAPL, AAPL (Form 610) and RMMLF JOA models provide fewer protections for non-operators, as they adopt a softer approach towards the duties and obligations of the operator. Unfortunately, none of the JOAs studied provides a simple right to request clarification of information that is provided. If a non-operator is an active partner and detects problems regarding the content or quality of the information, it would be helpful for it to be able to seek a reasonable explanation from the operator about such discrepancies. Without such a provision, the non-operator has no option but to attempt to resolve even simple matters through an audit, which could be costly, time consuming and probably not an appropriate mechanism for a technical matter.

This is important since any breach of the operator's duty in providing information about the joint operations will put the non-operators in a difficult position, for several reasons. First, if no information is available, it is extremely difficult for the non-operators to verify and analyse the operator's performance. Second, even though the non-operators may have no control or knowledge of the conduct of the joint operations, they will still share the joint liabilities of this enterprise, which could be very high (eg, health and safety liabilities, environmental liabilities, development liabilities). Finally, if the non-operator is keen to divest its participation, then the lack of information makes this particularly challenging.

An analogy can be drawn with the position of minority shareholders. The right to receive information is a basic right of minority shareholders, just as it is for any non-operator.[290] Under the UK Companies Act 2006, a minority shareholder has the

290 See notes 3 and 4.

right both to obtain information and data on company activities and to audit the respective records.[291] It could be argued that minority shareholders enjoy a strong position, as this is enshrined in legislation; but on the other hand, they are likely to receive information later in comparison to non-operators.

Information is the key element from the non-operators' perspective, as they are not conducting the joint operations themselves. It is essential to provide for different layers of participation and as much access to information as possible, so that non-operators can make valuable contributions towards the best practices of the JV. Without such information, a non-operator cannot assess the effectiveness or otherwise of the consortium, and thus cannot step in to help remedy the situation if the JV is threatened with failure.

(b) Operating committee (Opcom)

As the operator is responsible for the day-to-day operations of the JV, it is highly recommended – from the non-operators' perspective – that the JOA make provision for a body that can control the activities of the operator.[292] However, such control can be exercised only if the operator provides all necessary information in relation to its activities; without such information, this will be effectively impossible.[293] Consequently, the right to information is a basic right of non-operators and the basis for efficient control by another body.

This body is commonly referred to as the 'management committee' or the 'Opcom'.[294] The Opcom is the highest authority of the JOA, as it is responsible for controlling and supervising the overall operations of the JV.[295]

Each party will thus seek the strongest possible position on this decision-making body. The operator will seek to restrict the influence of non-operators, so that it can act freely according to its own judgement. The non-operators in turn will desire more control, so that they can ensure that their views are clearly addressed in the conduct of the joint operations. Peter Roberts describes these tensions in the following terms:

> *The very concept of the Opcom illustrates another of the great paradoxes in the JOA: while the operator is appointed by all of the parties with the intention that the operator shall have exclusive responsibility for the performance of the joint operations, the non-operating parties typically try to exert the greatest possible degree of influence over the operator through the Opcom. This tension between the operator and the non-operating parties runs through the JOA and the Opcom is the stage on which that conflict is played out.*[296]

While the Opcom is very important for all contracting parties, it has special

---

291 Companies Act 2006 (sections 145/151, 228, 229, 373, 459, 476).

292 See also Terence Daintith *et al* (n 16) pp1143–1145, Sandy Shaw (n 16) pp18–19, Anthony Jennings (n 16) pp24–25, Scott Styles (n 14) p278.

293 "The JOA will ensure that the operating committee is kept sufficiently well informed to exercise such supervision and control." Taylor and Tyne (n 54) p36.

294 Arguably the role of the Opcom members is comparable with that of shareholders or partners, as Gerry Bean observes: "In a JOA day-to-day management is in the hands of the operator. The operating committee sets policy and supervises the operator, but does the operating committee act more like a meeting of partners and less like a meeting of shareholders, or vice versa? It must be remembered that a meeting of partners may deal with both day-to-day matters and also with broader policy matters, and that different considerations may apply to these different matters." Gerard MD Bean (n 18) pp176–177.

295 See Chapter I, section 1.1(b).

296 Peter Roberts (n 5) p96.

significance for non-operators, as it may be the sole channel through which they can provide input on the conduct of the joint operations.

Claude Duval explains this as follows:

Because of the large sums of money involved and the frequent participation of NOCs in joint operations, non-operators will demand significant input and supervision over the decisions and actions of the operator. The principal means of controlling the operator is by creating an operating (or management) committee under the provisions of the JOA. Thus, despite the operator's exclusive charge over joint operations, the non-operators may have considerable influence.[297]

The Opcom provision is thus crucial to protect and strengthen the position and participation of non-operators in the JOA,[298] as all the main activities must be approved by the Opcom before the operator executes them.[299]

Another effective way to increase the participation of non-operators is through the establishment of sub-committees.[300] The role of a sub-committee is to provide the Opcom with technical advice on specific issues as required. These committees are a highly effective vehicle through which non-operators can contribute their own views and experience on various issues.[301] However, some operators might seek to prevent significant participation by non-operators, lest the sub-committees get diverted from their original purpose. In other words, they may fear that the non-operators will endeavour to exploit the sub-committees as a way to exert greater control over the joint operations, rather than as a vehicle through which to collaborate and provide input.[302] Claude Duval describes the conflict of interest within sub-committees as follows:

Some JOAs may allow the operating committee to establish subcommittees to act in an advisory capacity on technical or other matters. These subcommittees can use the particular expertise of non-operator employees to address difficult tasks. However, the operator may not look favourably on project subcommittees headed by non-operators which might infringe on the operator's "exclusive charge" over joint operations.[303]

As a consequence, the sub-committees are subject to the Opcom's supervision, so that they can be properly controlled by all parties.[304] In practice, however, most of the work in a JV is arguably carried out by the sub-committees,[305] with the Opcom's approval a mere formality.[306]

---

297 Claude Duval *et al* (n 122) p291.

298 "The principal vehicle by which the non-operating parties can secure representation of their interests before the operator is the Opcom." Peter Roberts (n 5) p95.

299 Bernard Taverne (n 90) p137.

300 "Such subcommittees can be used to facilitate the input of the expertise of the non-operating parties to a greater degree than might be usual under the Opcom." Peter Roberts (n 5) p99.

301 "[S]ome JOAs may allow the operating committee to establish subcommittees to act in an advisory capacity on technical or other matters. These committees can use the particular expertise of non-operator employees to address difficult tasks." Claude Duval *et al* (n 122) p293.

302 "The operator might be reluctant to allow the existence of subcommittees with significant non-operating party involvement, due to concern that the subcommittee might be used as a device by which the operator s ability to exercise control over the performance of the joint operations is somehow subverted." Peter Roberts (n 5) p99.

303 Claude Duval *et al* (n 122) p293.

304 Kenneth C Mildwaters (n 16) p413.

305 Chavez Golvala (n 6) p47.

306 "Much of the real work of operational decision making is done at sub-committee level and ratified at the Operating Committee level." Sandy Shaw (n 16) p18.

A similar mechanism through which non-operators can provide input is a project team. This is a body established within the consortium to gather non-operators' input on relevant matters such as work programmes and budgets and the award of contracts. However, it faces the same problems as a sub-committee: as the operator will not wish to grant extensive rights to the non-operators, the project team will usually be controlled by the operator.

Of the many issues relating to the Opcom (eg, minutes, notice of meetings, location of meetings), the voting procedures are by far the most critical for all parties (especially non-operators), as these will determine the extent to which non-operators can control the conduct of the joint operations.[307] The voting procedures are thus analysed in detail below.

The Opcom represents all contracting parties to the JOA,[308] with each party nominating one representative to the committee. As a general rule, a party can have a representative on the Opcom regardless of the size of its participating interest in the JV; this constitutes valuable protection for non-operators.[309] Peter Roberts recognises the importance of this when he states: "This principle of having one representative for each party represents the high-water mark of equality between the parties."[310]

Each representative has a percentage of the voting rights on the Opcom in proportion to its participating interest in the JV. This arrangement can also create tensions. From the very outset, there is a conceptual conflict, as each party can vote according to its own interests, which may be different from those of the JV.[311] On the other hand,[312] it can be argued that each party owes a fiduciary duty towards the JV whenever it exercises its voting rights on the Opcom – that is, a party should not vote for its own advantage against the interests of the consortium.[313] There is no straightforward answer to this dilemma,[314] but it is reasonable to suggest that both

307 "How the voting control mechanism which applies between the parties is exercised at the Opcom is a critical part of the composition of the JOA and can be used to enable the non-operating parties to exercise some control over the operator's ambitions." Peter Roberts (n 5) p99.

308 "This committee consists of representatives of each participant with the operator's representative serving as chair." Bernard G Taverne, *Co-Operative Agreements in the Extractive Petroleum Industry* (Kluwer Law International, The Hague 1996) pp68–69.

309 There are exceptions, as Kenneth Mildwaters explains: "In some cases it is provided that a Participant with an Interest of less than a stated percentage is not entitled to appoint its own representative and alternate representative to the Operating Committee." He explains that this is due to the proliferation of "relatively small companies" with acquired interests in Australian joint ventures. In such cases, one representative will represent more than one party. This provision may have practical reasons to stand but it is highly negative for non-operators as it precludes their direct participation in the main decision-making body of the JV. Kenneth C Mildwaters (n 16) p407.

310 Peter Roberts (n 5) p97.

311 "The JOA might state that at each Opcom each party is free to cast its vote entirely in accordance with its personal preference, and that there is no obligation on a party to vote in accordance with what might be regarded as the best interests of all the parties. Thus, a party could exercise its voting rights at the Opcom with an eye to affording some preference to a competing project or interest if it so wished. Whether such a provision should be expressed to apply in favour of the party-operator, in its capacity as the operator rather than as a party, should be considered. The existence of such a provision would be helpful in regulating the potential for the existence of fiduciary duties between the parties." Peter Roberts (n 5) p97.

312 For further information see Gerard MD Bean (n 16) pp176–208.

313 "In the Committee a venture is expected, and is permitted, to seek to promote its own personal interest as a participant in the venture. But he is not expected, and is not permitted, to there seek to promote his private interests to derive personal benefits not countered by the venture agreement. It is when undisclosed private interest, an undisclosed personal benefit, infects the Committee that the conflict rule comes into play." PD Finn, "Fiduciary Obligations of operators and Co-Venturers in Natural Resources Joint Ventures", 1984 AMPLA Yearbook pp160–170.

positions have merit and should co-exist insofar as possible. In other words, each party should seek to benefit itself and also the consortium. In reality, however, the former is far more likely than the latter – as Scott Styles argued – because the JOA is not a democracy, but simply a private contract.[315]

The JOA must specify which issues are subject to the Opcom's approval, but usually the range of issues will be as broad as possible.[316] Opcom decisions will commonly require approval by a certain percentage of the votes (the 'passmark'), and exceptionally may require unanimous approval. The former will be the 'default' provision to approve proposals at the Opcom level and the latter the exception.[317] Any decision taken by the Opcom is binding on all the contracting parties.[318]

The determination of the passmark and the issues that require unanimous approval are important topics during the JOA negotiations, as these can influence the extent of the control exerted by non-operators. However, the existence of non-consent and sole risk clauses can reduce the tension caused by these issues.

Taylor and Tyne explain how complicated the determination of the passmark can be and the issues involved as follows:

> *Fixing the passmark can be a difficult negotiating matter since, depending upon the particular passmark chosen, different combinations of parties will be able to pass or block resolutions of the operating committee. A typical passmark would be in a region of 70 per cent but the actual figure chosen in any particular JOA will depend upon a combination of factors. These will include the respective percentage interests of the parties to the JOA, the degree of confidence which the non-operators have in the operator (and vice versa), the likelihood of serious conflicts of interest between the parties, the view which each party takes of the relative importance of being able to block a resolution which it opposes as against preventing others from blocking a resolution which it supports and the existence or otherwise of rights of sole risk and non-consent under the JOA.*[319]

In other words, if a higher passmark is established, the operator will probably need to secure the agreement of one or more non-operators in order to reach this threshold. The following table illustrates how this can happen:

Example 1	**Company A**	**Company B**	**Company C**
Role	Operator	Non-operator	Non-operator
Interest	60%	20%	20%
Pass mark	70%		

314 See also Simon Fisher, "Formation and Structure" in WD Duncan, *Joint Ventures Law in Australia* (2nd ed, The Federation Press, Sydney 2005) pp165–171.

315 Scott Styles (n 14) p287.

316 "A list of the Operating Committee's powers and duties will be usually be listed in the JOA along with a 'catch all' or two to ensure that everything is covered." Sandy Shaw (n 14) p18.

317 Chris Thorpe, *Fundamentals of Upstream Petroleum Agreements* (CP Thorpe, UK 2008) pp127–-131.

318 Kenneth C Mildwaters (n 16) pp68–69.

319 Taylor and Tyne (n 54) p23.

In this example, the operator cannot achieve the passmark by itself, but will rather need to secure the cooperation of at least one non-operator to do so. If the issue requires unanimous approval, then any non-operator can block the proposal.

On the other hand, if the passmark is low, the operator can reach this by itself and consequently approve proposals without any major difficulty, as the following table illustrates:

Example 2	Company A	Company B	Company C
Role	Operator	Non-operator	Non-operator
Interest	60%	20%	20%
Pass mark	50%		

Some JOAs provide a secondary criterion for approving decisions at the Opcom level: even if a proposal has achieved the passmark according to the percentage of participating interests, the support of a certain number of parties must also be secured. This will prevent a situation where one party with a large participating interest can force through a proposal by itself.[320] Such a provision is thus very positive for non-operators, given that the operator commonly retains the largest interest in the JV.[321]

Taylor and Tyne also explain the reason for providing this secondary criterion as follows:

> *Such provision might be adopted where the parties to the JOA prefer a low passmark but are concerned at the prospect that, if a party holding a substantial percentage interest purchased the percentage interest of another party under the JOA, it might be able to pass resolutions of the operating committee without needing the support of any other parties.*[322]

Where this secondary level of protection is adopted, parties might abuse it by seeking to block decisions simply by not attending the relevant Opcom meeting. However, it is possible to prevent such behaviour by providing that any absence from the meeting shall be regarded as an affirmative or negative vote.[323]

It is also possible to provide for different levels of passmark, depending on the nature of the proposal and its significance for the parties. More contentious issues would require a higher passmark (eg, a declaration of commerciality or decision to stop production), and less contentious issues a lower passmark (eg, the acquisition of

---

320 "On the other hand, the assent of more than one party may be required, as in a provision stating that all approvals 'shall be determined by the affirmative vote of two or more parties then having collectively at least 51% of the participating Interests.' If one or more parties hold small percentage interests, say less than 10%, no one of them will have disproportionate power to veto decisions." Claude Duval *et al* (n 122) p292.

321 Peter Roberts (n 5) p101.

322 Taylor and Tyne (n 54) pp23–24.

323 Peter Roberts (n 5) p103.

data or the award of low-value contracts). Claude Duval describes this situation as follows:

The JOA can provide for different minimum percentages of approval (including unanimity) depending on the type of decision being voted on. Thus approval to unitize the contract area may require a different percentage agreement than approval of a development plan.[324]

The connection between the number of parties, the participating interest and the relevance of the proposals is crucial in determining the most appropriate voting procedure. Bernard Taverne explains the importance of these factors as follows:

The prescribed voting percentages depend firstly on the number of participating parties and the distribution of the participating interest amongst them and secondly on the nature and importance of the matters in respect of which decision has to be taken. If the number of parties is small and the interests are evenly distributed, important decisions, such as the approval of the annual programmes and budgets, the approval of the award of important contracts or the declaration of a commercial discovery, will usually require unanimity.[325]

Unanimous voting is another complex issue.[326] As mentioned previously, specific subjects – such as voluntary surrender, modification of the scope of the JOA or unitisation – usually require the approval of all parties.[327] In this case, the position of the non-operators is considerably stronger, as any non-operator (regardless of the size of its participating interest) can block the proposal; however, this can also lead to a deadlock[328] if no consensus is established.

Thus, while unanimous approval is beneficial for non-operators, it can also jeopardise the existence of the JV if the parties cannot reach agreement.[329] For this reason, it is important to provide alternatives to avoid deadlocks, such as by providing for alternative dispute resolution (eg, mediation, mini-trial, expert determination) or simply by lowering the passmark if a particular proposal is "repeatedly brought back to a committee".[330] However, the most common approach for the JOA is to provide that any deadlock will be resolved through exclusive operations.

Thus, in a traditional JOA negotiation, the operator will seek to institute a lower passmark and restrict the number of issues requiring unanimous approval. On the other hand, the non-operators will seek exactly the opposite: a higher passmark and more issues requiring unanimous approval.[331]

324 Claude Duval *et al* (n 122) pp292–293.

325 Bernard Taverne (n 90) p137.

326 The exceptionality of such procedure is required "to protect each of them from unexpected additional expense in terms of quantum or a change in the scope of the Operations, that is, matters which affect a Participant's basic rights and duties under the Joint Operating Agreement and in the petroleum title." Kenneth Mildwaters (n 16) p415.

327 "Some decisions however, such as those relating to voluntary surrender of part of the licensed area, will require unanimity." Taylor and Tyne (n 54) p23.

328 Chris Wilkinson defines 'deadlock' as "where two parties, each of whom is to hold one-half of the shares and neither of whom is willing to surrender control to the other." Chris Wilkinson (n 103) p171.

329 "[T]he obvious disadvantage with unanimous voting is that the deadlock between the parties is always a possibility, and (taken to the extreme) that deadlock might completely frustrate the performance of the joint operations. It is helpful, therefore, to ensure that if the JOA contains a unanimous voting formulation, the JOA also contains a deadlock resolution mechanism." Peter Roberts (n 5) p100.

330 Chavez Golvala (n 6) p47.

331 Sandy Shaw (n 16) p18 and Peter Roberts (n 5) p100.

It is very unlikely that non-operators will obtain control of the joint operations, but it is important that they secure preventative control over critical issues, so the operator is forced to eek their consent on such matters.

Scott Styles argues that the passmark is not a democratic instrument, but rather reflects the relative strength of the parties during negotiations.[332] It is important to maintain a certain equilibrium, in this regard: if the passmark is very low, the role of the Opcom is effectively redundant; but if the passmark is very high, this will create extra bureaucratic hurdles which will compromise the effectiveness of the JV.[333] Thus, when negotiating on the exact percentage, the parties should bear in mind the importance of reasonable terms for all stakeholders in the interests of an efficient, clear and balanced consortium.

Peter Roberts describes the connection between the voting procedure and efficacy of the JV as follows:

However, despite the existence of such a committee, the extent to which the ambitions of the non-operating parties can be accommodated in this regard will vary according to the terms that have been agreed in any particular JOA. Thus, at one end of the scale the Opcom (if indeed an Opcom exists at all – see below) might do little more than be notified of the operator's activities, while at the other end of the scale the operator might be precluded from engaging in any activity without first having secured the Opcom's express approval.[334]

Therefore, it can be said that the Opcom is a crucial instrument to protect the non-operators' position, as it allows for their proactive participation in the JV and ultimately allows them to exert a degree of control over the conduct of the joint operations.[335]

However, the mere existence of an Opcom is not in itself sufficient to secure the non-operators' position, as the vehicle can once again be dominated by the operator.[336] In order to make a real difference, the Opcom must be accompanied by balanced provisions to secure the non-operators' control over and participation in the joint operations.

---

332 "The JOA is a private contract, not an experiment in participatory democracy and the actual pass mark is a matter for negotiation and agreement between the parties, the outcome being dependent on the relative contractual strengths of the parties and the degree of trust they have in each other." Scott Styles (n 14) p287.

333 Chris Thorpe demonstrates the importance of maintaining the equilibrium of the Opcom provision as the JOA is a document with a long duration and the situation of the parties might change. "The many arduous negotiations over operating committee passmarks have a melancholy aspect but also sometimes a humorous one. The melancholy aspect is that parties argue on the basis of a naked self-interest. When you hold 40% and you are arguing for a passmark of 'more than 60%', it is difficult to marshal any persuasive argument in support of your position. You just want it that way, and the reason is obvious. The humorous aspect can be seen when a party that has achieved the most advantageous passmark subsequently assigns part of its interest and finds itself, as a result of its own negotiating prowess in the worst possible position." Chris Thorpe (n 317) p129.

334 Peter Roberts (n 5) pp95–96.

335 In some cases, using its vote to block a particular proposal might be the only way the non-operator can participate and express its views on the joint operations, as Kenneth Mildwaters explains: "After all, a blocking vote may be the only protection afforded to a Participant holding a minority Interest." Kenneth C Mildwaters (n 16) p414.

336 "Thus, despite the operator's exclusive charge over joint operations, the non-operators may have considerable influence, although experience teaches that the operating committee can either be a 'rubber stamp' for the operator or a strong 'board of directors' depending on the group's dynamics and personalities." Claude Duval *et al* (n 122) p291.

Consequently, in the JOA negotiations, non-operators should seek to ensure that the Opcom provides for the following:

- representation of all parties, regardless of the size of their participating interest in the JV;
- establishment of sub-committees allowing for effective participation of non-operators and/or project teams;
- establishment of a voting procedure based on participating interest and number of parties;
- establishment of a voting system that subjects crucial issues to unanimous approval, and other issues to passmarks depending on importance;
- establishment of deadlock resolution procedures which are not significantly detrimental to the non-operators' position.

There follows an analysis of the Opcom provisions in each JOA model form or, where no provision is made for the existence of an Opcom, an explanation of why this is so and who controls the joint operations instead.

AAPL model forms: AAPL Form 810 does not provide for the existence of an Opcom. It could be argued that this model allows the operator to act without any major interference from the other parties. The main protection available to non-operators under this model form is the non-consent clause, which allows a party not to participate in a joint operation.[337]

However, it is not entirely correct to say that non-operators cannot exert control over the conduct of the joint operations, as other provisions require their approval for certain operations.[338] According to AAPL Form 810, "there are four general classes of activities or operations under this Agreement: (a) those requiring approval by Vote, (b) those requiring approval by Election, (c) those requiring approval by unanimous agreement, and (d) those within the discretion of the operator."[339]

This system involves a mix of voting procedures commonly regulated by the Opcom. The parties should decide on the relevant percentage required to approve a specific proposal, which can range from a simple passmark to unanimous approval.[340] A distinction is also made between the percentage of participating interest and the number of parties involved. In other words, the AAPL model Form 810 adopts a similar flexibility to the AIPN model. This is probably the high water mark for non-operators under this model form (in cases where a high passmark is implemented).

However, it does not provide a resolution for deadlocks. Although this might place non-operators in a strong position, it could also jeopardise the whole consortium if the deadlock is not resolved swiftly. Likewise, no provision is made for the effective participation of non-operators in the joint operations, as there is no sub-committee

337 Taylor and Tyne (n 54) pp21–23, Peter Roberts (n 5) p96, Terence Daintith *et al* (n 16) p1143.

338 "Although the AAPL JOA does not countenance the creation of an OpCom, the non-operating parties nevertheless have some measure of control over the operator's ability to exercise absolute control through the implementation of a voting control mechanism which could afford a non-operating party at least a partial ability to direct the performance of the joint operations." Peter Roberts (n 5) p102.

339 AAPL Form 810 § 8.1.

340 AAPL Form 810 §10.1, 11.1, 11.2.2, 12.2.1, 12.3.2, 12.7.6, 12.8, 13.1.1. 13.1.2.

structure through which non-operators can provide input on the operations and help to shape the overall policies of the consortium. The model form does provide for the existence of project teams, which have a similar remit to sub-committees,[341] but these bodies are placed under the direct control of the operator.[342] Thus, while non-operators have a channel through which to provide input, it is left for the operator to decide whether to take this feedback into consideration. That said, AAPL Form 810 nonetheless allows non-operators a certain degree of control over the joint operations.

AAPL Form 610 also does not provide for the establishment of a management committee,[343] except for a limited period where the operator cannot be removed due to insolvency legislation.[344] However, the situation of non-operators under this obsolete model form is far worse, as there is no elaborate voting system such as that included in AAPL Form 810. Non-operators can merely elect to participate in a specific proposal or refuse to participate by exercising their right of non-consent. In other words, there is no provision which gives them a degree control over the operations conducted by the operator, but only a right to opt out of operations.

Consequently, the position of non-operators under both AAPL model forms is weak, as they cannot shape the overall policies and operations of the consortium, and there is no effective channel for their input. However, their position is considerably worse under the traditional Form 610, which affords no control over the joint operations. Both models require unanimous approval for certain operations, but do not provide for the resolution of deadlocks.[345] The AAPL model forms thus arguably position the non-operators as mere investors, which increases the fiduciary duties as previously outlined.[346]

RMMLF model: The RMMLF, like the other American JOA models, does not provide for the existence of a management committee. The operator has sweeping powers under this model, which provides that the operator "shall direct and have control of all operations conducted hereunder and shall have exclusive custody of all materials, equipment and other property owned by the parties".[347]

The model does provide that the operator should consult non-operators about matters considered relevant in its sole and "best" judgement.[348] Clearly, this is detrimental to the non-operators' perspective as it affords too much discretion to the operator.

Like the Canadian model, the RMMLF model merely allows non-operators to decide whether to participate in or opt out of a particular operation[349] – that is, they

341 AAPL Form 810 § 6.2.2.2, 12.3, 12.8.
342 AAPL Form 810 § 2.58.
343 "[T]he widely used A.A.P.L Form 610 makes no provision for an operating committee. Instead non-operators look, for protections against operators' proposals to which they object, to wide powers of non-consent, unlike the position in the North Sea." Terence Daintith *et al* (n 16) p1143.
344 Such exceptional and transitional situation is analysed in another Chapter 3 section 3.2 (Removal of the operator).
345 AAPL Form 810 § 8.1 and AAPL Form 610 Article VI (A).
346 Scott Styles (n 14) pp286–287.
347 RMMLF JOA §4.1.
348 RMMLF JOA §5.1 (B).
349 RMMLF JOA §5.5., 9.2.

can decide only whether to share in the costs and participate in the operation, or alternatively to exercise their right of non-consent. Non-operators cannot block a proposal or even effectively participate in ongoing activities through sub-committees or project teams.

Non-operators in North America are thus likely to end up in a weaker position compared to those in other regions (eg, the United Kingdom, Greenland, Norway) or under the International model. The Opcom is a clear and effective forum through which non-operators can participate in the decisions that will determine the conduct of the joint operations. However, such participation will only be effective if the non-operators have *de facto* positive or negative control in this decision-making body.

CAPL model: The CAPL model adopts a similar approach to AAPL Form 610: it provides neither for the existence of an Opcom nor for an elaborate voting system.[350] It does expressly state that: "The operator will consult with the Parties periodically about the exploration, development and operation of the Joint Lands ... and management of the Joint Property."[351] However, the mere obligation to consult does not afford non-operators a high degree of control, as the operator can simply choose to reject their views and continue with its own plans.

The model further provides that after consultation, the operator should "create a written forecast outlining all anticipated Joint Operations during the next 12 months period and their estimated cost".[352] However, it is clear that this procedure is for information purposes only.

It is thus arguable that non-operators have no real control over the joint operations under the CAPL model. Their only real option is to exercise their right of non-consent.[353]

The CAPL model thus does not give non-operators a high degree of participation in and control over the joint operations at a management level. It clearly recognises the operator's duty to consult the non-operators, but without further explanation, which renders this clause ineffective in practice.

British model:[354] The British JOA model does provide for the existence of an Opcom to control and supervise the activities of the JV.[355] Its provisions are similar, but not identical, to those of the AIPN model.

As under the AIPN model, each party can nominate a representative to the Opcom, regardless of the size of its participating interest.[356] This provision secures the greater participation of all the contracting parties.

350 "The AAPL and CAPL forms of JOA do not provide for an operating committee at all." Taylor and Tyne (n 54) p22.
351 CAPL OP §3.01.
352 CAPL OP §5.04.
353 CAPL OP §7.01.
354 Historically the British model did not have an Opcom, as it was based on the AAPL JOA Form 610. In the mid-1970s the UK included an Opcom provision for the first time, within the BNOC pro-forma model. In the current OGUK JOA model, the Opcom is provided for in clause 9. See: Terence Daintith *et al* (n 16) p1143.
355 OGUK JOA §9.
356 OGUK JOA §9.2.

Like the AIPN model, the British model also provides for the creation of sub-committees for advisory purposes. However, in contrast to the AIPN model, it does not expressly determine the right of each party to nominate a representative to such sub-committees.[357]

The voting procedure under the British model is also similar to that under the AIPN model, as the parties must again negotiate a passmark for specific operations.[358] As mentioned previously, this system might weaken the non-operators' position if they cannot secure a high passmark in the negotiations. On the other hand, the British model requires unanimous approval for certain matters, which clearly affords non-operators a degree of control over the joint operations than the AIPN model.[359]

Although the relevant passmark is agreed between the parties the parties,[360] the British model includes no provision on the minimum number of parties required to approve a proposal. This means that the operator may be able to push through proposals alone if its participating interest, as a percentage of the votes, exceeds the relevant passmark. In order to prevent such a situation from arising, this model should also specify the minimum number of parties (ie, at least two) required in order to approve a proposal. However, such a provision would prove problematic for consortia comprised of only two parties, as unanimous agreement would thus be required for all proposals – a favourable situation for the non-operator, but not for the operator.

Additionally, the model does not specify how the parties should proceed in the event of a deadlock. Instead, it provides only that "the agreement, approval or consent of the Joint Operating Committee is not to be unreasonably withheld or delayed in respect of any matter".[361] So what happens if a party unreasonably withholds approval? Or, even if a party has reasonable grounds for withholding approval, what happens where unanimous approval is required? The model seeks to provide a solution in the form of the minimum work obligation, but only where the Opcom makes no objection within 28 days. In such a case there will be some measure of resolution for the minimum work obligation. In general terms, it seems that the standard dispute resolution process would apply and the public court would resolve the matter; however, this might be time consuming and expensive, and could put at risk the whole consortium.[362] The most reasonable interpretation is that the solution for deadlocks in Opcom decisions is through exclusive operations.

In general terms, the key difference between the British model and the AIPN model is the flexibility afforded by the latter. At first glance, this flexibility does not appear positive for non-operators, as they will have to negotiate on which issues require a higher passmark and which require unanimity. However, if the non-operators can secure a strong position in the negotiations, this flexibility might eventually increase their powers to an extent that they would be unlikely to enjoy in current operations outside mature provinces. Like the AIPN model, the British model

357 OGUK JOA §9.7.
358 OGUK JOA §9.8.
359 OGUK JOA §9.8.3.
360 OGUK JOA §9.8.2.
361 OGUK JOA §9.8.5.
362 OGUK JOA §29.

does not specify a passmark, but rather leaves it to the parties to agree on a case-by-case basis.

The British model also does not provide for a high degree of participation by non-operators on sub-committees – although it does afford them a greater degree of control by stipulating that certain issues require unanimous approval by all parties.

Like the AIPN model, therefore, the British JOA model is relatively favourable towards no-operators in allowing them to exert control over the joint operations. However, there is limited scope for non-operators to input on decisions and no provisions on how to deal with deadlocks (except as an exclusive operation), which could ultimately jeopardise the JV.

Norwegian model: The Norwegian model form establishes a management committee (ie, an Opcom) to control and supervise the conduct of the joint operations.[363] The principles which govern the Opcom are balanced and allow for participation and control by all parties involved.[364]

The management committee comprises one representative of each party of the consortium.[365] It is chaired by a representative of the operator.[366] The composition is fairly balanced, as all parties can participate in the decision-making process. However, the operator will inevitably enjoy greater control via the chairman's seat.

Clear provision is made for the existence of sub-committees. Each party has the right to nominate a representative to each sub-committee, although the parties remain free to decide otherwise. Each sub-committee has a purely advisory role, unless the Opcom decides otherwise.[367] This is a balanced approach to the extent that equal representation is secured.

Voting procedures are addressed not within the body of the JOA itself, but rather in the introduction to the agreement (the JOA is in fact an attachment to this introduction). Voting is based on the participating interest of each party,[368] with decisions being taken according to a combination of the number of parties voting in favour and the participating interests of the parties. The most valuable provision for non-operators states that one party by itself cannot constitute a quorum. This allows the non-operators to exercise negative control over the joint operations.[369]

Certain matters require unanimous approval, such as "relinquishment of acreage within the licence area or surrender of the Production Licence".[370] Voting procedures are not a private matter between the parties, but are also relevant to government authorities. Thus, if any change occurs to the voting rules, the parties must obtain governmental approval.[371]

Another advantage for non-operators is the provision that "The management

363 Norwegian JOA §1.1.
364 Norwegian JOA §1.3.
365 Norwegian JOA §1.1.
366 Norwegian JOA §1.2.
367 Norwegian JOA §1.3.
368 Norwegian Agreement Concerning Petroleum Activities §3.1.
369 Norwegian Agreement Concerning Petroleum Activities §3.2.
370 Norwegian Agreement Concerning Petroleum Activities §3.4.
371 Norwegian ACPA §3.5.

committee shall make no decision which could render an unreasonable advantage to certain Parties or others to the detriment of other Parties or the joint venture."[372] This is a balancing provision which favours the consortium and not a specific party, as it applies to both sides (ie, operator and non-operators).

The Opcom must not take a decision that is contrary to the petroleum regulations; the JOA authorises the government or the operator to reject any such decisions.[373] This provision on state control is standard and reasonable, but the operator's final control nonetheless raises some concerns, as it gives the operator the right to reject a decision of the supreme body of the JOA. The operator might potentially abuse this right of veto by extending its interpretation of the provision in certain cases. It would be more reasonable to leave the exercise of such control exclusively to the state, given that the Opcom is the supreme body of the JOA.

In conclusion, the Norwegian JOA model form is reasonably beneficial for non-operators, as it requires their participation in any decision regarding the joint operations. It also strikes a fair balance, as no decision in the Opcom can exclusively benefit one party – a provision that will give comfort to the operator. An interesting feature is that the voting procedure is provided outside the JOA itself, in a short introduction to the consortium agreement. The main flaw with this model form is the lack of provisions on the resolution of deadlocks, which might create problems for the parties down the line (even though there are provisions for sole risk operations), especially regarding minimum work obligations and decisions that require unanimous approval. A further problem is the greater power that the operator has to 'ratify' the decisions of the Opcom.

Australian model:[374] The Australian JV model also provides for the existence of an Opcom (referred to as a 'management committee'), to supervise the operations of the JV and determine its major policies.[375]

Representation on the committee is similar to that under the British and International JOA models, as each member of the JV can nominate a representative to the committee regardless of the size of its participating interest.[376]

In contrast, the voting procedure is quite different from that under other JOA models. First, the operator cannot vote on the Opcom as an operator, but only as a party. This provision has little practical significance, except that it may reduce the fiduciary duties owed.[377] Second, the voting procedure does not factor in the number of parties voting, but considers only the percentage of participating interest – which means that a proposal could ultimately be pushed through by a single party.[378] Third,

372 Norwegian ACPA §3.2.

373 Norwegian ACPA §3.2.

374 AMPLA JOA §5 – The JOA model form maintains the same structure as the JV model, with few changes:
- It stipulates a minimum PI in the JOA.
- The powers of the Opcom are augmented on several issues relating to procurement.
- The JOA authorizes a defaulting party to receive documents related to Opcom meetings (but it still cannot participate or vote in meeting).

375 AMPLA JV §5.1.

376 AMPLA JV §5.1 (a).

377 AMPLA JV §5.5 (b).

378 AMPLA JV §5.5 (a).

as a rule, the passmark is a simple majority, with unanimous approval required for certain matters, such as surrender, decommissioning and management fees – although these are mentioned as mere examples, rather than obligations.[379] As under the other models, no provision is made for the resolution of deadlocks.

The Australian model also provides for the creation of sub-committees where the Opcom so decides.[380] These sub-committees provide advisory guidance to the Opcom. However, their composition is determined by the Opcom, which does not guarantee the participation of all parties.

If the voting restriction on the operator could be extended to all cases (except where unanimous approval was needed), this model would arguably invert the traditional situation, as it would place the non-operators in a dominant position in the Opcom. The operator would be severely restricted in its capacity to vote in the Opcom, and the non-operators could exercise overall control over any sub-committees. However, the operator remains the chair of the Opcom and would also prepare most of the proposals to be approved by the Opcom.

If such a procedure were implemented, it would mitigate the strength of the operator by reducing its rights in the JV. This solution would suit ongoing JOA operations, as it would equalise the power between the operator and non-operators by reducing the rights of the operator so that a balanced agreement could be reached that provided for a higher degree of participation by non-operators. On the other hand, it would not suit mature province operations, as the provisions of the existing JOAs in themselves are not truly balanced.

However, as it stands, this model fails to provide for a high level of participation by non-operators, as there is no requirement on the minimum number of parties to approve decisions, so the operator's strong position (resulting from its larger participating interest) will likely be determinative.

Finally, the voting restrictions on the operator have little effect in practice, as the operator can still vote as a party to the JV. As a consequence, non-operators face the same problems as in any other JOA, and can exercise effective control only if they secure a higher passmark to block decisions.

AIPN model:[381] The AIPN form recognises the Opcom as the highest authority of the JOA, stating: "To provide for the overall supervision and direction of Joint Operations, there is established an Operating Committee."[382]

Representation on the Opcom is well balanced, as each party can nominate a representative regardless of the size of its participating interest.[383] However, some parties might raise concerns about the extension of the authorities of such representatives.[384] As

379 AMPLA JV §5.5 (c) and schedule 1.
380 AMPLA JV §5.7.
381 AIPN JOA model form 2012 – No relevant change occurred in the Opcom provision, with only minor adjustments to style and wording.
382 AIPN JOA §5.1.
383 AIPN JOA §5.1.
384 "Companies have occasionally expressed concern about the authority of a Party's representative to the Operating Committee to bind that Party to participation in any type of operation. The issue was raised for discussion but no one on the drafting committee felt a change was necessary or practical." David F Asmus, "The 1995 Model Form International Operating Agreement" (1996) 14 *J Energy & Nat Resources L* 14, p22.

mentioned, this approach is advantageous for non-operators, because it allows for the participation of all parties in the main decision-making body of the JOA. It is particularly beneficial for smaller participants.

The Opcom can decide on the creation of sub-committees, which in principle should have an advisory role only, although the parties can change this by unanimous agreement. The most important part of this provision states that: "Each Party shall have the right to appoint a representative to each subcommittee."[385] This is a valuable way to gather non-operators' input on each sub-committee, as all parties can nominate a member to such sub-committees.

All of the above features form part of the AIPN's compulsory provisions and must therefore be included in any JOA draft. However, the AIPN model is unique in providing flexible terms: in several instances, different alternatives are available in the model draft, with the parties free to choose that which best suits the deal. For instance, in terms of the voting procedure, there are two main options.[386] The first is quite simple, involving a single passmark for all proposals. The second is more complex as it provides three different scenarios ('A', 'B' and 'C') with different percentages for each scenario. The parties can choose which issues will require a higher passmark and which a lower passmark. Commonly, scenario A represents a simple majority, scenario B requires a higher passmark (eg, 70%) and finally scenario 'C' requires unanimous approval.

This second alternative affords stronger protection to non-operators, as they can exercise greater control over complex and sensitive issues and less control where an issue is less important to them. However, the flexibility of this model might also affect them negatively, as the current dominant position enjoyed by operators might result in the implementation of lower passmarks. Arguably, such flexibility suits operations in mature provinces, where the parties are more likely to be in equal negotiating positions, but not traditional operations where the non-operators are more likely to sign unbalanced terms. Thus, for current operations, a defined percentage – or at least a defined range of minimum and maximum percentages – would give more comfort to non-operators and would also re-establish the equilibrium between the parties.

The AIPN model lacks provisions on the resolution of deadlocks. It is likely that these would be dealt with as conflicts and could thus take a long time to resolve, except in the case of minimum work obligations, as the model provides that the ultimate decision in this regard rests with the operator.[387] The AIPN aims to allow for sole risk operation as a resolution process – this might be an option to resolve some problems, but not all of them.[388]

With regard to the voting procedure, it is significant that each alternative is based on both the percentage interest and the number of participants.[389] However, there is no requirement on the minimum number of parties required to approve a proposal,

---

385 AIPN JOA §5.4.
386 AIPN JOA §5.9.
387 AIPN JOA §6.1 (D).
388 See section 3.1(d).
389 AIPN JOA §5.9.

so once again, one party might be able to push through a proposal by itself. Consequently, if the parties do not agree that the support of more than one party is required to approve a decision, this situation will clearly benefit the operator: its higher participating interest will afford it unfettered authority over the JV, as it will be able to dictate Opcom decisions by itself, even though it might be a minority in terms of the number of parties.

The AIPN also provides for the possibility of voting by notice, with the aim of increasing flexibility and speed when voting on a particular proposal. In theory, this could benefit the whole consortium, as certain proposals may require urgent determination; however, the problem with this provision is that it affords discretion to operator to determine whether a proposal is urgent.[390]

It is thus clear that the AIPN model secures a relatively strong position for non-operators, but only if they can negotiate a higher pass mark. If this is not the case, the Opcom may in practice be just a formality, as the operator will be able to conduct the joint operations in accordance with its own views, regardless of any opposition from the non-operators. However, if the JV's interaction with government authorities involves some kind of committee,[391] the non-operators will also have a seat and vote on that committee – or at least the right to attend meetings.

In addition, the AIPN model fails to provide for the establishment of a project team – which could allow for greater participation by all parties in certain activities of the consortium, such as the preparation of the work programme and budget, authorisation for expenditures and the award of contracts – in the standard form, even though there are references in the guidance notes.[392] This exclusion probably relates to the fact that there exists a clear provision for sub-committees.

Greenlandic model: Like the AIPN, British, Norwegian and Australian models, the Greenlandic model also provides for the existence of the Opcom.[393] Each party can nominate a representative to the Opcom, regardless of the size of its participating

---

390 PR Weems, M Bolton, (n 24).

391 "In some countries such as Egypt, the Government may for purposes of development establish a board of an operating company or supervisory committee to which the contractor is entitled to appoint more than one representative. A Non-operator with large Participating Interests may feel that it is entitled to appoint one of its personnel to one of those positions. After a brief discussion, the drafting committee concluded that the allocation of available positions was far less important to most Parties than how the representatives holding those positions voted. Article 4.2(B)(10) of the 1990 Model Form already makes the operator's dealings with the Government subject to the decisions of the Operating Committee, so no change was made." David F Asmus (n 384) pp14, 21.

392 "Some members of the AIPN have for years argued that the Model Form should include provisions allowing the non-operators to require the establishment of project teams consisting of both operator and non-operator personnel for the implementation of various stages of Joint Operations. Two proposals were tabled to the drafting committee, one of which would have allowed any non-operator to cause the creation of a project team and the other of which would have required an operating committee vote. Additional language would be necessary because of the specific authority that the Model Form grants the operator over the selection of employees and contracting and the strict limitations the Model Form places on the creation of non-advisory subcommittees. While many members of the drafting committee recognised the benefits that might be gained by using expert personnel furnished by each Party, they felt that imposition of such an arrangement on the operator would amount to 'removal of operator by stealth'. In addition, many members were wary of allowing fewer than all Parties to establish subcommittees with actual decision-making powers. The project teams concept was shelved until the next Model Form revision." *Ibid* p22.

393 Greenlandic JOA §4.1.

interest. The same applies to any sub-committee that is subject to regulation by the Opcom.[394]

Once again, the pass mark and the number of parties required to approve a proposal are left open for negotiation.[395] This model also faces the same problems as those previously outlined in this regard. However, like the British model, The Greenlandic model does require unanimous approval.[396] This is a valuable guarantee that certain proposals cannot be pushed through without the consent of non-operators.

The Greenlandic model does deal with deadlock situations, but only in relation to related to minimum work obligations or surrender of acreage.[397] The result is likely to favour the operator rather than the non-operators, as the former retains the greatest participating interest in the JV and thus will be free to resolve such matters. The unanimous approval required under this model is therefore arguably illusory, as in the end the party with which the decision rests is that which holds the highest participating interest. On the other hand, it may be argued that the interests of the consortium as a whole are greater than those of any particular party, so it is necessary to provide for special measures where there is a danger that the entire investment might be lost.[398] Both arguments are valid, so a provision that balances the protection of the consortium against the parties' individual interests would be the best way forward.

It may thus be said that the Greenlandic model adopts a similar approach to the AIPN model regarding representation on sub-committees and deadlock resolution, and a similar approach to the British model regarding the voting procedure.[399]

Conclusion: The Opcom is a valuable instrument for the protection of non-operators, allowing them a degree of control over the joint operations and affording a great opportunity to gather their input to maximise the efficiency of the JV. However, not all JOA models provide for such management committees in all JOAs, as the following table illustrates.

---

394 Greenlandic JOA §4.2.
395 Greenlandic JOA §4.7.2.
396 Greenlandic JOA §4.7.2.
397 Greenlandic JOA §4.7.4.
398 "Also some decisions, like relinquishment of Licence can only be made unanimously and for critical decisions, like surrender of parts of the Licence Area, fall back provisions may be necessary to ensure that the decision can be reached." Sandy Shaw (n 16) p19.
399 AIPN JOA §5.4, OGUK JOA §9.7.
400 "North American JOA forms prefer a position which gives greater obvious latitude to the operator." Peter Roberts (n 5) p96. Ernest Smith describes the same situation: "In contrast to the broad discretion given the operator in Canada and U.S. onshore JOAs, international JOAs provide for an operating committee that exercises some degree of supervisory control over operations." Ernest E Smith *et al* (n 16) p542.
401 Hew Dundas describes the weak position of a non-operator in North America as follows: "The degree of control by the Operating Committee over the operator represents a major difference between UK and North American practice. Springing from BNCOC S 1977 requirement to be able to manage its interest in every joint venture in which it was involved but with limited manpower resources, the UKCS JOA places the operator firmly under the control and direction of the Operating Committee, whereas the American model forms give the operator rather wider discretion." Hew Dundas (n 16) pp4–5.

North American models			
JOA models/provisions	**AAPL**	**RRMLF**	**CAPL**
Opcom	No	No	No
Limitation for participating interest	–	–	–
Sub-committee/project team	Yes	No	No
Voting procedures	Yes	No	No
Deadlock resolution	Partial*	Partial*	Partial*

**Via exclusive operation (if allowed)*

Other models					
JOA models/provisions	**OGUK**	**Norway**	**AMPLA**	**AIPN**	**Greenland**
Opcom	Yes	Yes	Yes	Yes	Yes
Limitation for participating interest	No	No	No/Yes	No	No
Sub-committee/project team	Yes	Yes	Yes	Yes	Yes
Voting procedures	Yes	Yes	Yes**	Yes	Yes
Deadlock resolution	Partial*	Partial*	Partial*	Partial*	Partial*

**Via exclusive operation (if allowed) **Based only on participating interest*

In North America, the operator has far more discretion in the conduct of the operations, as non-operators cannot exercise adequate control over the joint operations,[400] and thus cannot collaborate and give their input on such operations.[401] However, it may be argued that as North American operations, being onshore or in shallow waters, are generally less expensive and risky than those elsewhere in the world, there is no need to provide for greater participation and control by non-operators – an argument that is not valid for complex or deepwater operations (eg, Gulf of Mexico, Alaska or the Arctic).

On the other hand, the remaining models[402] afford non-operators greater control over the joint operations through the existence of the Opcom, as this body is the

402 Terence Daintith *et al* (n 16) p1143.

highest authority that determines the overall policies and supervision of the JOA.[403] In other words, the existence of an Opcom can give non-operators greater comfort, as it can allow them to input on the conduct and supervision of the joint operations. However, this is possible only if the relevant provisions also secure their effective participation on the Opcom; otherwise, it will be a redundant body which increases the administrative burden without any real benefit for the non-operators.

To conclude, non-operators in North America enjoy less control over the joint operations than non-operators in any other region analysed in this book.[404] While different JOA models afford varying degrees of protection to non-operators, in terms of voting systems or participation on sub-committees, they all fail to provide for the effective participation of more than one party and the adequate resolution of deadlocks,[405] even though there are provisions for exclusive operations. Under the current JOAs, therefore, operators can conduct joint operations without any major interference from non-operators. While some JOAs may secure the non-operators' participation in critical matters by requiring unanimous approval, they do not allow for the non-operators' full collaboration in the JOA.

(c) *Costs and expenditures*[406]

As mentioned previously, the purpose of a JV is to enable the parties to share the risks and costs associated with the joint operations. This is one of the most crucial aspects of the JOA, as the ultimate aim of each party is to maximise its profits. Decisions on expenditure are thus crucial for all stakeholders.

It is important to remember the fact that the structure of the JOA is based on the conduct of the operations solely by the operator, who is the person responsible for acting on behalf of the consortium. Muhammed Mazeel describes the operator's powers in relation to incurring expenditure as follows: "The operator shall charge the Joint Account with all costs and expenditures incurred by the operator to perform as operator in connection with the Joint Operations."[407] However, in conducting the operations, the operator must comply with the relevant petroleum legislation and any other applicable regulations, as well as with the procedures established in the JOA.[408]

While the operator executes the operations alone on behalf of the consortium, all parties will contribute to the expenditures according to their participating interest.[409] There is one exception to this general rule:[410] sometimes – usually in cases

403 The Greenlandic and Australian models have not been fully analysed by academics, but several authors have recognised the higher degree of participation and control provided in the British JOA model.

404 See also Terence Daintith *et al* (n 16) p1143, Hew Dundas (n 16) pp4–5, Scott Styles (n 14) pp269–270, Ernest E Smith *et al* (n 16) p539.

405 For example, Greenland JOA §4.7.4.

406 For further analysis see Taylor and Tyne (n 54) pp36–46, Peter Roberts (n 5) pp105–119, Terence Daintith *et al* (n 16), Sandy Shaw (n 16) pp19–20.

407 Muhammed Mazeel, *Petroleum Fiscal Systems and Contracts* (Diplomica Verlag, 2010 Hamburg) p59.

408 John Wilkinson (n 16) pp49–40, Anthony Jennings (n 16) pp24–30, Chavez Golvala (n 6) pp47–48.

409 "The operator's costs are borne by the whole group according to their participating interests." Chris Thorpe (n 317) p126.

410 "Expenditures on joint operations are as a general rule shared by the licensees proportionately with their percentage of interest shares, though in practice there are exceptions to this rule. Disproportionate sharing of costs may however result in tax benefits. An example of disproportionate sharing is the carried interest. This is an arrangement whereby a party to the joint venture is entitled to have all or part of its percentage share of expenditures borne by one or more parties." Terence Daintith *et al* (n 16) p1145.

involving an NOC and/or a farmout agreement – one or more parties cover another party's expenditure for a certain period.[411] This is known as 'carried interest'. However, a detailed examination of this exceptional situation is beyond the scope of this book.

From a non-operator's perspective, it is extremely important to exert control over decisions on capital spent in conducting the joint operations.[412]

Terence Daintith recognises this when he states that: "Financial control over expenditure is a main concern of non-operators and therefore an effective method of forecasting and controlling expenditures is vital."[413] Sandy Shaw concurs: "Another major means of controlling operations is by control on expenditures."[414] Expenditure control is crucial for both proactive and passive non-operators, as even mere investors will seek to secure their investments by controlling costs.

On the other hand, the operator will seek discretion to determine expenditures without the delay of formal procedures and/or approval by the non-operators. This is therefore another tension point between operators and non-operators.[415]

An important principle regarding expenditure is the fact that the operator must neither profit nor suffer loss from its activities as operator of the consortium.[416] As mentioned, this is another reason why the operator has traditionally the highest participating interest in the JV, so that non-operators do not fear that the operator is less than fully committed to the project.

The non-operators will wish to exercise control over expenditures incurred by the operator so that they can verify that their investments are being used diligently and prudently.[417] Several procedures apply in this regard;[418] the analysis in this book concentrates on the work program and budget, authorisation for expenditures and procurement. However, the essence of expenditure regulation is governed by the accounting procedures.[419] These are commonly provided as an attachment to the JOA,[420] since a separate document is required to address fully all relevant issues, as well as the right of audit, which is a valuable instrument in this regard.[421] An analysis of the accounting procedures is beyond the scope of this book; suffice to say that

411 For further information, see Claude Duval *et al* (n 122) p297, Terence Daintith (n 16) p1146.

412 "[T]he day-to-day control of the Joint Operations rests with the operator. In practice this reduces the position of the non-operators to one major duty and one major right. The major duty is to pay pro rata for all expenditure authorized by the JOA and to contribute pro rata towards any liabilities incurred by the Joint Operations. The non-operator's major right is to uplift pro rata their share of production arising out of the Joint Operations." Scott Styles (n 14) p288.

413 Terence Daintith *et al* (n 16) pp1143–1150.

414 Sandy Shaw (n 16) p19.

415 As "The non-operating parties will be keen to exercise some measure of control over the costs which the operator will incur and how the operator will enter into contracts on their behalf in the performance of the joint operations. This is an area in which the contracting parties will be particularly apparent." Peter Roberts (n 5) p105.

416 See Chapter 2, section 2.2(b) and Chapter 3, section 3.2(b).

417 See Chapter 2, section 2.2(b).

418 "The other way in which an operator can be supervised is through the control of expenditure, which is achieved in a number of different ways." Chavez Golvala (n 6) p47.

419 This procedure is hotly debated during JOA negotiations as it will determine how cash calls or invoices for expenditures are handled. Taylor and Tyne recognise this situation as follows: "Probably the most important function of the accounting procedure is to specify the costs and expenses which the operator may charge to the joint account and the basis upon which these costs and expenses are to be calculated." Taylor and Tyne (n 58) pp43–44.

420 Taylor and Tyne (n 54) p43.

they represent a fundamental mechanism through which to exercise effective control over the joint operations.

Work programme and budget: In acting on behalf of the JV, one of the operator's main duties is to prepare the work programme and budget, which must be approved by the Opcom[422] (where applicable) or by the other parties.[423]

The extent of this obligation[424] remains in question. The nature of the agreement is self-explanatory: as the parties will jointly share the costs, it is logical that they should together decide how these will be incurred.[425] This is the purpose of the work programme and budget, as it establishes how monies will be spent. In other words, the operator can proceed with any form of expenditure only if it is provided for in the work programme and budget. Taylor and Tyne describe this obligation as follows:

As a general rule, the operator is not permitted to conduct any joint operation (or otherwise incur expenditure on the joint account) unless and until a programme and budget for it has been approved by the operating committee.[426]

However, the operator will seek greater flexibility so that it is free to incur expenditures outside the work programme and budget.[427] As a general rule, unauthorised expenditures are not allowed. However, it is impossible to predict the exact budget for the entire operations, as several factors might require adjustments and might be beyond the control of the parties (eg, market fluctuations in the cost of materials, geological conditions or technical difficulties).[428] The work programme and budget is thus an estimate[429] which can be modified where justified.

A detailed work programme and budget can help the non-operators to exercise greater control over operations so that less discretion is afforded to the operator. Peter Roberts recognises this situation as follows:

So that the parties can make a suitably informed decision at the OpCom about the WP&B which the operator is proposing, the JOA typically requires the operator (to the

421 "Control is also exercised over operations through the use of the Accounting Procedure, which will form a part of the JOA. It is a critical facet of the JOA and will demand as much time in negotiation as other key aspects. The purpose of the Accounting Procedure is to establish and detail the workings ... of the Joint Account, determine what costs the operator may charge to the Joint Account and how they are calculated and to ensure that generally accepted accounting procedures are adhered to." Sandy Shaw (n 16) p21.

422 References to the Opcom within this sub-heading apply to the JOA models which have such provision. Otherwise, 'the Opcom' should be read as referring to the approval or determination of the contracting parties.

423 Bernard G Taverne (n 308) pp66–67.

424 Hew Dundas (n 16 p5), Claude Duval *et al* (n 122) p290, Ernest E Smith *et al* (n 16) p543, Terence Daintith *et al* (n 16) p1140.

425 "Despite the appointment of the operator with responsibility for performance of the joint operations ... the operator will not have an unlimited ability to incur expenditure which will be back-charged to the parties in respect of operations under the JOA." Peter Roberts (n 5) p105.

426 Taylor and Tyne (note 54) p36.

427 "Some companies regularly seek to provide the operator with a revolving fund that can be spent on whatever operation the operator chooses relating to Joint Operations, whether or not contained in an approved Work Programme and Budget; those expenditures can be submitted for approval of the Operating Committee and the amount available to the operator is then restored. The drafting committee did not support advance authorisation of expenditures for matters that are not contained in an approved Work Programme and Budget." David F Asmus (n 384) pp14, 22.

428 Taylor and Tyne (n 54) p41.

429 "The approved budget for an annual programme is inevitably an approximate estimate of the anticipated level of expenditures involved." Terence Daintith *et al* (n 18) p1145.

extent that it is able) to provide a sufficiently detailed outline of its intentions through the content of the WP&B. Consequently, the WP&B will usually be broken down so as to recite individual line items of proposed activity and expenditure (by reference to the proposed works and the relevant costs and the intended timings and durations for the commission of those works). These line items in the WP&B will go on to be applied in respect of permitted overspends by the operator ... and in respect of the grounds for rejection of an AFE in certain circumstances ..., so care should be taken in their preparation.[430]

The operator is generally required to comply with the precise determination of the work programme and budget as approved by the Opcom. Exceptionally, however, the work programme and budget can be modified. In this regard, it is important to distinguish between modifications made by the Opcom and modifications made by the operator. As the highest authority of the JOA, the Opcom can generally modify the approved work programme and budget at any time, so long as the relevant pass mark is reached.[431] The operator also has a certain degree of flexibility to deviate from the work programme and budget without seeking the Opcom's approval where this deviation is no more than a fixed percentage (commonly 5–10% of the approved budget). However, if the amount of additional expenditure exceeds this percentage, the operator must obtain the Opcom's approval.[432]

Peter Roberts describes such limited discretion given to the operator conducting operations as follows:

In contrast to the idea of close control of the operator's freedom to incur expenditures, the JOA might also afford some latitude to the operator by providing that certain operational circumstances might dictate a right of the operator to overspend against an agreed budget which has been set within a WP&B ... A more prosaic example of this right would be a standing right for the operator to overspend against any particular line item in a budget, up to a defined finance limit.[433]

There is only one situation in which the operator can modify the work programme and budget without the Opcom's consent. In the event of an emergency, such as a spill, explosion or fire,[434] an immediate response is required, so there is no time to obtain the consent of the other parties. Nevertheless, the operator must inform the non-operators immediately of the emergency.[435]

In all other cases the operator must follow the work programme and budget to the letter or request a revision through the Opcom.

However, problems might arise where a high pass mark has been implemented in the Opcom, as the non-operators may therefore have the power to reject the operator's proposed revision to the work programme and budget. In such cases, the operator will generally have to amend its proposal and resubmit it. This in turn may

430 Peter Roberts (n 5) p108.
431 *Ibid.*
432 Claude Duval *et al* (n 122) p298.
433 Peter Roberts (n 5) p109.
434 "Generally, the operator is authorized to fund any activities which shall safeguard lives or property or prevent pollution." Claude Duval *et al* (n 122) p298.
435 Kenneth C Mildwaters (n 16) p561.

lead to a deadlock situation, as described in the previous section.[436] So what happens if the non-operators keep rejecting the operator's proposal? If it involves a minimum work obligation (and exclusive operations are forbidden),[437] then the situation is drastic, as it might result in the termination of the petroleum title and thus of the JV itself, and might also affect future applications with regard to the host government.[438]

It is thus important to adopt a resolution process for work programme and budget deadlocks in order to protect the petroleum licence and JV. As mentioned,[439] several procedures could be implemented to address this issue, such as mediation, mini-trial or expert determination, in order to determine if the parties have complied with the terms of the JOA.

Anthony Jennings outlines the need for flexible solutions to avoid deadlocks in this regard as follows:

In awarding a licence or PSA, a government will often impose a requirement to drill obligation` wells in the exploration phase and the JOA will need to be tailored in certain aspects, for example in the voting procedure, authority for expenditure (AFE), and assignment provisions to cater for these. Because failure to drill obligation wells is a fundamental breach of the licence, PSA or other concession agreement or contract, it is vital that a mechanism exists for getting the wells drilled.[440]

Jennings later provides a solution to this problem as follows:

Provision may have to be made in the JOA for the normal voting procedure to be overridden by another that will give the operator ultimate control in the event of failure to agree the location or budget.[441]

This seems the easiest solution to protect the interests of the consortium, but it does not prevent abuse by the operator, as the final decision on minimum work obligations rests with the operator. In other words, this is not a balanced solution, but rather the most practical alternative.

Another solution, which is a little more reasonable, is to allow the proposal that wins the greatest support to prevail. Claude Duval describes this situation as follows:

IPAs [International Petroleum Agreements] generally require minimum work obligations and the annual work programs and budgets of the JOA must accord with these obligations. The JOA usually requires all parties to participate in the minimum work obligations. If the parties disagree about the operator's proposal to satisfy these obligations, the JOA contains provisions to resolve this dispute expeditiously so that the

436 Peter Roberts (n 5) p109.

437 For the host government, the minimum work obligations are highly important, as observed by Howayda Fawzi: "For the purpose of identifying a prospective discovery area, the oil company will be required to carry out an exploration programme, containing certain work and expenditure commitments, which ensures that the area is thoroughly explored. Compliance with the exploration programme is of vital importance for the host country, whether the programme resulted in commercial discovery or not. In short, it represents a major source of information to the government about the area in question." Howayda Hassan Fawzi, *The Evolution of the Legal and Contractual Framework for Exploration and Production of Oil in Sudan and the United Kingdom, A comparative approach to developing and developed countries* (PhD Thesis presented to the University of Dundee, 1996).

438 For further information about MWO see David AW Maloney, "Australia's Offshore Petroleum Work Programme Bidding System" (2003) 21 *J Energy & Nat Resources L* p127.

439 See Chapter 3.

440 Anthony Jennings (n 16) p27.

441 *Ibid.*

underlying IPA is never put at risk for failure to conduct these obligations. Typically, the proposal receiving the largest vote will be selected.[442]

While this option might once again secure the existence of the petroleum title and ultimately the consortium, it also puts the non-operators in a difficult position, as the operator is likely to have the final decision on such crucial issues. In extreme cases, if the operator presents an inadequate work programme and budget due to either negligence or bad faith, this will nonetheless be passed at the end of the process because the operator has the final decision in resolving a deadlock. However, it is still more reasonable as it gives power to the largest participating party, rather than the operator itself.

On the other hand, the option described by Jennings could be improved if provision were made for the final decision to alternate between the parties (ie, through rotation). While this arrangement could prove interesting in the long term, it is still not optimal in the short term, as one party will still have greater power at first.

A radical alternative would be to prohibit the operator from voting on any proposal that it has prepared exclusively by itself. The operator would thus be forced to seek the non-operators' input and to prepare the work programme and budget very carefully. While such a provision would balance the positions of the parties, it is unlikely that an operator would accept such terms in practice.

A more moderate alternative is to provide that after a specific number of rejections, the operator will lose the power to prepare the work programme and budget, with this reverting instead to the non-operators on an *ad hoc* basis. However, in this case the operator might also simply block the non-operators' proposal and the problem will therefore persist.

The optimal solution is thus a balanced provision obliging the operator to prepare a reasonable proposal in collaboration with the non-operators, which no party can reject without reasonable grounds. If there are reasonable grounds to reject the proposal, then alternative dispute resolution mechanisms could be used to resolve the deadlock.[443]

While the work programme details the activities that the JV will perform, the latter estimates the cost of such activities.[444] The budget is also commonly divided into the capital budget and operating budget: the former outlines the costs of the main activities, such as seismic and drilling costs,[445] while the latter relates to manpower and overhead costs.[446] Overheads can potentially be a contentious issue, as the operator may wish to maximise its revenues by establishing these as high as possible.[447] Consequently, the non-operators should verify carefully whether the accounting procedures restrict the extension of the application of overheads.[448]

---

442 Claude Duval *et al* (n 122) p291.
443 See Chapter 3.
444 Scott Styles (n 14) p288, Sandy Shaw (n 16) p20.
445 *Ibid.*
446 *Ibid.*
447 Taylor and Tyne (n 54) p44.
448 "Sensitive questions arise with regard to the audit of company overhead." Terence Daintith *et al* (n 16) p1146.

The work programme and budget must cover a specific timeframe. This will relate to a specific phase of the project, such as exploration, development or production.[449]

As a general rule, the operator must prepare a work programme and budget on an annual basis,[450] though not necessarily for each phase of the project.[451] During the exploration phase, a minimum work programme must be established according to the petroleum title.[452] The parties may thus prepare a single work programme and budget to cover the whole exploration phase, subject to amendment if further work is necessary to progress towards the development phase.[453] Similarly, before moving to the development phase,[454] approval of the work programme and budget is commonly required by the host government,[455] so some parties might opt for a multi-year work programme and budget to deal with that situation.[456] The production phase is more straightforward: the JOA parties will likely accept an annual work programme and budget without further amendment.

Whether the programme of activities is prepared annually or for longer periods will have no real practical implications for non-operators, so long as the Opcom has the power to amend any approved work programme and budget.[457] That said, an annual work programme and budget will ensure a greater degree of participation by non-operators, as the exploration and development phases can take a couple of years, during which time the non-operators should have more opportunities to provide input on each proposal of the work programme and budget.

From the non-operator's perspective, the establishment of a work programme and budget is an excellent opportunity to exercise control over the allocation of expenditure.[458] However, this will be possible in practice only if the non-operators have effective control in the Opcom.

As the operator will prepare programmes and budgets for the execution of the joint operations, it is essential to provide for the non-operators' input in this process.[459] Indeed, this might reduce the chances of deadlock on work programme and budget proposals, as all parties would participate in their preparation.

---

449 Some scholars and JOAs add another phase, 'appraisal', between the exploration and development phases. For further information see Taylor and Tyne (n 54) pp36–41 and Sandy Shaw (n 16).

450 Bernard G Taverne (n 90) p136, Chris Thorpe (n 317) 126, John Wilkinson (n 16) pp41–42.

451 Chavez Golvala (n 6) p47.

452 Model Clause 16 (1) – Petroleum Licensing (Production) (Seaward Areas) Regulations 2008.

453 However, practice may vary in the exploration phase as some parties might still prefer to approve an annual program and to address the minimum work program accordingly. See Taylor and Tyne (n 54) pp36–37.

454 Peter Roberts (n 5) p109.

455 Model Clause 17 (1) and (2) – Petroleum Licensing (Production) (Seaward Areas) Regulations 2008.

456 PR Weems, M Bolton (n 24).

457 The same principle applies for multi-year programmes as activities might evolve to require revision of such programmes: Chavez Golvala (n 6) p47.

458 "Control of expenditures is achieved through the procedures established to agree programmes and budgets, and subsequent release of approved funds. The operator will have the delegated authority to implement all agreed programmes and budgets. Hence, the approval of programmes and budgets is of key importance to partners in controlling operations and their exposure to costs." Sandy Shaw (n 16) p19.

459 "The operator will be under a duty to consult with and keep the Participants informed of matters relating to the Operations. This will include all matters which may warrant the taking of insurance, either jointly or severally by the Participants, information of logging, coring and testing and copies of analyses of well logs and cores." Kenneth C Mildwaters (n 16) p561.

In summary, a non-operator should seek a JOA which contains a work programme and budget provision with the following characteristics:

- approval of the work programme and budget by all or most of the parties;
- scope for the Opcom to amend the work programme and budget at any time;
- provision for deadlock resolution without jeopardising the consortium or weakening the non-operators' position;
- participation of – or at least consultation with – the non-operators during the process of amendment of the work programme and budget;
- clear direction on the extent to which an operator can modify a work programme and budget approved by all the parties;
- imposition of a duty on the operator to notify the other parties, as soon as possible, of any modification of the work programme and budget; and
- the inclusion of detailed information in work programme and budget proposals.

However, while the work programme and budget provision constitutes valuable protection for the non-operators, this mechanism is absent from some JOA model forms.[460] The following paragraphs will examine how each JOA model deals with such provisions, and where no work programme and budget provision is included, why this is so.

AAPL models: AAPL Form 610 does not include a work programme and budget provision. It gives wide discretion to the operator to "conduct and direct and have full control of the all operations on the contract area".[461] The only procedure available to non-operators is a request for estimated expenditure.[462]

However, this right is available only to parties that have already consented to the operation – not before the operation is approved. Is it thus possible to affirm that under this model form, non-operators cannot exert control over expenditures? At first glance, the answer would appear to be yes, as the operator's total control of the operations clearly weakens the non-operators' position in this regard. Another mechanism – the authorisation for expenditure, examined in the following section – allows non-operators to exert a degree of control.

AAPL Form 810 includes a provision on the work programme and budget which is referred to as the 'annual operating plan'. However, the mechanism adopts a soft approach as it is for informational purposes only.[463] In other words, this is a purely bureaucratic mechanism: there is no effective participation by non-operators, except for the right to make suggestions, additions or deletions to the annual operating plan. However, the operator is not obliged to incorporate any such input from non-operators.[464] The operator's strong position is very clear under this model, which

460 Peter Roberts confirms this fact: "[T]he WP&B formulation is not universally adopted within all JOAs." Peter Roberts (n 5) p105.
461 AAPL JOA Form 610 article V (A).
462 AAPL JOA Form 610 article V (D) (8).
463 AAPL JOA Form 810 § 6.4.1 and 6.4.2.
464 AAPL JOA Form 810 § 6.4.3.

provides that "the operator has the exclusive right and duty to conduct (or cause to be conducted) all activities or operations under this Agreement".[465]

Under AAPL Form 810, therefore, non-operators are treated as mere investors: they have access to information, but no effective participation in the activities performed by the JV. However, the authorisation for expenditure mechanism – which will be addressed later – included in this model is an efficient and effective method through which the non-operators can nonetheless control expenditures.

RMMLF model: This historical model form does not include a work programme and budget provision. Paragraph 4.1 simply states that the operator "shall direct and have control of all operations conducted hereunder and shall have exclusive custody of all materials, equipment and other property owned by the Parties."[466]

The operator thus has a very strong position and broad discretion to conduct the joint operations under this model form. However, the non-operators may nonetheless have an opportunity to participate in the preparation of the work programme, as the operator must "[c]onsult freely the other Parties concerning operations hereunder and keep them advised of all matters arising in operations hereunder which the operator deems important in the exercise of its best judgement".[467]

Once again, however, the operator is not obliged to incorporate the non-operators' input. It could further be argued that the term 'freely' suggests that it is left to the operator's discretion whether to consult the non-operators.

It is thus apparent that the RMMLF JOA model affords the non-operators no real control over the work programme and budget. However, the non-operators can exert control over expenditure through the authorisation for expenditure mechanism, to be discussed later.

CAPL model: The Canadian model adopts a similar approach to the US JOA model forms, as there is no work programme and budget provision. The operator has wide discretion to conduct the operations.

This model secures greater participation by the non-operators than the US JOA models, as it specifies that the operator "will consult" with the non-operators "periodically".[468] The operator is thus obliged to consult with the non-operators, which is a valuable provision for them. Once again, however, the operator is not obliged to accept any input from the non-operators. There is, therefore, no scope for real participation by the non-operators, as there is no guarantee that they can effectively contribute to the work programme and budget.

The Canadian model is thus similar to the US JOA models, as it gives the operator broad discretion to conduct the joint operations, with no opportunity for the non-operators to exercise effective control over the work programme and budget. However, it does include an authorisation for expenditure mechanism – which, as is seen below, is another procedure through which expenditure can be controlled.

465 AAPL JOA Form 810 § 5.1.
466 RMMLF JOA § 4.1.
467 RMMLF JOA § 5.1 (B).
468 CAPL OP § 3.01.

British model: The OGUK model form contains a work programme and budget provision. The operator is obliged to set annually the work programme and budget for the following year, which must be approved by the Opcom.[469] Additionally, the Opcom has powers to revise any work programme and budget previously approved.[470]

The British JOA model form provides, as a general rule, that the operator cannot incur any expenditure until it is approved by the Opcom. However, it allows more flexibility for the operator, as it states:

> *Notwithstanding the above, where commitments are required prior to approval of the Programme and Budget, the Joint Operating Committee will use reasonable endeavours to approve such commitments in advance of approving the Programme and Budget and in time to allow such commitments to be made and any commitments so approved shall form part of the approved Programme and Budget to which they relate.*[471]

In general terms, this provision is positive, as certain issues require more urgent resolution than others, so ultimately this will benefit the consortium as a whole. However, there is a risk that the operator might pressure the Opcom to approve preferred items, as there is no clear regulation on who determines the specific commitments which must be approved before the work programme and budget and how this right can be controlled.

The model provides a practical solution for avoiding deadlocks in relation to the minimum work programme,[472] which affords extensive discretion to the operator. The programme proposed by the operator will be deemed to be approved unless an alternative plan is approved by a simple majority of votes. Thus, if the non-operators cannot control the Opcom, the operator will effectively be in a position to determine the work programme and budget by itself in the majority of cases. There are no provisions on the resolution of deadlocks in relation to anything other than the minimum work programme. This might prove problematic, as the consortium will run into problems if it does not meet the rigorous deadlines imposed in the licence. However, it implies that sole risk is the solution for other cases.

The British JOA model form further provides that the operator may overspend beyond the terms specified in the budget. As the extent to which it may do so is not specified, the parties are free to determine this during the negotiations.[473] The operator is not obliged to notify the non-operators of any overspending, but must only obtain the Opcom's approval if the limit is exceeded. There is a clear obligation to notify the non-operators whenever the operator is required to take action to deal with emergencies.[474]

There is no direct obligation that the operator must seek the non-operators' input

---

469 OGUK JOA model § 10, 11, 12, 13 and 14.
470 *Ibid.*
471 *Ibid.*
472 OGUK JOA model § 9.9.1.
473 OGUK JOA model § 10.5, 11.4, 12.4 and 13.4.
474 OGUK JOA model § 6.10.2.

when drawing up the work programme and budget, and even direct consultation is not required.[475] On the other hand, the operator's general duties do require that it "shall freely consult with the Participants and keep them informed of matters concerning the Joint Operations".[476] This provision gives grounds for non-operators to request participation in the discussions on the work programme and budget, but does not force the operator to incorporate their views. The word 'freely' also affords more discretion to the operator.

This approach is not positive for non-operators, as their participation is restricted to Opcom approval of the work programme and budget. If the operator has overall control of the Opcom, the non-operators are left as mere observers, as they can influence neither the drafting of the work programme and budget nor the determinations of the Opcom. The non-operators' position is somewhat stronger if they can block decisions and thus have negative control of the Opcom, as they therefore have the power to block approval of the work programme and budget. However, the operator has more discretion to deal with issues concerning the minimum work programme.

On the other hand, this model does specify in greater depth what must be included by the operator in any work programme and budget proposal.[477] Such a provision is very valuable for the non-operators as they will have a stronger basis to vote on the Opcom, somewhat offsetting the fact that the non-operators cannot effectively participate in the preparation of the work programme and budget proposals, which is controlled by the operator.

In conclusion, the British JOA model puts non-operators in a relatively weak position, as it affords extensive discretion to the operator in preparing the work programme and budget and dealing with minimum work programme issues. More positively, however, more detailed information must be provided in each work programme and budget proposal, and non-operators can veto a work programme and budget proposal if they can effectively block it in the Opcom.

Norwegian model: The operator is responsible for preparing the work programme and budget proposals, which must be submitted to the management committee.[478] However, this model clearly requires the participation of the non-operators as follows: "When preparing proposals for work programs and budgets, the operator shall involve the Parties before the proposal is submitted to the management committee for final adoption."[479] This is a valuable provision for the non-operators, as it gives them a chance to participate in discussions on the work programme and budget.

Any party can propose amendments to the approved work programme and budget to the management committee,[480] which has authority to revise any

475 OGUK JOA model § 10, 11, 12, 13 and 14.
476 OGUK JOA model § 6.9.1.
477 OGUK JOA model § 10.4.
478 Norwegian JOA model § 3.3.
479 Norwegian JOA model § 12.2.
480 Norwegian JOA model § 12.2.

provisions approved in the work programme and budget.[481] Thus, any non-operator has the right to call for amendments. However, such a right is also commonly provided in the Opcom regulations, as any party can add topics to the agenda for an Opcom meeting within a specific timeframe.[482]

This model further includes detailed provisions on proposals regarding both the work programme and the budget.[483]

The provisions on budget proposals state that the operator must "explain the allocation procedures for charging costs".[484] However, the most important provision concerns the structure and content of the budget items, which must be specified according to the activity to be performed by the JV.[485] This is a valuable approach for non-operators, as it allows them to exert control over the overall work programme and budget.

This model also provides a certain flexibility for the operator, as it is allowed to exceed the budget line by up to 10%, but in no case by more than 5%.[486] In emergencies, the operator can incur expenditure outside the approved work programme and budget in order to protect life, health or property.[487] The operator also has the power to spend up to Nkr3 million per year, subject to adjustment by the management committee. However, the operator must provide the management committee, "with no undue delay", with written notice detailing all expenditure unforeseen or which might exceed the approved work programme and budget.[488]

A situation is considered an emergency "if there is not sufficient time to present the matter to the committee", which implies that the operator must consult the non-operators if it is going to prepare an emergency plan – a valuable protection for the non-operators. It is not clear whether the Nkr3 million allowance is included in the relevant percentages or is a supplementary sum. While the wording "may also" might suggest the former, a logical analysis would indicate the latter.

A major flaw in this model is the lack of a resolution process for deadlocks. On the other hand, it does allow for sole risk operations, which might be a way of resolving deadlock, but this is forbidden in situations which include a minimum work obligation.[489] It is important to ensure that any alternative adopted does not provide excessive powers to the operator to deal with such issues; flexibility and balance are vital in this regard. The Norwegian JOA model thus secures a fairly positive position for non-operators and, significantly, a higher level of participation in the preparation of the work programme and budget. However, it fails to provide a resolution process for deadlocks, which could jeopardise the existence of the consortium.

481 Norwegian JOA model § 12.2.
482 Norwegian JOA model § 2.1.
483 Norwegian JOA model § 12.1.
484 Norwegian JOA model § 12.3.
485 Norwegian JOA model § 12.4.
486 Norwegian JOA model § 12.5.
487 Norwegian JOA model § 12.5.
488 Norwegian JOA model § 12.5.
489 Norwegian JOA model § 18.3 (d).

Australian model:[490] The Australian model requires that each year, the operator prepare the work programme and budget for the following year, which must be approved (including any amendments)[491] by the Opcom.[492] However, there is no indication that the operator need seek the non-operators' participation in the preparation and discussion of work programme and budget proposals.

The model says little on what must be included in work programme and budget proposals; there are no specific requirements in this regard, but only general terms.[493] However, it does provide for the resolution of deadlocks, giving the operator the authority to manage certain operations until the Opcom has reached agreement.[494] While this is a valuable provision which should help to secure the existence of the consortium, it also affords too much discretion to the operator, as the obligation to "maintain the Tenements in good standing" is overly broad. The non-operators are thus likely to face serious problems in exerting control over such operations.

Under the Australian model, the operator is allowed to exceed the budget approved by the Opcom by up to 10%, and in emergencies it need not obtain the Opcom's approval to incur expenditure.[495] This approach is very common in the petroleum industry, but what is interesting is the distinction between reporting to the non-operators in emergencies and overspending.[496] The former must be "promptly" reported to the non-operators, while the latter must be reported as soon as reasonably practicable. This is precisely what a non-operator would wish for, since emergencies often significantly affect the whole consortium; it is thus vital that non-operators are aware of emergencies and can take part in decisions on how to tackle them. As overspends are not so urgent, it is possible to take a little longer to report them.

The Australian model thus affords reasonable protection to non-operators, as they will receive full reports on any spending beyond the scope of the approved work programme and budget. In the event of deadlocks, the model also requires the Opcom to meet as many times as necessary to find a solution; meanwhile, the operator will do the minimum required to maintain the good standing of the assets. However, this wording might give too much discretion to the operator to continue conducting the joint operations until an agreement is reached.

The major flaw of this model is the lack of participation by non-operators in the preparation of the work programme and budget. As the non-operators cannot participate in the discussion process, the sole control available to them is Opcom approval. However, this is effective only if the non-operators can block approval of the work programme and budget in the Opcom.

---

490 AMPLA JOA model § 8.2 – The JOA model form introduced a few modifications in the WPB provision. The Opcom may request the operator to prepare and submit a WPB. The model form allows for multi-year programmes. Discretion to perform activities pending the Opcom reaching a decision is reduced.

491 AMPLA JV model § 8.2. (b).

492 AMPLA JV model § 8.1.

493 AMPLA JV model § 8.1.

494 AMPLA JV model § 8.1.

495 AMPLA JV model § 8.3.

496 AMPLA JV model § 8.3.

AIPN form:[497] The AIPN form includes a work programme and budget provision which allows non-operators to exert further control over these key elements of the joint operations.[498]

As usual, the operator has the duty to prepare the work programme and budget.[499] However, the form clearly establishes the need to obtain Opcom's approval in this regard, and the Opcom's authority to revise any work programme and budget that has already been approved.[500]

The operator is also required to consult with the Opcom or applicable sub-committees on the content of work programme and budget proposals.[501] This provision allows the non-operators to provide input on such important issues. However, the provision only mentions "consult" – meaning that the operator is not obliged to incorporate the non-operators' suggestions. In addition, the AIPN model allows for multi-year work programme and budgets, which might prove problematic.[502] On the other hand, it also requires the inclusion of a reasonable amount of detail in work programme and budget proposals, making it easier for non-operators to exert control when voting in the Opcom.[503]

This model allows the operator to overspend by 10% on each approved item in the budget, although it cannot exceed 5% of the total work programme and budget approved for the year.[504] If the operator exceeds these percentages, it must obtain the approval of the Opcom.[505]

However, this restriction does not apply in emergencies (eg, explosion, sabotage and crude oil spills); in these situations the operator can incur expenditure without obtaining the Opcom's consent.[506] Nevertheless, the operator must "as soon as reasonably practicable, report to non-operators the details of such event and any measures the operator has taken or plans to take in response thereto".[507] While this provision would appear sufficiently flexible to protect both the operator's and non-operators' interests, this is not entirely true. "As soon as reasonably practicable" is not the best timing for urgent measures. The operator should rather be required to report immediately after the event; an immediate response from non-operators might allow them to input on decisions to deal with catastrophic events. Moreover, the non-operators' approval should be sought for any plan to address any

497 AIPN model form 2012 – Clause 6 underwent several changes. Some of them were purely stylistic but a more significant change was the addition of obligations on the operator to provide more detailed information in the WPB. This is a classic issue to contrast the WPB with the AFE. As discussed later, the WPB usually does not provide much detail and this model tries to address this deficiency. The real novelty is the provision of a specific WPB for decommissioning activities.

498 AIPN clause 6.

499 AIPN § 4.2 (B) (5).

500 AIPN § 6.1 (E).

501 AIPN § 6.4 (A).

502 "The drafting committee discussed the problems raised by multi-year Minimum Work Obligations, where the Parties' continued failure to agree can push an entire multi-year Minimum Work Obligation into the last calendar year when the work is ultimately required to be completed, but the drafting committee made no curative changes." David F Asmus (n 384) pp14–16.

503 AIPN § 6.1 (F) and 6.2 (A).

504 AIPN § 6.8 (A).

505 AIPN § 6.8 (B).

506 AIPN § 6.8 (C) and 13.5.

507 AIPN § 4.2 (B) (13).

emergencies – as the consequences of such measures will affect all contracting parties, it is reasonable to allow for their participation at such a critical moment.

This model includes a process for the resolution of deadlocks in relation to the minimum work programme, which will be decided by the party with the highest participating interest.[508] This provision obviously favours the strongest party in the JV.[509] While it is valuable in preserving the integrity of the petroleum title, and thus the consortium, it clearly gives more powers to the operator, as this will likely retain the largest participating interest. This procedure also departs from the usual voting processes, as it does not consider the number of parties, but only the percentage of interest.[510] Nonetheless, it is a significant improvement on earlier editions of this model, as the operator previously had even more discretion to perform the minimum work obligations if consensus was not reached in the Opcom.[511]

The AIPN form obliges the operator to provide "detailed" information about the joint operations which will be performed in general.[512] It further obliges the operator to provide certain detailed information at different stages of the operations.[513] These provisions put the non-operators in a strong position, as they give them two layers of protection.[514]

It is thus apparent that the AIPN JOA model affords reasonable protection to non-operators, so long as they can exert effective control over the Opcom. They enjoy valuable participation rights in the preparation of the work programme and budget. However, the operator is not obliged to incorporate their suggestions, so if the operator has absolute control of the Opcom, effective participation by the non-operators may be precluded. In addition, this model fails to secure immediate notification of non-operators in the event of emergencies. It also fails to provide for the establishment of a project team, which could facilitate a higher level of participation in the preparation of work programme and budget proposals. However, this could be dealt with by the creation of a sub-committee to deal with the task.

Greenlandic model: Under the Greenlandic model, the operator must prepare and submit the relevant work programme and budget for approval by the Opcom.[515] As usual, the Opcom also has the authority to amend any approved work programme and budget.[516]

There is no requirement to seek the non-operators' input, or even to consult them, during the preparation of work programme and budget proposals. However, a general provision states that: "The operator shall freely consult with the Parties and

508 AIPN § 6.1 (D).
509 AIPN § 6.1 (D).
510 AIPN § 5.9.
511 "Article 6.1(D) of the 1995 Model Form provides that if the Operating committee cannot agree on a Work Programme and Budget that satisfies the Minimum Work Obligations for the calendar year in question, then the proposal receiving the largest Participating Interest vote is chosen, with the operator breaking any tie votes. In contrast, the 1990 Model Form permitted the operator to select the work necessary to satisfy the Minimum Work Obligations in the event that a passmark vote could not be obtained." David F Asmus (n 384) p14.
512 AIPN § 6.1 (A) (B) (C).
513 AIPN § 6.1 (F) and 6.2 (A).
514 See Chapter 3, section 3.1(a)
515 Greenlandic JOA § 5.1, 5.2, 5.3.1, 5.3.2, 5.4.1, 5.4.2, 5.5 and 5.6.
516 Greenlandic JOA § 5.11.

keep them informed of matters concerning the Joint Operations."[517] This affords the operator extensive discretion to determine such consultation, even for activities where this might be necessary.

The operator may thus opt not to consult with the non-operators; in turn, this lack of participation by the non-operators might increase the risk of proposals being rejected by the Opcom. However, this situation is far more complicated during the exploration phase, as there is no requirement to provide sufficient detail on proposals.[518] In other words, the first time that non-operators are likely to see a work programme and budget proposal during this phase is in the Opcom, and the information provided in proposals will be extremely limited. This means that the non-operators will effectively be voting on something that they are not entirely sure about – clearly a dangerous situation. On the other hand, during the development phase more detail is required for proposals; thus, even though the non-operators cannot participate in the discussion process, at least they have sufficient information to take an informed decision in the Opcom.[519] In contrast, in the production phase there is once again no need to provide detail on proposals; but this is far less risky and complex than in the exploration phase.[520]

The Greenlandic model recognises the importance of dealing with deadlocks, adopting the same approach as the AIPN in relation not only to minimum work obligations, but also to surrender of acreage. However, the end result is the same, as it gives more powers to the strongest party in the JV to break the impasse.[521] While this is a practical solution for work obligation deadlocks, it affords too much discretion to the strongest party in the consortium (ie, the operator). The operator can thus abuse this power by creating artificial obstacles to getting work obligations approved in the Opcom, where it can decide such matters unilaterally. Again, this seems to apply the exclusive operation approach to Opcom deadlocks.

Under this model, the operator can also incur expenditure which is not authorised in the work programme and budget in case of emergencies, or overspend by up to 10% or a defined sum.[522] The operator must promptly notify the non-operators of any emergency (including actions taken).[523] However, in the case of overspending, the operator is not required to notify the non-operators; instead, this is dealt with in the accounting procedures.

The Greenlandic model thus affords extensive discretion to the operator, as:

- the operator is not obliged to allow the non-operators to participate in preparing work programme and budget proposals or tackling emergencies;
- the largest party ultimately decides what happens in relation to minimum work obligations; and
- little detail need be included in work programme and budget proposals, except during the development phase.

517 Greenlandic JOA § 3.10.
518 Greenlandic JOA § 5.1 and 5.2.
519 Greenlandic JOA § 5.4.1.
520 Greenlandic JOA § 5.4.1.
521 Greenlandic JOA § 4.7.4.
522 Greenlandic JOA § 5.10.
523 Greenlandic JOA § 3.11.

The only effective way in which non-operators can participate is through Opcom approval, if they have sufficient control to block decisions; otherwise, the operator has full control over the work programme and budget.

An interesting debate concerns whether a carried partner (commonly the NOC) should be allowed to vote while it does not assume any risks or expenses; however, this is outside the scope of this book.

Conclusion: An initial distinction can be drawn between the North American JOA models and all other forms. The North American models do not provide for the control of operations through a work programme and budget, so the operator enjoys total discretion under those models. However, the remaining models clearly provide for the control of the operations through the work programme and budget.

Similarly, while the North American models do not provide for the existence of an Opcom, all other JOAs do. It is thus possible to suggest that the existence of an Opcom is directly connected to the existence of a work programme and budget.

The British, Norwegian, Australian, International and Greenlandic JOA models contain work programme and budget provisions. In general terms, they share a similar approach, as outlined below.

	OGUK	**Norway**	**AMPLA**	**AIPN**	**Greenland**
Opcom approval	Yes	Yes	Yes	Yes	Yes
Flexible terms	Yes	Yes	Yes	Yes	Yes
Parties' participation	Weak	Strong	Weak	Reasonable	Weak
Deadlock resolution	Partial	None	Partial	Partial	Partial
Detailed information	Strong	Strong	Weak	Reasonable	Reasonable

The AIPN and British models provide non-operators with this essential participation and control. In contrast, the Canadian model contains no such provision and the AAPL adopts a soft approach, providing that non-operators can only suggest modifications to the operator when formulating the work programme. It may thus be asked whether non-operators in JOAs based on the North American models are left in a dramatically weaker position than non-operators in JOAs based on the British or AIPN models, as they have no real rights in this regard. However, the work programme and budget is not the only instrument through which costs can be controlled, as is revealed in the following section.

For those JOAs that include work programme and budget provisions, the main problem is that most do not allow non-operators to participate in the preliminary process of elaborating work programme and budget proposals, except the AIPN and Norwegian JOA models, which strongly emphasise the importance of collaboration at this stage. This is negative for the consortium as a whole, as the non-operators could provide valuable input regarding best practices and efficiencies. The lack of participation also increases the risk of rejection by the Opcom in cases where the non-operators can block proposals. This might lead to deadlock, which can prove problematic for the consortium. While some JOAs try to address the issue of deadlocks, they focus primarily on minimum work obligations, which are imposed by the licence. The mechanisms they adopt for the resolution of deadlocks show a clear preference for the easiest solution: that is, affording greater discretion to the strongest party in the JV.

The operator's historically dominant position affords it extensive powers to conduct the joint operations. A more balanced scenario would make an important distinction between the preparation and implementation of work programme and budget proposals. Greater participation by all parties at the preparation stage would not only minimise the risk of rejection by the Opcom, but also promote efficient and effective operations. The best way to obtain the non-operators' input would be to establish a dedicated sub-committee or project team for work programme and budget proposals, to which all parties would nominate a representative. This would give the non-operators the opportunity to contribute to work programme and budget proposals, even if they cannot control Opcom decisions.

Alternatively, to maximise efficiencies, implementation of the work programme and budget could remain within the operator's powers, with costs controlled through other means such as information provided, audit rights and authorisations for expenditure.

Another way to compensate for the non-operators' lack of participation in the preparation of work programme and budget proposals is to increase the level of detail required to be included in such proposals. This would allow non-operators to reach a more informed decision on such proposals. The level of detail required under the current JOA models varies significantly.

However, the most effective way to control work programme and budget proposals in any JOA is through Opcom approval. In practice, this is effective only if the non-operators have at least negative control of the Opcom – that is, if they can block decisions. If the operator has overall control of the Opcom, the non-operators cannot participate at all, but can only observe the decisions taken by the operator; the only alternative available is the right of non-consent or sole risk (if available).

Peter Roberts recognises the downside of controlling work programme and budget proposals through the Opcom as follows:

It will also be apparent that the ability of the Opcom to control the operator's freedom to act through the approval of the WPB will not be an issue where the operator has effective control of the Opcom through holding the requisite passmark voting level.[524]

As noted, however, there are several mechanisms through which to exert control over costs; another is the authorisation for expenditure, analysed below.[525]

524 Peter Roberts (n 5) p108.
525 *Ibid.*

Authorisation for expenditure: An authorisation for expenditure is exactly as the term would suggest – a request made by the operator to the non-operators requiring authorisation to proceed with a specific expenditure, which is outlined in the document.[526]

From the non-operators' perspective, this is a very effective way to control costs, as it allows for case-by-case analysis.[527] The authorisation for expenditure is even more precise than the work programme and budget, as it is not an estimated calculation of expenditure, but rather specifies the exact expenditure that will be incurred.[528] However, some scholars consider that the authorisation for expenditure is merely an estimate or prediction of the expenditure.[529] Both perspectives are correct, to a certain extent. The authorisation for expenditure is far more precise than a work programme and budget; but specific situations might still require overspending, a supplementary authorisation for expenditure or even revision of the work programme and budget, as events that are beyond the control of the parties might occur.

Work programme and budgets are thus effective instruments for non-operators, but only if they are combined with authorisations for expenditure, so that costs can be effectively controlled. This combination is an efficient mechanism to counterbalance the operator's discretion over expenditure in the joint operations.

Claude Duval clearly illustrates the connection between the work programme and budget and authorisation for expenditure provisions as follows:

> *The AFE often must identify the operation to be funded by referring to the line item in the approved work program and budget. It must describe the work in some detail, give the operator's best estimate of the total funds required, and then outline the proposed work schedule with a timetable of expenditures.*[530]

Therefore, if a work programme and budget is in place, the authorisation for expenditure will refer to the line item approved in the work programme and budget and thus provide for detailed control of a specific operation. The more detail that is provided in the work programme and budget, the easier it will be to exert control in the authorisation for expenditure.[531]

If the work programme and budget is the sole mechanism for controlling expenditure, this will afford too much discretion to the operator and too little control to the non-operators.[532]

---

526 Bernard G Taverne (n 308) p67.

527 "From the non-operators point of view, an AFE procedure gives them a far tighter control on expenditures than is possible by virtue of budget for any given stage of the Licence Operations." Taylor and Tyne (n 58) p42.

528 "The approved budget for an annual programme is inevitably an approximate estimate of the anticipated level of expenditures involved. A more precise means of financial control is the AFE, which is prepared by the operator when it has ascertained more accurately the likely costs of particular services or operations." Terence Daintith *et al* (n 16) p1145.

529 "An AFE is an estimate of expenditures on an item in a budget. The AFE may identify the major contracts or contingencies involved, and most operators will seek to minimize the number of AFEs required, including as much as possible within a single AFE: for example, drilling and related activities for an exploration may well be in a single AFE. Under the terms of the accounting procedure after the AFE is approved a co-venturer will generally be bound to meets its share of any cost overruns as the AFE is only an estimate." Gerard MD Bean (n 16) p17.

530 Claude Duval *et al* (n 122) p298.

531 *Ibid.*

532 Taylor and Tyne (n 54) p42.

Ernest E Smith outlined the need for authorisations for expenditure in his comments on *Haas v Gulf Coast Natural Gas Co.*[533] In that case the defendant non-operators persuaded the court that there was insufficient evidence to prove that the plaintiff operator followed the authorisation for expenditure procedures in order to demonstrate the legality of its operations. However, Professor Smith raised questions about what is to be considered compulsory in the authorisation for expenditure. Is it the operation *per se*? Or is it the details of the expenditure (including costs)? Professor Smith cited *Cleverock Energy Corp v Trepel*,[534] which confirms that a non-operator's consent relates to the operation as a whole, and not to the amount of expenditure. From this perspective, therefore, an authorisation for expenditure is an estimated cost.[535] However, this opinion is not unanimously accepted.[536] Moreover, why would it be possible to override expenditures without prior approval if the authorisation for expenditure had to specify every detail of the overall operations? There is no straightforward answer to this question. However, the authorisation for expenditure certainly affords more control to the non-operators, as it is a more precise instrument than the work programme and budget.

The importance of this mechanism for non-operators is thus clearly apparent. However, what will determine its efficacy in practice is the purpose of the authorisation for expenditure, which must be defined by the parties.

There are two main purposes of the authorisation for expenditure: information and control. The former is a purely bureaucratic procedure, as the operator need only issue an authorisation for expenditure to inform the non-operators about an operation per se; no further approvals are required.[537] The latter goes far beyond this, as it provides an effective system to verify whether each operation proposed by the operator is efficient and in the best interests of the consortium. However, the parties can choose whether the level of control is broad or limited. Broad control requires that the operator obtain the Opcom's approval for the specific operation; limited control restricts the need for Opcom approval, as there are limited grounds on which the authorisation for expenditure may be rejected.

Peter Roberts describes this situation when he states that three kinds of authorisation for expenditure might be implemented: authorisations for expenditure for information, authorisations for expenditure for approval and authorisations for expenditure for conditional approval. The first require no approval, but only the

533 *Haas v Gulf Coast Natural Gas Co*, 484 SW 2d 127 (Tex Civ App – Corpus Christi 1972) in Ernest E Smith *et al* (n 16) pp583–592.

534 *Cleverock Energy Corp v Trepel*, 609 F 2d 1358, 1360–61 (10th Cir. 1979), cert denied, 446 US 909) in Ernest E Smith *et al* (n 16) pp583–592.

535 Ernest Smith quotes JO Young, "Oil and Gas Operating Agreements: Producers 88 Operating Agreements, Selected Problems and Suggested Solutions" (1975) 20 *Rocky Mtn Min L Inst* 197, p207 as follows: "When it is considered that the AFE normally cannot be anything more than an estimate of costs and that consent to drilling a well is made consent to all necessary expenditures in connection therewith, we must conclude that normally a non-operator's consent to an AFE constitutes a consent to the operation and not to a specific amount of expenditure ... [But] where the overrun is not minimal, the operator may have an implied duty to advise the non-operators and provide a chance to nonconsent the additional cost." Ernest E Smith *et al* (n 16) p589.

536 See Taylor and Tyne (n 54) p42, Terence Daintith (n 16) p1145, and Sandy Shaw (n 16) p19.

537 "Where AFE approval is not required, however, an equivalent statement of the expenditure to be incurred must usually be given to the parties by the operator for information." Taylor and Tyne (n 54) p43.

provision of information on costs. The second and third require the Opcom's total or limited approval.[538]

Authorisations for expenditure for information only are negative from the non-operators' perspective, as the work programme and budget gives no precise details on the joint operations, so the operator will end up with broad discretion to execute the joint operations.[539] In contrast, authorisations for expenditure for approval are positive from the non-operators' perspective, as they give the non-operators a second, more precise mechanism to control the costs of the joint operations.[540]

However, where the JOA also contains a work programme and budget provision, non-operators might experience difficulties in introducing an authorisation for expenditure mechanism. The operator will seek to minimise the need to seek further approval in the form of authorisations for expenditure,[541] while the non-operators will seek to increase their control of expenditure by requiring further approvals through this mechanism.[542] As a consequence, as Sandy Shaw states, "the requirements for AFE approvals ... is another area of negotiation".[543]

An informative authorisation for expenditure system is the easiest solution, as the operator should have no objection to this approach. However, it is also the worst solution for non-operators, as the work programme and budget will contain no detail about the joint operations. If the authorisation for expenditure system is not fully implemented, the JOA will afford too much discretion to the operator and the non-operators will have little control over costs in the joint operations.

The implementation of an approval authorisation for expenditure system – whether broad or limited – will be considerably more difficult. The strongest argument against this system is that it gives the non-operators another chance to approve or reject an operation that has already been approved in the work programme and budget.[544] A system of limited approval might seem easier to implement, as there is a clear and restricted basis on which to analyse the proposed authorisation for expenditure.[545]

---

538 Peter Roberts (n 5) p108.

539 "The parties can elect that all AFEs are for informational purposes only and require no further approvals for the underlying operation being funded. (Note that the operation has already been approved in the current work program and budget.) This alternative gives the operator the most freedom." Claude Duval *et al* (n 122) p298.

540 "Other alternatives are similar to that used in the UK Model JOA which requires that the operator obtain operating committee approval before making any expenditures or incurring any commitments for work subject to the AFE ... This two-step approval process allows greater control over the operator. However, it can be criticized as inefficient and subject to abuse by non-operators who commit to fund an activity in the annual budget, knowing that they can withdraw this commitment later." *Ibid.*

541 "In addition to the concept of programmes and budgets for each stage of operations, most UKCS JOAs also incorporate the concept of AFEs, although many operators will seek to minimize the need for specific approval from the operating committee for expenditure already approved in a budget." Taylor and Tyne (n 54) p42.

542 "Most non-operators, however, will be in favour of a requirement that an AFE be approved by the operating committee before any significant expenditure is incurred, even where the expenditure concerned has been included in an approved budget." *Ibid.*

543 "A low passmark bestows a dominant position on a relatively high PI-holding party (because of the ability of that party to compel a proposal which it favours), and a high passmark bestows a disproportionately large amount of management influence on a relatively low PI-holding party (because of the ability of that party to block a proposal which it does not favour)." Peter Roberts (n 5) p100.

544 Taylor and Tyne (n 54) p43.

545 Hew Dundas disagrees with this perspective: "Some JOAs provide for deemed approval of an AFE unless the Operating Committee vote against it within a specific time limit, but the practice of deemed approvals is considered dubious by most UKCS practitioners." Hew Dundas (n 16) p9.

However, this argument is not fully correct, as the work programme and budget is merely an estimate or prediction of the work and costs required for the joint operations; only the authorisation for expenditure allows for the precise verification of the proposed work and costs. Thus, the absence of an approval authorisation for expenditure mechanism is akin to a scenario in which both parties decide on the destination of a journey, but the operator alone decides on the route to get there.

In some negotiations, this issue might therefore become a deal breaker, as the operator is unlikely to give the non-operators a second chance to approve specific operations, while the non-operators will wish to avoid giving too much discretion to the operator. However, certain options can achieve a middle ground between these opposing views, such as:

- a financial cap;
- a distinction between operational and capital budget;
- an exclusion of items;
- a lower passmark in the Opcom;
- a deemed approval in the Opcom;
- special provisions for over-expenditure; and
- special provisions for emergencies.

Introducing a financial cap is a simple solution, as an authorisation for expenditure will require further approval from the Opcom only if this financial cap is exceeded.[546] However, the difficulty with such an approach – especially from the non-operators' perspective – is the determination of the financial limitation, as the operator commonly retains the strongest position in the negotiations on this point. Moreover, as smaller operations will not be subject to control, larger operations might be broken down into several smaller operations to prevent further control by the non-operators. In addition, if a financial cap is implemented, this will vary depending on the phase of the project.[547]

With regard to the distinction between operational and capital budgets, the former are ongoing costs of the joint operations which require specific approval by the Opcom, while the latter should be set out in an informative authorisation for expenditure.[548] This approach is based on the fact that the capital budget has already been approved in the work programme and budget, so the non-operators should control ongoing costs that are not directly related to the joint operations, such as overheads.[549] While this allows for effective control of ongoing costs, the non-operators will have little control over the most costly operations, as these will be dealt with in the capital budget.

546 "Some operators (and some non-operators) take the view that once a party has approved a work programme and budget then that party should not have a second chance at the AFE stage to opt out of the programme or prevent it being implemented in accordance with the budget." Taylor and Tyne (n 54) p42.

547 *Ibid* p43.

548 "One possible solution to the conflict of interests which arises in relation to the AFE procedure is to classify some categories of expenditure as requiring subsequent AFE approval with other categories simply requiring approval at the budget stage. Such classification may be on the basis of the type of expenditure (eg, only capital as opposed to operating expenditure is subject to AFE approval)." *Ibid.*

549 For more information, see Gulzhan Nurakhmet, "What is the Role of Overhead Cost Recovery in Production Sharing Contracts?" at www.dundee.ac.uk/cepmlp.

The exclusion of items might resolve specific problems, but this approach is unlikely to achieve the desired balance in all situations, as it is difficult to predict in advance which items should be excluded. The operator will seek to exclude as many items as possible, while the non-operators will seek the opposite. As the operator enjoys stronger bargaining power than the non-operators, it is likely to prevail.

Chris Thorpe clearly recognises this conflict of views as follows:

What expenditures are subject to AFE control is often a contentious issue in a JOA negotiation. The operator often argues that only specific major items of expenditure should require an AFE, so that it can spend minor and routine expenditures on the basis of the approved programme and budget without further approval. The non-operators often argue that all expenditures must be AFE'd. Some sort of compromise must be found.[550]

Kenneth Mildwaters highlights the danger of failure of performance of any minimum work obligation when he says: "In the event that the holders of the Licence do not carry out the work programme set out in the Licence the Secretary of State for Energy may revoke it."[551] Later, he stresses that priority must be given to performance of the minimum work obligations in the work programme and budget and in authorisations, and states: "To avoid breaching the conditions set out in the Permit it is therefore usual for the proposals to be drafted in general terms in so far as work is concerned and conservatively in so far as expenditure is concerned."[552]

The same principle applies for emergencies, as JOAs facilitate an immediate response without delay.[553] However, the systems commonly adopted in existing JOAs are inefficient and fall far short of best practices in the industry,[554] as the non-operators have no power to participate in decisions regarding such emergencies. It is true that the liabilities of the parties remain the same regardless of the non-operators' participation in actions to address such emergencies. However, in the event of an emergency, it is important to impose a duty on the operator to notify the non-operators immediately, so that the non-operators can assist accordingly.

The exclusion of items is relatively beneficial for the consortium in practical terms, as the operations can be conducted more efficiently. However, it is disadvantageous to the non-operators, as they will have little or no control over the initial activities of the JV, which could ultimately determine the success or failure of the consortium (the minimum work obligations). They may further be excluded from crucial decisions which could affect the existence of the consortium (eg, decisions on emergencies), as occurred with the Deepwater Horizon accident in the Gulf of Mexico. In other words, it is difficult to find a balance between the exclusions sought by the operator and those acceptable to the non-operators.

Another important mechanism to minimise the use of authorisations for expenditure is allowing overspending. This affords the operator a certain flexibility conducting the joint operations, as – up to a certain limit (commonly 10%)[555] – the operator can exceed

550 Chris Thorpe (n 317) p137.
551 Kenneth Charles Mildwaters (n 16) p169.
552 *Ibid* p171.
553 *Ibid.*
554 *Ibid* p561.
555 See Terence Daintith (n 16) p1145 and Peter Roberts (n 5) p111.

the budget as approved without the needing to obtain the Ofcom's approval.[556] However, some JOAs do not allow for overspending without the Opcom's formal approval,[557] while others provide that this right applies only under certain conditions.[558]

The flexibility afforded by allowing for overspending in the form of approved authorisations for expenditure is essential to the consortium. However, while the dynamics of the oil and gas industry might require that the operator enjoy certain discretion in conducting the operations, this discretion should be clearly regulated and controlled by the non-operators in order to prevent abuse.

In this regard, Claude Duval raises an interesting scenario, where the operator seeks to exceed the overspending limit:

[A]n operator may not know that the limit has been exceeded until the operation is near completion and over-expenditures can exceed the limits set in just a day or two of additional drilling time. Is the operator then liable for any unapproved over-expenditures, even if it would not be good oil field practice to stop the operation until approval is obtained? Arguably, these additional, but prudent, over-expenditures should be charged to the joint account, even if they exceed the prescribed limits in the JOA.[559]

This is a complex situation, although Claude Duval suggests a solution to the problem. In such a case it is important to analyse whether the operator has acted diligently and in accordance with good practice; otherwise, the operator will have unlimited discretion to exceed the specified limits. If the operator is conducting the operations carefully and diligently, it will likely predict any difficulties in complying with the overspending limits and revise the specific budget and seek the non-operators' approval in time – or at least report the situation accordingly. The operator might then request a further extension to prove he is acting with due diligence and according to best practice.

Claude Duval clearly recognises this as follows:

If the limits on costs overruns are expected to be exceeded, the operator must either seek committee approval and revise the work program and budget or prepare a supplemental AFE for such approval.[560]

There seems to be agreement that best practice in the oil and gas industry clearly requires an operator to be diligent and aware of all circumstances that might delay or harm the joint operations, and report those circumstances as soon as possible to the non-operators so that they can plan how best to address them. However, as mentioned previously, emergencies are excluded from the overspending limitation.

Another alternative to the use of authorisations for expenditure is to reduce the

---

556 "[S]ubject to the operator's right to incur over expenditures within certain narrow limits expressed as percentage of total budget and as a percentage of the individual budget item being overspent." Bernard G Taverne (n 308) p68–69.

557 "Some JOAs, including the BNOC proforma JOA, do not permit over-expenditure without further approval." Terence Daintith (n 16) p1145.

558 "One solution to cost overruns is to provide automatic non-consent by each operator on reaching (for example) 125% of the original AFE. All costs would then be paid by the operator who may then be allowed to recoup the extra costs with interest before the non-consenting parties execute back-in rights. The exact point at which the overrun is reached is not critical because the non-consent is automatic. This places a heavy onus on the operator to estimate the costs precisely but it allows cost-to-date computations to be made with the benefit of hindsight." Hew Dundas (n 16) p9.

559 Claude Duval (n 122) p298.

560 *Ibid.*

pass mark required in the Opcom for the approval of operations. The justification for this is that authorisations for expenditure deal with operations which, in theory, have already been approved in the work programme and budget. This approach reduces the approval burden, while at the same time affording some measure of control to the non-operators.[561] In theory, therefore, this alternative appears to strike a balance between the operator's and non-operators' positions. However, the practical result of this approach strongly favours the operator, as the operator is usually in a dominant position during the negotiations. If the operator has overall control of the Opcom, a reduction in the pass mark will have no practical effect, as the operator is likely to be in a position to approve any decision either with or without such a lower pass mark, as illustrated in the following table.

Example 1	**Company A**	**Company B**	**Company C**
Role	Operator	Non-operator	Non-operator
Interest	80%	10%	10%
Ordinary passmark	70%		
Lower passmark	40%		

If the non-operators have control of the Opcom, a reduction in the pass mark might also make no difference, as the result will remain the same as for any other approval in the Opcom, as illustrated below.

Example 2	**Company A**	**Company B**	**Company C**
Role	Operator	Non-operator	Non-operator
Interest	40%	30%	30%
Ordinary passmark	60%		
Lower passmark	50%		

Thus, this approach might suit only a situation where the consortium has many parties and the lower pass mark would reduce the number of non-operators needed for approval, as illustrated below.

561 "The voting requirements on an AFE as submitted by the operator will be as prescribed for routine operational decisions because it concerns expenditures and commitments under an approved budget." Bernard G Taverne (n 308) p67.

Example 3	Company A	Company B	Company C	Company D	Company E
Role	Operator	Non-operator	Non-operator	Non-operator	Non-operator
Interest	40%	20%	20%	10%	10%
Ordinary passmark	80%				
Lower passmark	60%				

A similar option is to provide that authorisations for expenditure will be deemed approved unless a specific number of negative votes is cast.[562] Sandy Shaw recognises this as follows: "In most JOAs approval of the AFE is subject to the same passmark as the original programme and budget, although some JOAs provide for deeming of approvals unless a specific percentage of negative votes is received."[563]

However, this approach presents the same problem as outlined previously, in that a pass mark is required. If the number of negative votes required is too high, the non-operators might not succeed in blocking authorisations for expenditure. However, if the number of negative votes is too low, the non-operators might succeed in blocking everything. Therefore, this system might suit only a situation where the consortium involves several parties and the application of the authorisation for expenditure mechanism can be minimised without unduly benefiting any one party. A requirement that non-operators approve every authorisation for expenditure is unlikely to be accepted by the operator, as it would give too much control to the non-operators[564] – even though this would be the optimal mechanism for any non-operator to control the expenditure of the joint operations.[565]

Equally, an informative authorisation for expenditure system is unlikely to be accepted by the non-operators. Therefore, a balance will usually achieved through a combination of several of the mechanisms outlined above, such as financial caps, exclusion of items and limited approval.

Sandy Shaw describes the need to strike a balance between the operator's and non-operators' interests as follows:

As the budget is very much a forecast of spending, the ability to review expenditure by

562 Peter Roberts (n 5) p110.

563 Sandy Shaw (n 16) p20.

564 "This two-step approval process allows greater control over the operator. However, it can be criticized as inefficient and subject to abuse by non-operators who commit to fund an activity in the annual budget, knowing that they can withdraw this commitment later." Claude Duval *et al* (n 122) p298.

565 Scott Styles stresses the importance for non-operators of full AFE implementation, as follows: "The need for the operator to secure agreement on AFEs greatly strengthens the influence of the non-operators over the development of Joint Operations as it means there can be no cash call on the non-operators without sufficient consent to achieve the stipulated pass mark." Scott Styles (n 14) p288.

> *way of the AFE is of value to the non-operators in controlling the way in which available funds are committed and limiting the operator's discretion. On the other hand, the non-operators should not be allowed to delay or prevent operations pursuant to an agreed programme and budget by unreasonably manipulating the AFE procedure.*[566]

As outlined, the difficulty in creating an authorisation for expenditure mechanism exists only in JOAs where a work programme and budget system is established. However, this is not the case for the North American JOA models.[567]

An important concern for smaller non-operators in particular is when the operator is under an obligation to issue an authorisation for expenditure. The industry commonly provides that the operator must issue "an invoice for approved expenditures in that month".[568] However, this might be too short a period if the amount of expenditure involved is high. It would thus be better for smaller non-operators if expenditure over a certain limit required more advance notice, so that they had sufficient time to make the necessary preparations.[569]

As mentioned, full implementation of the authorisation for expenditure mechanism requires approval by the Opcom (where applicable) or the non-operators. So what happens if the non-operators can block the proposal? The first option in such case is for the operator to revise the proposed authorisation for expenditure so that it can be re-submitted to the Opcom.[570] The second is to propose the relevant work as an exclusive operation.[571]

On the other hand, if an authorisation for expenditure is approved, what happens next? In this case, as a general rule, each party contributes according to its share in the JV. However, there are exceptions, such as implementation of a carried interest.[572]

As with the work programme and budget, it is possible to amend or revise the authorisation for expenditure where the Opcom (if applicable) or non-operators so determine. However, this will not affect any authorisation for expenditure that has been approved prior to such decision.[573]

Finally, non-operators should seek an authorisation for expenditure mechanism that requires the approval of all contracting parties. However, this might not be possible in all JOAs; where it is not, non-operators should seek a mechanism that allows them to exercise effective control over expenditure, but at the same time affords some flexibility to the operator in conducting the joint operations. Any method that minimises the application of the authorisation for expenditure mechanism could achieve this purpose, but non-operators should analyse any such

---

566 Sandy Shaw (n 16) p20.

567 Peter Roberts (n 5) p111.

568 Chris Thorpe (n 317) p128.

569 *Ibid.*

570 "If, where the JOA gives the Opcom the ability to reject an AFE, the OpCom does reject it, then the activity which was suggested in the relevant AFE will prima facie no longer be capable of being undertaken as a joint operation. Consequently, at that point the likely reaction is that the operator will re-submit a revised AFE to the Opcom in order to secure the Opcom's approval." Peter Roberts (n 5) p110.

571 "If the operating committee fails to approve an AFE, the operation is deemed rejected, and any party may propose to conduct that operation as a sole risk operation." Claude Duval (n 122) p298.

572 Terence Daintith (n 16) pp1145–1146.

573 Kenneth C Mildwaters (n 16) p569.

limitations carefully, to ensure that the operator does not end up with too much discretion. It is also important to establish a connection between authorisation for expenditure approval and the information provided, so that overspending (above a certain limit) requires a supplementary authorisation for expenditure.

Additionally, non-operators should seek a reasonable timeframe between the issue of an authorisation for expenditure and payment of the relevant costs, as smaller non-operators may need external funding to cover major costs and may thus find it difficult to comply with the payment provision quickly.[574]

There follows an analysis of the application of authorisations for expenditure in each JOA standard model form. It is also made clear that sometimes there is a benefit in not having a work programme and budget provision. Arguably, the exclusive use of authorisations for expenditure is in many cases a better system to control expenditure than a combination of work programme and budget and authorisations for expenditure. However, full implementation of the latter system would afford the optimum degree of control to non-operators.

AAPL models: AAPL Form 810 clearly obliges the operator to issue an authorisation for expenditure before incurring any expenditure.[575] However, there are mechanisms in place to minimise the impact of this system.

The main criterion to determine the application of this system is the amount of expenditure involved. If the expenditure exceeds a financial cap, the operator must obtain the non-operators' approval; but if the expenditure is below the financial cap, the operator can simply inform the parties of the expenditure without any further requirements.[576] This is an interesting provision that balances the interests of the operator and the non-operators. However, the financial cap is left unspecified, so the parties can negotiate and establish the most suitable level for the deal. In practice, the non-operators are unlikely to secure a positive outcome in current operations, as the operator will be able to overrule the non-operators through its dominant position.

This model form also recognises the need to afford a certain degree of flexibility to the operator in conducting the joint operations, and thus authorises the operator to overspend on an approved authorisation for expenditure up to a certain limit.[577] The operator must issue an authorisation for expenditure for information purposes, so that the non-operators are made aware of any overspending. As mentioned, this flexibility is fairly common in the existing JOA model forms. However, the interesting provision is the express obligation to issue a supplementary authorisation for expenditure if the limit is exceeded.[578] If the operator predicts that the overspend limit will be exceeded, it must issue a supplementary authorisation for expenditure for the additional costs.

Another procedure to minimise the potentially negative impact of an

574 *Ibid.*
575 AAPL Form 810 § 6.2.
576 AAPL Form 810 § 6.2.
577 AAPL Form 810 § 6.2.1.
578 AAPL Form 810 § 6.2.2.

authorisation for expenditure was established for situations such as emergencies and *force majeure* events, which are excluded from such scrutiny.[579] This flexibility is important to maintain the good standing of the petroleum title. However, there is no obligation to seek the non-operators' input on any action to address emergencies, as the form provides that the operator must take such decisions based on "its opinion as a reasonable and prudent operator".[580] The operator's only obligation to the non-operators is to "report to the Participating Parties, as promptly as possible, the nature of the emergency, the action taken, and the Costs incurred".[581] However, when the emergency or *force majeure* is over, the operator must then issue a supplementary authorisation for expenditure to continue or to finish any of these operations.[582]

Form 810 further provides for a special 'long lead development system,'[583] which gives extensive rights and discretion to the operator, as it requires fewer specifics than a normal authorisation for expenditure. This mechanism might make it more difficult for the non-operators to exert effective control over the expenditure. However, unanimous consent is required to proceed with this special system.[584]

Minimum work obligations are not excluded from the authorisation for expenditure mechanism. This is a positive provision for non-operators, as they can thus participate in decisions on such crucial operations, which usually occur in the early stages of the consortium. However, if a deadlock occurs in relation to approval, this could jeopardise the existence of the JV, as it could frustrate performance of the licence obligations.

The authorisation for expenditure mechanism is thus very important in AAPL Form 810, as the work programme and budget has an informative purpose only.[585] The authorisation for expenditure is the only procedure through which non-operators can exert control over expenditure. Procedures that restrict the use of this mechanism should thus be as weak as possible. Indeed, such procedures are reasonably balanced, as they allow the non-operators to control the majority of operations while also affording a certain degree of discretion to the operator in its operations. However, the critical issue is the determination of the financial cap, as this will determine whether the authorisation for expenditure mechanism has an informative or approval purpose.

AAPL Form 610 also imposes a duty on the operator to issue an authorisation for expenditure before incurring any expenditure.[586] However, the provisions and mechanism applied in this historical model form are much simpler.

The authorisation for expenditure is limited based on financial terms, which must be defined by the parties.[587] There is no clear determination on overspending, unlike in Form 810, which sets out specific financial limits for each phase of the JV.

579 AAPL Form 810 § 6.2.3.
580 AAPL Form 810 § 6.2.
581 AAPL Form 810 § 6.2.
582 AAPL Form 810 § 6.2.3.
583 AAPL Form 810 § 6.2.4.
584 AAPL Form 810 § 6.2.4.1
585 AAPL Form 810 § 6.4.1.
586 AAPL Form 610 article I (A).
587 AAPL Form 610 article VI (C) (2).

Additionally, emergencies can be excluded from the authorisation for expenditure mechanism, provided that the operator notifies the non-operators of the situation as soon as possible.[588]

The main differences between Form 810 and Form 610 are that:

- the operator does not have the flexibility to overspend in different phases of the JV under Form 610; and
- Form 610 makes no mention of work programme and budget, although Form 810 adopts this for information purposes only.

The need for the parties' approval under Form 610 is much stronger, but only if the parties have not exercised their right of non-consent.[589]

It is thus apparent that the authorisation for expenditure system in Form 610 affords less flexibility to the operator, allowing the non-operators to exert more control over the joint operations. Form 810 also provides non-operators with a reasonable amount of control of expenditure through the authorisation for expenditure mechanism. The AAPL model forms thus secure a high degree of control over expenditure, even though they provide for neither an Opcom nor a work programme and budget.

RMMLF model: The RMMLF JOA model includes a concise, but effective, provision on authorisations for expenditure. The major limitation on the use of this mechanism is the financial consideration involved. The parties must define this financial limit in US dollars; if this limit will be exceeded, the non-operators' approval is required.[590] The only exception to this a rule relates to emergencies – the operator does not need to obtain non-operators' approval before incurring expenditure in an emergency. However, the operator must report such emergencies to the non-operators "as promptly as possible".[591]

The RMMLF model thus gives non-operators a higher degree of control over expenditure through a simple authorisation for expenditure mechanism (provided that the financial cap is not set too high). However, why would a dominant operator accept such tight control by non-operators? The answer lies in the fact that the operator still enjoys a stronger position, as once the authorisation for expenditure has been approved, the non-operators can exert no further control over the conduct of the operations.

Problematically for non-operators, the authorisation for expenditure contains only an estimated cost: "[T]he operator shall not, without the consent of all Parties chargeable with the Costs thereof, undertake any single project reasonably estimated to require an expenditure in excess of …"[592] Thus, the non-operators approve an estimated cost only, and there is no regulation of further adjustments. The wording of this clause requires non-operators to approve the operation itself, but not the

588 AAPL Form 610 article VI (C) (2).
589 AAPL JOA Form 610 article VI (B) (8).
590 RMMLF JOA §5.5.
591 RMMLF JOA §5.5.
592 RMMLF JOA §5.5.

details provided in the authorisation for expenditure. Thus, once the operation has been approved, the operator has unfettered discretion once again.

Thus, while the limitation on expenditure seems to favour the non-operators in theory, the lack of any provisions on overspending is in fact disadvantageous to the non-operators, as this is left unregulated. Once an operation has been approved, the operator has extensive powers to conduct the joint operations.

Canadian model: The Canadian model provides for an authorisation for expenditure mechanism.[593] However, this will only apply if a financial cap is reached, set at C$50,000.[594] This limit has little real impact in practice, as oil and gas operations usually involve very large sums and it is more important to exert control over major costs than minor ones. In other words, discretion over minor expenditure makes the JV more efficient.

Where the expenditure exceeds the financial cap, the operator must issue an authorisation for expenditure, which must be approved by all non-operators.[595] This is by far the best control provided in this model form, which makes no provision for a work programme and budget.[596]

The financial cap is not the only limitation on the authorisation for expenditure mechanism: exclusions of items and overspending are also allowed. The former mainly exclude emergencies and expenditure required by regulations.[597] In both cases, the operator must report to the non-operators any anticipated costs, together with details of the event, nature, scope and schedule for payments.[598] This is a positive provision, allowing non-operators to participate in decisions concerning such events; however, as it is informative only, there is no obligation to seek the non-operators' input on such decisions. The emergency exclusion is fairly common in the oil and gas industry, but the regulatory exclusion is far too broad, as it might even encompass minimum work obligations. Non-operators might thus face critical problems in the interpretation and application of this clause, as the operator might seek to avail of it as often as possible.

The overspending provision allows overspending almost without limitation: as the authorisation for expenditure approves the operation itself, any overspending will require no further approval, but only an informative authorisation for expenditure.[599] This is simultaneously both positive and negative for non-operators. At first glance, their position appears strong, because they must approve the operation through an authorisation for expenditure. The lack of a work programme and budget in this model gives more powers to the non-operators to control operations through the authorisation for expenditure mechanism.

On the other hand, however, once the non-operators have approved the

593 CAPL OP Form 610 §3.01 (B). The new version provides more information related to AFEs (specially for horizontal wells) in CAPL OP form 610 §3.01 (D) (E).
594 CAPL OP Form 610 §3.01 (B).
595 CAPL OP Form 610 §7.01 (A).
596 Peter Roberts (n 5) p110.
597 CAPL OP Form 610 §3.01 (B).
598 CAPL OP Form 610 §3.01 (B).
599 CAPL OP Form 610 §3.01 (C).

operation through the authorisation for expenditure, the operator has extensive rights to incur any overspending, with few limitations, such as the completion of wells. In this respect, the non-operators' position is weak, as they are relegated to the status of mere observers by informative authorisations for expenditure.[600]

This model form further provides that the operator must commence an operation within 120 days of approval of the relevant authorisation for expenditure.[601] If the operator fails to do so within this timeframe, the validity of the authorisation for expenditure expires.

The Canadian model thus provides non-operators with strong control over expenditure, but only at an early stage. The operator generally has more discretion once an authorisation for expenditure has been approved, as this approves the operation as a whole, not the precise costs involved. The non-operators might subsequently experience difficulties in controlling the joint operations.

British model: The British model includes an authorisation for expenditure mechanism, but its implementation depends on the phase of the project.

During the exploration phase, the operator must issue an authorisation for expenditure for the Opcom's approval before incurring any capital expenditure or seismic expenditure that exceeds a financial cap in the approved work programme and budget.[602] The precise amount of this financial cap is unspecified, so the parties can agree on the amount that is most appropriate to the deal. In practice, where there is a power imbalance, this approach is likely to benefit the operator. However, the approved authorisation for expenditure can be revised or amended by determination of the Opcom.[603]

Emergencies are excluded from the authorisation for expenditure mechanism.[604] The operator's sole obligation in this regard is to report such circumstances to the non-operators, as well as the expenditure incurred so far. The British model does not require the participation of non-operators in such decisions.

Minimum work obligations are not excluded from the authorisation for expenditure mechanism; but if the Opcom does not reject such a proposal within 28 days of its submission, it is deemed automatically approved.[605] The impact of the authorisation for expenditure mechanism is further minimised by a provision that allows overspending by up to 10% of the amount approved in the authorisation for expenditure or a specific amount in pounds sterling, whichever is lower.[606]

The same provisions apply during the development, production and decommissioning phases.[607] However, there are some limitations on the right to

600 "It is customary in Canada for the operator to submit a revised informational AFE if costs exceed 10% of the original AFE, but not in the UK where JOA provisions in this are much stricter – refer footnote *infra*. But in the absence of gross negligence or wilful neglect, a non-operator is not likely to prevail in a suit to challenge the reasonableness of costs in excess of an AFE." Hew Dundas (n 16) p9.

601 CAPL OP Form 610 §7.01 (A).

602 OGUK JOA §10.2.

603 OGUK JOA §10.3.

604 OGUK JOA §6.10.2.

605 OGUK JOA § 10.4.

606 OGUK JOA § 10.5.

607 OGUK JOA § 11.2, 11.3, 11.5, 12.2, 12.3, 12.4, 13.2, 13.3 and 13.4.

reject an authorisation for expenditure in the decommissioning phase, as the model provides that approval shall not be "unreasonably withheld or delayed where the AFE is consistent with the approved Decommissioning Programme and Budget".[608]

It is thus clear that there is concern about minimum work obligations and decommissioning obligations, as more restrictions are imposed on the non-operators' control of expenditure in relation to such matters. As a general rule, however, the British model affords strong control to the non-operators through a combination of work programme and budget and authorisation for expenditure provisions. But in practice, this control is effective only if the non-operators have some measure of control over the Opcom; otherwise, the control is illusory. In addition, the non-operators cannot participate in decisions on emergencies, which might be disadvantageous in a catastrophic situation that affects the whole consortium.

Norwegian model: The Norwegian JOA model contains both a work programme and budget provision and an authorisation for expenditure mechanism.[609] In theory, these are positive provisions for non-operators, but it is necessary to analyse the interplay between these mechanisms of control.

Initially, the body that approves the work programme and budget is the same body that approves the authorisations for expenditure – the Opcom. As mentioned, while the existence of the Opcom is an effective way of exerting control over the joint operations, the efficacy of such control is directly connected to the voting procedures. If a lower pass mark is established, the operator will usually have total control of the Opcom, which will essentially sideline the non-operators.

The Norwegian model form provides flexibility by allowing for overspending by up to 10% of the sum approved in the authorisation for expenditure and by excluding formal procedures in case of emergencies.[610] Both situations must be reported to the Opcom so that the non-operators are informed accordingly; but the model does not require Opcom participation in emergencies, which might be disadvantageous for non-operators. In addition, the model gives no further details on the use of the authorisation for expenditure mechanism, beyond the requirement for Opcom approval.[611]

However, the Norwegian model does include another mechanism of controlling expenditure, referred to as the 'master control estimate', which gives non-operators a better estimation of the planned costs of the JV.[612]

The Norwegian JOA model thus gives non-operators strong control of expenditure through a combination of an authorisation for expenditure mechanism, a master control estimate and finally a work programme and budget provision. However, the model does not require the non-operators' participation in decisions on emergencies, which might cause them to suffer substantial loss – a risk highlighted by the 2010 oil spill in the Gulf of Mexico.

608 OGUK JOA §13.2.
609 Norwegian JOA § 12.5.
610 Norwegian JOA § 12.5.
611 Norwegian JOA § 12.5.
612 Norwegian JOA § 12.6.

Australian model: The Australian JV model includes no authorisation for expenditure mechanism.[613] All control over expenditure is exercised through the work programme and budget; there is no further obligation on the operator to obtain consent from the Opcom,[614] but only a procedural obligation to provide monthly statements on chargeable expenditure.[615] This is a typical obligation in accounting procedures and thus is not analysed further.

The non-operators must therefore rely on the work programme and budget provision to exert control over expenditure; however, this will be difficult, as the work programme and budget does not contain the same level of detail as authorisations for expenditure. Thus, non-operators are not afforded a high degree of control over expenditure under this model.

AIPN model:[616] The AIPN model also contains an authorisation for expenditure provision, but this is optional only.[617] As under most JOAs, only expenditure that exceeds a specific financial cap, defined by the parties, requires an authorisation for expenditure.[618] The financial cap is similar to the British model, as it changes depending on whether the project is in the exploration, development or production phase. However, the AIPN model does not provide for specific authorisations for expenditure for decommissioning.

It also affords the operator some flexibility in the form of provisions on overspending and excluded items.[619] The former allow overspending by up to 10% of the line item, but no more than 5% of the approved work programme and budget.[620] If this limit will be exceeded, the parties can decide whether the operator must revise the work programme and budget and resubmit it for Opcom approval[621] or need only submit a supplementary authorisation for expenditure to the Opcom for approval.[622] In addition, the operator is not obliged to issue an authorisation for expenditure for minimum work obligations and emergencies.[623] These exclusions were introduced

613 AMPLA JOA § 8.3 – This is one of the most substantial differences between the JV for mining and the JOA under the AMPLA model. The JOA model provides for an AFE. In short, this provision secures the non-operators' position as follows.
- All authorisations for expenditure must be approved by the Opcom (generally by a majority vote).
- Each authorisation for expenditure should contain a fair amount of detail.
- Failure to vote is deemed to be a rejection.
- If an authorisation for expenditure is rejected by the Opcom, then any interested party might continue as a sole risk.
- The operator may only commence work once it has been approved through an authorisation for expenditure.

614 AMPLA JV § 8.1 and 8.2.

615 AMPLA JV § 8.5.

616 AIPN model form 2012 § 6 7 and 6.8. The new JOA model form retained a similar structure to the older version. The most relevant modification was the addition of a fourth option for authorisation for expenditure – a mixture of the other options, it refers to an authorisation for expenditure for information and an authorisation for expenditure for approval, but subject to limitations.

617 AIPN § 6.7.

618 AIPN § 6.7 (A).

619 AIPN § 6.7 (A), 6.8 (A) and (C).

620 AIPN § 6.8 (A).

621 AIPN § 6.8 (B) alternative 1.

622 AIPN § 6.8 (B) alternative 2.

623 AIPN § 6.7 (A) and 6.8 (C).

only in the 2002 edition, as from 1990 to 1995 an authorisation for expenditure was also required for minimum work obligations.[624]

The AIPN model also contains a unique provision on the scope of the authorisation for expenditure. This recognises three main types of authorisation for expenditure:[625] informative,[626] approval[627] and limited approval (ie, Opcom approval is required on restricted grounds only).[628] The parties are free to negotiate on the option that is most appropriate for the JOA.

From the non-operators' perspective, the second type is the most attractive, as it creates a robust second layer of protection regarding control of expenditure. It allows the non-operators to provide input on the content of the work programme and budget, and subsequently to control each specific item of expenditure on a case-by-case basis through the authorisation for expenditure mechanism. The first type, by contrast, gives the operator more freedom to execute the work programme and budget, which is usually an estimate of the overall expenditure. The third type is the most balanced scenario, as it represents a compromise between the interests of the operator and those of the non-operators.

While a limited approval mechanism is not optimal for non-operators, it does protect them from abuse and unreasonable expenditure, while at the same time giving comfort to the operator that authorisations for expenditure will not be rejected so long as they are based on the approved work programme and budget and reasonable grounds.

The AIPN model further requires the inclusion of fairly detailed information in authorisations for expenditure.[629] This is a positive provision for non-operators, as they can exert effective control over expenditure by comparing the line item approved in the work programme and budget with the proposed authorisation for expenditure.

The AIPN model thus provides:

- an excellent authorisation for expenditure mechanism for non-operators (total approval);
- an excellent authorisation for expenditure mechanism for operators (informative); and
- a reasonable authorisation for expenditure mechanism for both parties (limited approval).

However, this could lead to imbalanced provisions where the parties' negotiating powers are unequal. In current operations, the operator is likely to secure better terms. In any event, the best case scenario for non-operators (ie, total approval) will

624 "Article 6.6(A) no longer requires the operator to issue AFEs for Minimum Work Obligations and for general and administrative costs, provided these items are separately listed in the approved Work Programme and Budget. At present, only well workovers are completely exempt from the AFE requirement." David F Asmus (n 384) pp11, 14.

625 AIPN § 6.7 (B).

626 AIPN § 6.7 (B) alternative 1.

627 AIPN § 6.7 (B) alternative 2.

628 AIPN § 6.7 (B) alternative 3.

629 AIPN JOA item 6.7 (C).

in practice be effective only if they can exert some measure of control in the Opcom; otherwise, this will amount only to a bureaucratic procedure which in reality affords them no control over expenditure. The weakest point of the AIPN approach towards authorisations for expenditure is the fact that this mechanism is itself optional, rather than compulsory.

Greenlandic model: This model form also contains an authorisation for expenditure mechanism.[630] The most notable feature of the mechanism is the absence of a financial cap, meaning that all expenditure is subject to the Opcom's approval.[631]

However, the impact of the authorisation for expenditure mechanism is once again minimised by provisions on overspending and the exclusion of items.[632] The former allows for overspending by up to 10% of the approved authorisation for expenditure or a specified amount of capital, whichever is lower. The latter provides that authorisations for expenditure are not required in the event of emergency. However, the operator must promptly notify the non-operators of any emergencies. While this is positive for non-operators, the operator is not obliged to seek their input on important decisions in an emergency that will affect and bind the consortium as a whole.

There is also a mechanism to avoid deadlocks if a party fails to vote: "Failure of any Party to approve or disapprove, along with reasons for such disapproval, by the expiry of the first notice period, shall constitute deemed approval by such Party." In other words, if a non-operator does not clearly indicate its rejection of an authorisation for expenditure (including its reasons), the operation shall be considered approved by default. This is a negative provision for non-operators, as it restricts their rights; but it is positive for the effective and efficient operation of the consortium.

However, the model further provides that: "Each AFE shall describe the expenditure, give an estimate of the cost and estimated phasing by Quarter for the current Year and by Year thereafter of such expenditures."[633] An operator might seek to use this wording to obtain greater flexibility for each approved authorisation for expenditure. On the other hand, non-operators might argue that the estimate relates only to the overspending allowance, and that beyond this limitation the operator must seek further approval from the Opcom.

Non-operators thus enjoy strong control over expenditure under the Greenlandic model form, as a highly effective combination of work programme and benefit and authorisation for expenditure provisions affords them a high degree of control over additional expenditure. However, in practice, such control can be exercised only if the non-operators can control the Opcom, whether positively or negatively.

Conclusion: The authorisation for expenditure mechanism – which is largely beneficial to non-operators – is common to all JOA model forms, except the

630 Greenlandic JOA § 5.10.
631 Greenlandic JOA § 5.10.
632 Greenlandic JOA § 5.10.
633 Greenlandic JOA § 5.10.

Australian model. Those models that do include authorisation for expenditure provisions may be divided into two categories. The first combine work programme and budget provisions with the authorisation for expenditure mechanism; the second provide for the control of expenditure exclusively through the authorisation for expenditure mechanism. This latter category encompasses the North American models; the former includes all remaining JOA models.

Remaining models					
JOA model/provision	OGUK	NOR	AMPLA[650]	AIPN	GRE
Opcom	Yes	Yes	Yes	Yes	Yes
Work programme and budget	Yes	Yes	Yes	Yes	Yes
Authorisation for expenditure	Opcom	Opcom	No	Optional	Opcom
• Approval	Opcom	Opcom	No	Optional	Opcom
• Financial cap	Yes	Yes	No	Yes	Yes
• Exclusions	Yes	Yes	No	Yes	Yes
• Details	Yes	Yes	No	Yes	Yes

North American models			
JOA model/provision	AAPL	RRMLF	CAPL
Opcom	No	No	No
Work programme and budget	Partial	No	No
Authorisation for expenditure:	Yes	Yes	Yes
• Approval	Total	Total	Total
• Financial cap	Yes	Yes	Yes
• Exclusions	Yes	Yes	Yes
• Details	Yes	No	Yes

Under the North American models, non-operators cannot participate in decisions on operations, since no provision is made for a work programme and budget or an Opcom. All remaining JOA models, which clearly provide for work programmes and budgets and Opcoms, place non-operators in a stronger position to exert control over the joint operations in this regard.

However, the situation is different regarding authorisations for expenditure, as the North American JOAs afford non-operators a higher degree of control of expenditure than other JOA model forms in this respect.

Firstly, as mentioned, the work programme and budget is only a rough estimate which is prepared on an annual (or phase) basis; authorisations for expenditure are more precise and detailed in comparison. A work programme and budget alone is thus insufficient to secure adequate control over expenditure, so the authorisation for expenditure mechanism is a valuable complement in this regard. There has been a tendency, with each committee revision of the AIPN model, to require the provision of more detailed information in both instruments, but more information must be provided in authorisations for expenditure than in the work programme and budget.

Second, with all JOAs that provide for a work programme and budget, a dilemma arises, in that the operator will regard it as unfair to give non-operators a second chance to reject an operation that has already been approved in the work programme and budget. Several procedures have thus been established to minimise the burden that this places on the operator's ability to conduct operations, from informative authorisations for expenditure to limited approval authorisations for expenditure. By contrast, the JOAs that contain no work programme and budget provisions (ie, the North American JOA models) avoid this dilemma and can fully implement the authorisation for expenditure mechanism with only minor restrictions to ensure the efficiency and security of operations.

Third, the JOAs that do not include work programme and budget provisions also do not provide for an Opcom, so the parties vote as individual entities instead of towards a specified cumulative pass mark. They therefore have a higher degree of control over expenditure, as each authorisation for expenditure must be approved by the non-operators as individual parties. In contrast, where Opcom approval is required, the non-operators must rely on their control in the Opcom to exert control over expenditure; if the operator has control of the Opcom, the non-operators are effectively powerless to influence expenditure.

The major difference between the JOAs is thus the body responsible for approving authorisations for expenditure. In the international, British, Norwegian and Greenlandic models, Opcom approval is required; in the North American models, the non-operators' approval is required. Thus, for the first time in this analysis, it is possible to suggest that the North American models place non-operators in a stronger position than the other models, as authorisations for expenditure must be approved by each individual non-operator, instead of by a body on which the operator is also represented. This is easy to understand in practical terms: if the operator retains the largest participating interest in the JV or if a low pass mark exists, the operator can overcome this hurdle without any major difficulty, as it will have the final decision in the Opcom. Some authors would disagree with this view, such as Hew Dundas:

> *[T]he UKCS norm is for AFE to require Operating Committee approval prior to the operator making any commitment, while the North American approach is generally that AFEs are provided to non-operators more by way of information and do not require prior approval.*[634]

634 Hew Dundas (n 16) p9.

Arguably, however, the above statement is not entirely correct: while a joint operation can occur only if the non-operators approve the relevant authorisation for expenditure, this does not mean that the operator cannot proceed nonetheless with the operation as an exclusive operation. It is thus possible to affirm that under the North American JOAs, joint operations will take place and bind the non-operators only if the relevant authorisations for expenditure are approved; the non-operators thus enjoy a higher degree of control.

The lack of a work programme and budget provision also increases the non-operators' power to control expenditure, as a full authorisation for expenditure mechanism must be implemented, with little flexibility. The combination of a work programme and budget provision with an authorisation for expenditure mechanism is unlikely to achieve a higher degree of control for non-operators, but rather a balancing of control between these different mechanisms. This is a problem that existed even in the early editions of the AIPN JOA model forms, and it still exists today.[635]

Importantly, these provisions do not commonly apply to minimum work obligations imposed under the applicable petroleum legal regime or to emergency procedures, since the operator is obliged to act in such situations and any objection to an authorisation for expenditure could jeopardise the existence of the JV.[636] While a degree of flexibility thus seems reasonable under such circumstances, non-operators should have more than just a right to be informed, given that these decisions could affect the future of the consortium itself. However, none of the JOAs provides for adequate participation in emergencies. Ideally, the parties would agree a 'quick response' mechanism to tackle future emergencies.

The question of whether an authorisation for expenditure should be regarded as a flexible estimate or a fixed quote is controversial. The most reasonable interpretation is that the authorisation for expenditure is strict with regard to the procedures determined in the JOA, but flexible to the extent that the JOA allows for modifications. Thus, once an authorisation for expenditure has been approved, the operator can modify it only up to the level authorised in the JOA; otherwise, the authorisation for expenditure will be subject to further approval. An authorisation for expenditure is thus an estimate, in the sense that it can be subject to amendment or revision; but the rules are strict, as any amendment is subject to the approval of the non-operators or the Opcom, as appropriate.

In practice, operators should avoid the inclusion of multiple operations in a single authorisation for expenditure, as it will be far more difficult to control expenditure. However, the operator may be tempted to do so in order to reduce the level of control that non-operators can exercise through the authorisation for expenditure mechanism.[637]

Thus, non-operators are in a difficult position: where a high degree of control is exercised through the work programme and budget, this might at the same time reduce the chances of full implementation of the authorisation for expenditure

---

635 David F Asmus (n 384) p10.
636 Peter Roberts (n 5) pp105–119, Terence Daintith (n 16) pp1143–1150.
637 Taylor and Tyne (n 54) pp42–43.

mechanism. The operator might regard this mechanism as a second chance to reject an operation that has previously been approved in the work programme and budget. In this case, non-operators face a dilemma. On the one hand, they could gain an advantage by participating in major decisions on the joint operations through the work programme and budget, but lose control of the details. On the other hand, they could exert far more control over individual operations through the authorisation for expenditure mechanism, but lose the power to provide input on the overall content of the activities. Non-operators should thus consider carefully the kind of control that they are seeking, to ensure that the most suitable terms are in place.

In practical terms, therefore, the operator will seek to avoid the implementation of an authorisation for expenditure mechanism – or at least to minimise the use of this mechanism by including multiple operations in a single authorisation for expenditure.[638] The non-operators will seek the opposite, so that they can exercise more control over expenditure.[639] A balance should be the goal of all parties, so that efficiency can be improved.

The implications of contracting procedures for control of expenditures will be analysed in the following sections.

Procurement: As previously outlined, the operator acts on behalf of the JV in performing the joint operations.[640] Through its agent status, the operator has the power to award contracts on behalf of the consortium. However, in certain circumstances the operator may be authorised to award contracts in its own name, rather than on behalf of the consortium.[641]

For the purposes of this book, the operator's agent status is the initial focus, as this is how contracts are usually awarded. Where relevant, however, the award of contracts outside the scope of agency is addressed. This section also analyses the relationship between the JOA parties, rather than the relationship between the JOA parties and third parties (ie, contractors).[642]

The complexity of oil and gas operations and the lengthy duration of the petroleum title usually require expert services, which the operator is unlikely to be able to provide exclusively by itself.[643] The operator therefore performs the joint operations through the award of contracts to other parties during the lifespan of the consortium. Gerard Bean describes this situation as follows:

---

638 *Ibid.*

639 "In practice some operators will seek to minimise the number of AFEs required by including as much work as possible within a single AFE, but this tendency should be firmly resisted by the non-operators since it works against their interest by diluting the prime purpose of AFEs through allowing overruns on one section of the work to be offset against underruns elsewhere." Hew Dundas (n 16) p9.

640 See Chapter 2.

641 Kenneth C Mildwaters (n 16) p539.

642 For further information about the relationship with third parties, see Helen Franklin, "Irretrievable Breakdown? A Review of Operator/Contractor Relationships in the Offshore Oil and Gas Industry" (2005) 23 *J Energy & Nat Resources L* p1.

643 "With the trend towards multi-venture contracting, shared facilities and the contracting-out of traditional operator services, the more usual provisions on contracting may not be sufficient. In negotiating new JOAs or in going forward with changes in methods of operations, one should be aware of how the contracting provisions will apply and whether the non-operators will be sufficiently protected and informed." Sandy Shaw (n 16) p20.

The JOA will require the operator to supervize and conduct the operations on behalf of the co-venturers and will enable it to do so by the employment of agents or independent contractors. During the exploration phase of the project the employment of independent contractors such as seismic operators, geophysicists, and drilling contractors will be important.[644]

Control of the procedures through which the operator awards contracts (commonly referred to as 'procurement') is thus a key mechanism through which to control expenditure in the JV.[645] There is no doubt about the importance of this mechanism of control.[646]

Usually, a procurement provision will set out the rules that the operator must follow before hiring or acquiring any goods or services in relation to the JV. The difficulty lies in deciding on the details of this process, as it is up to the parties to determine the relevant procedures.

As a consequence, the extent of the parties' control over procurement is a potential source of tension. The operator will seek to retain as much discretion as possible, so that it can act freely without major interference from the other parties. The non-operators, by contrast, will seek to impose as many restrictions as possible, in order to ensure that procedures are transparent and efficient. This tension is noted by several scholars in the field, such as Taylor and Tyne,[647] Sandy Shaw[648] and Charez Golvala.[649]

The operator has many options in performing the joint operations. The first, as Peter Roberts observes, is to perform the operations itself.[650] This is not generally a concern for non-operators – although, as previously mentioned, it is important to verify that the overheads charged by the operator are reasonable and accord with the accounting procedures.[651]

The third-party route (ie, outsourcing the performance of contracts to third parties) is of much greater concern for non-operators, as most of the operations will be performed by third parties that can provide the necessary expertise for highly technical and risky operations.[652]

The affiliate route (ie, outsourcing to companies affiliated with the operator) is not a main concern for non-operators, although it might be important in specific situations where the operator is a major company with several subsidiaries and can deliver services through its affiliates.[653]

Of the above procurement routes, the award to third parties is the most common, as oil and gas operations inevitably involve expert and highly technical services.

There is no doubt about the necessity of awarding contracts *per se*, and non-

644 Gerard MD Bean (n 16) p15.
645 Peter Roberts (n 5) p115.
646 Taylor and Tyne (n 54) p45, Golvala (n 6) pp47–48, Anthony Jennings (n 16) p29, Peter Roberts (n 5) p115.
647 Taylor and Tyne (n 54) p45.
648 Sandy Shaw (n 16) p20.
649 Chavez Golvala (n 6) pp47–48.
650 Peter Roberts (n 5) pp111–112.
651 *Ibid.*
652 *Ibid.*
653 *Ibid.*

operators should have no objection to the operator doing so.[654] However, there are several concerns for the non-operators regarding the mechanism which will determine the award of contracts.[655]

Peter Roberts outlines the main concerns for non-operators as follows:

- form of contract;
- identity of supplier;
- contracting capacity;
- involvement of the Opcom; and
- involvement of affiliates.[656]

A practical solution to minimise conflict between the parties is to specify a financial limit beyond which a competitive tender process must be used. This system gives the operator wide discretion over less important contracts and the non-operators more control over important contracts. According to academics and experts in the field – such as Taylor and Tyne,[657] Scott Styles[658] and Bernard Taverne[659] – in practice, operators use this financial cap to reduce use of the procurement mechanism by non-operators to control expenditure. However, any indexation regarding market rates or inflation is disadvantageous for non-operators, as it will reduce their level of participation.[660]

As previously mentioned, the usual route for procurement is the award of contracts by the operator (on behalf of the JV) to third parties. However, if this is not expressively restricted in the JOA, the operator might also provide services or goods from its own resources,[661] or through its affiliates.[662] This could result in a conflict of interest.[663]

The operator will prefer to award contracts to its affiliates whenever possible, to give it greater control over the operations and maximise its profits from the project.[664]

The operator will further seek flexibility in procurement procedures, which might differ from those for the usual award of contracts. Peter Roberts describes this situation as follows:

> *In the JOA the operator may therefore seek to afford priority to contracts for the provision of affiliate services in the performance of the joint operations. The operator may require that such affiliate services be provided with the greatest possible degree of flexibility and informality.*[665]

654 *Ibid* p113.
655 Sandy Shaw (n 16) p20.
656 Peter Roberts (n 5) p113.
657 Taylor and Tyne (n 54) p45.
658 Scott Styles (n 14) p280.
659 Bernard Taverne (n 90) p136.
660 Taylor and Tyne (n 54) p46.
661 Peter Roberts (n 5) p115.
662 Bernard Taverne (n 90) p136.
663 Taylor and Tyne (n 54) pp45–46.
664 Peter Roberts (n 5) p115.
665 *Ibid.*

However, the non-operators will have a different view on the award of contracts to affiliates of the operator.[666] Peter Roberts highlights cost and quality as the two main concerns of non-operators in this regard.[667]

It might appear reasonable to suggest that an element of profit could be allowed in the provision of services by the operator itself or its affiliates. However, this would clearly contradict the governing principle that the operator must neither profit nor suffer loss from conducting the joint operations. This would create an exception to that principle, which might encourage the operator to seek to award as many contracts to its affiliates as possible, in order to maximise profitability. However, the operator might also suffer losses from its operations and might try to restrict its liabilities for possible failure of performance. In this case, if profit is acceptable, should the operator lose the benefit of restricted liabilities? It seems reasonable to accept the market price for such services; but at the same time it is also reasonable to require full standards of performance without any restriction of liability, such as would be expected of any third-party provider.

In practice, contracts are awarded to third parties more commonly than to affiliates. However, sometimes an affiliate of the operator will have the most appropriate financial and technical resources to provide the relevant services. If an affiliate is selected, the operator will ultimately benefit. The non-operators are thus usually keen to preclude or carefully control such awards. However, such a restricted approach might not be in the best interests of the consortium.[668]

Consequently, balance is crucial in determining the application of the procurement procedure, so that all parties' interests are safeguarded without harming the efficient operation of the consortium. The affiliate route might even be positive for non-operators, as it is likely to raise issues relating to the operator's fiduciary duties towards them.

Thus, the non-operators should not object to the affiliate route, as this could bring benefits for the consortium; but they should carefully verify whether this will secure a high standard of services at no more than the fair market price. Non-operators should have the right to participate in the procurement process, not only to verify compliance with the regulations, but also to assist the operator in achieving optimal performance. Non-operators will additionally be keen to verify that the operator is complying with all relevant regulations, such as the EU Procurement Directive in European jurisdictions (to the extent it is applicable or not exempted by the European Commission), any local content regulations which might be established in the petroleum title, and any other regulations.[669]

Non-operators should therefore seek a JOA with balanced and efficient procurement procedures, in order to secure high standards of operations at a fair market price. The JOA should also allow for a certain degree of flexibility in the conduct of the joint operations; a financial cap would achieve this purpose, affording flexibility to the operator while at the same time giving the non-operators control

666 *Ibid* p116.
667 *Ibid.*
668 *Ibid* p116.
669 *Ibid* p113.

over important services. Additionally, non-operators should not rule out the affiliate route, as it might bring benefits to the consortium, especially in time-sensitive situations. However, this should be carefully controlled in order to prevent abuse by the operator. Finally, the participation of the non-operators in important roles might increase the efficiency of the JV.

AAPL models: AAPL Form 810 gives broad discretion to the operator, which has almost absolute control over the operations.[670] Procurement follows the same principle, as the operator has almost unfettered control in this regard.[671]

Non-operators are placed in a difficult position under this JOA model form, as there is little regulation of the award of contracts to affiliates of the operator (except for drilling operations) and reference only to competitive contracts.[672] As there is no clear explanation of the extension of such terms, it is difficult for non-operators to exercise control thereunder. Under this model form, the operator awards contracts as an independent contractor, not as an agent of the non-operators. This increases the operator's liabilities regarding such operations. However, as previously mentioned, it is difficult to deny the existence of agency, as performance of the operations will ultimately benefit all parties to the consortium. A third party might therefore initiate a lawsuit to recognise the liabilities of non-operators, even if this has been expressly excluded in the contract.

Non-operators have little or no input on procurement under AAPL Form 810. Even if the project team participates in the process, its role will be informative only, as the operator has the final word on such matters. The non-operators must rely on the operator's duty to "timely commence and conduct all activities or operations in a good and workmanlike manner, as would a prudent operator under the same or similar circumstances".[673]

AAPL Form 610 also gives total control over the operations to the operator, which can decide at its own discretion the number of contracts that might be necessary to perform the joint operations.[674]

However, this model clearly requires a high standard of service performance, as follows: "All wells drilled in the Contract Area shall be drilled on a competitive contract basis at the annual rate prevailing in the area." This is probably one of the most important differences between the two JOA model forms, as the competitive basis is compulsory under Form 610, but only a possibility under Form 810.

The most significant difference is the provision on contracting with affiliates or using the operator's own resources, as this clearly refers not only to competitive contracts, but also to the best available rates and to agreement between the parties.[675] Thus, if the operator wishes to perform any operation using its own resources or through an affiliate, it must obtain the non-operators' approval of the rates to be

670 AAPL Form 810 §5.1.
671 AAPL Form 810 § 5.1.
672 AAPL Form 810 § 5.3.
673 AAPL Form 810 § 5.2.
674 AAPL Form 610 article V, C.
675 AAPL Form 610 article V, D, 1.

charged, which must be transparent and competitive. The historical Form 610 thus affords a high degree of control to non-operators where the operator awards contracts to affiliated companies or performs operations using its own resources. In addition, it is important to note the fact that Form 610 also requires the operator to "conduct its activities under this agreement as a reasonable prudent operator, in a good and workmanlike manner, with due diligence and dispatch, in accordance with good oil field practice".[676]

The AAPL forms thus place the operator in a strong position, as it is free to decide on the award of contracts without any significant interference from the non-operators.[677] However, the historical JOA model form places non-operators in a stronger position than the modern form in the case of offshore operations. These findings are surprising, as the higher costs and risks involved in offshore operations should mean that non-operators have a commensurately higher degree of control and participation in such operations. The new Form 810 makes provision for a 'project team', but this remains under the control of the operator; non-operators have no real powers. On the other hand, the historical Form 610 clearly regulates the award of contracts (especially to affiliates of the operator), in order to ensure that the providers contracted are competitive, qualified and responsible. However, neither form allows for effective participation by non-operators. They fail to establish a clear and transparent procedure for tendering, and for the disclosure of relevant information to the non-operators.[678]

The North American JOA models avoid over-elaborate procurement procedures,[679] as these could present an administrative burden in conducting the operations. They give the operator almost completely free rein, making it difficult for non-operators to exert any control over expenditure in this regard.

RMMLF model: This model form places the operator in the strongest position by far, stating very clearly that the "operator shall direct and have control of all operations conducted hereunder and shall have exclusive custody of all materials, equipment and other property owned by the Parties."[680] It later continues: "The number of employees to be used in operations conducted by the operator hereunder and their selections, as well as their hours of labor and compensation, shall be determined by operator."[681]

Non-operators can only hope to be consulted by the operator during the procurement process, as follows:

> *Consultation of the Parties. Consult freely with the other Parties concerning operations hereunder and keep them advised of all matters arising in operations hereunder which operator deems important in the exercise of its best judgement.*[682]

676 AAPL Form 610 article V, A.
677 AAPL Form 810 § 5.2.
678 The Canadian model has a similar approach (§3.3. (B)), as there is no clear and effective way to control this process and it does not allow for the effective participation of the non-operators.
679 Taylor and Tyne (n 54) 45.
680 RMMLF JOA §4.1.
681 RMMLF JOA §4.4.
682 RMMLF JOA §5.1 (B).

However, the reality is that consultation is by no means obligatory and is subject to the operator's discretion. There is thus nothing that controls the conduct of the operations, the award of contracts or the rules or principles that the operator must follow.

This model neither confirms nor denies the operator's agent status, but there is no doubt that the operator is acting on behalf of the other parties to the consortium. Therefore, the RMMLF model is the worst JOA from the non-operators' perspective, as it does not allow them to exert any control over the operator's conduct of the operations or to provide any guidance on the procedures to be followed when awarding contracts. In this case, the position of non-operators is akin to that of mere investors.

Canadian model: The Canadian model gives the operator considerable powers to award contracts at its own discretion,[683] providing as follows:

> *[The operator] will supply or cause to be supplied all material, labour and services reasonably necessary for Joint Operations. It will determine the number of employees and contractors required for Joint Operations, their selection, their hours of labour and their compensation, and they will be regarded as the operator's employees and contractors.*[684]

However, it also requires the operator to follow "good contracting practices in the oil and gas industry", and to take decisions based on criteria such as "reliability, safety, environmental protection, technology, cost, quality of service, delivery time and other factors relevant to the contract".[685] This is a valuable provision for non-operators, as it gives them clear grounds to compare and verify whether the operator is complying with the principles imposed in the JOA.

The operator must further award contracts on a competitive basis. This is beneficial for non-operators, as higher standards can be secured at fair market prices. However, exceptions to these requirements apply in the following situations:

- where the operator provides services through its own resources or through affiliates;
- in case of agreement between the operator and a supplier;
- for operations to comply with local regulations compliance; and
- for operations below a financial cap.[686]

The final two exceptions above are reasonable, as less expensive services do not require the same attention as major operations and regulatory compliance must always be secured. In contrast, the first two exceptions may weaken the non-operators' position in the JV – especially the provision on services provided by the operator from its own resources or through affiliates.

The operator is considered an independent contractor under the Canadian model.[687] As previously mentioned, however, it is difficult to deny the operator's

683 CAPL OP §3.03.
684 CAPL OP §3.03 (A).
685 CAPL OP §3.03 (B).
686 CAPL OP §3.03 (B).
687 CAPL OP §3.03 (A).

agent status, as it is the sole party responsible for conducting the joint operations (including procurement) on behalf of the whole consortium. Moreover, the provision on the exceptions to the competitive obligation mentions the existence of a "bona fide arm's length contract", which is a basic characteristic of an agency relationship.[688] Thus, the JOA generally seeks to avoid agency duties, which could benefit both the non-operators in terms of liabilities to third parties and the operator in terms of its duties towards the non-operators. Later, however, it recognises the operator's agent status, for the sole benefit of the operator. The non-operators might thus endeavour to have the operator's agency duties confirmed in court in order to safeguard their rights, while the restriction of liabilities might be also challenged in court by any third-party contractor.

This model form further requires the operator to "conduct all Joint Operations diligently, in a good and workmanlike manner, in compliance with the Title Documents and the Regulations and in accordance with good oilfield practice".[689]

The Canadian model thus affords extensive discretion to the operator to decide on the award of contracts. However, it also establishes reasonable guidelines that the operator must follow when awarding contracts, in order to secure high standards of operations. The exclusion of some operations might prove problematic for non-operators, as it might give the operator too much power and the non-operators little scope to verify the operator's standards. The worst feature of this mechanism is the lack of participation by non-operators, as the operator can decide unilaterally on the award of contracts. In such cases, the sole right available to non-operators, is the operator's general obligation to consult them periodically.[690]

British model: The British model authorises the operator to award contracts for goods and services where the expenditure has been approved by the work programme and budget and through the authorisation for expenditure mechanism.[691] This connection between procurement and both mechanisms for controlling expenditure is beneficial for non-operators – but only if all of these mechanisms effectively allow them to control and participate in the joint operations.

This model also clearly recognises the operator's agent status, as it states that the operator acts as the agent of the consortium in dealings with contractors.[692] It further seeks to exclude the non-operators from liability to third-party contractors, which is discussed elsewhere in this book.[693]

The key mechanism that restricts the operator's discretion to award contracts is based on a series of financial caps. The parties must determine three different mechanisms and three corresponding financial caps for procurement purposes.

The first mechanism deals with goods and services provided by the operator or an affiliate.[694] The parties must decide on the applicable financial cap; the relevant

688 CAPL OP §3.03 (B).
689 CAPL OP §3.04.
690 CAPL OP §3.01 (A).
691 OGUK § 6.5.1.
692 OGUK § 6.5.8.
693 OGUK § 6.5.
694 OGUK § 6.5.2 (b).

contract will require Opcom approval where this cap is exceeded. The financial cap is a useful instrument through which to achieve a balance between the interests of the operator and those of the non-operators, but the amount must be determined with care and precision. A lower financial cap might inhibit the conduct of the joint operations, but a higher financial cap might afford too much discretion to the operator.

The second mechanism concerns the financial cap for multi-field operations.[695] The operator must obtain Opcom approval before awarding contracts where the cap is exceeded. However, the level of information that must be provided to the Opcom (eg, on sensitive or confidential issues) may be reduced at the operator's discretion.

The third mechanism provides for a financial cap for third-party contracts, which must satisfy certain criteria in order to be awarded. This last mechanism is divided into two categories. The first category requires a higher level of participation by the non-operators; competitive tender; and the Opcom's approval.[696] The second category requires a lower level of participation by the non-operators and Opcom approval only where the operator awards the contract to an entity which is not the best qualified in the competitive tender.[697]

The main difference between the first and second categories is the financial cap. The first category affords the non-operators a higher degree of control over major expenditure, while the second reduces the non-operators' control for moderate expenditure (ie, contracts for amounts above the minimum requirement to tender, but below the first category). This seems an intelligent system, affording flexibility to the operator while at the same time safeguarding the non-operators' position. However, the main flaw with such a complex system is the lack of guidance regarding goods and services provided by the operator from its own resources or through affiliates. The non-operators could argue that clause 6.5.6 requires the operator to put any contract up for tender outside the scope of the previous clauses.[698] However, this is a weak provision, as it also provides that the operator is not obliged to put a contract out to tender if it considers, at its own discretion, that it is impractical or inefficient to do so.

The British model also requires the operator to perform the joint operations in accordance with basic principles and standards in order to secure higher standards of performance.[699]

It is thus clear that the British model provides for greater participation by the non-operators, especially in relation to higher expenditure. The operator is also subject to a general duty to consult the non-operators about the joint operations, but this is clearly not an obligation, as the word 'freely' is used.[700] In addition, the provision refers to a 'project team', but without further details.[701] A project team would be a valuable body through which to gather non-operators' views and input

695 OGUK § 6.5.3.
696 OGUK § 6.5.4.
697 OGUK § 6.5.5.
698 OGUK § 6.5.6.
699 OGUK § 6.2.2.
700 OGUK § 6.9.1.
701 OGUK § 6.11.1 (a).

on the joint operations. The model also establishes an intelligent and effective system procurement system based on the level of expenditure involved. However, a major flaw in this model is its failure to control the provision of services by the operator from its own resources or through affiliates.

Norwegian model: At first glance, this model would seem to favour the operator, as it is responsible for "carrying out and administer[ing] the day to day management of the joint venture activities".[702] However, as previously mentioned, the operator is not the highest authority of the JOA; rather, this is the Opcom. Thus, as a general rule, the operator's proposals must be approved by the Opcom.[703]

This is also the case for the award of contracts, as the operator must prepare the procurement strategy for significant expenditure, which must be approved by the Opcom.[704] This provision gives the operators a high degree of control over relevant contracts, while at the same time affording flexibility to the operator, as minor contracts will be subject to fewer requirements. The operator must provide detailed information to the Opcom in relation to significant purchases.[705]

The combination of the work programme and budget system and this detailed procurement provision is positive for non-operators, as they can take meaningful decisions at the Opcom level. What is remarkable about the Norwegian model is the exclusion of the 'manager' from such decisions, as follows:

The Manager shall not be party to information nor exercise any voting rights on decisions regarding sources of procurement to the activities. When calculating the individual Party's proportional voting right when voting over sources of procurement, the Manager's voting right shall be distributed among the other Parties in proportion to their Participating interests so that the total voting rights in such cases are distributed as follows:

X ....%
Y ....%
Z ....%

In such cases, a decision is adopted by the management committee when at least y% of these Parties representing at least x% of the Participating interest have voted in favour of the proposal.[706]

This provision could have balanced the positions of the parties if the operator were the manager. However, in the Norwegian case the manager is the state's representative in matters concerning licences and JOAs.

This model form recognises the potential for conflict of interest when contracts are awarded to affiliates, as it requires that a report be presented to the Opcom before such an award.[707] However, this provision does not clearly require Opcom approval for such contracts; the process is informative only. In such cases the non-operators'

702 Norwegian JOA § 3.1.
703 Norwegian JOA § 3.3.
704 Norwegian JOA § 13.1.
705 Norwegian JOA § 13.1.
706 Norwegian ACPA §3.2.
707 Norwegian JOA § 13.4.

control depends on the financial cap: if this limit is exceeded, the operator will not participate in the vote on the relevant contract. Nevertheless, the model clearly provides that the operator "shall in its capacity as such neither have profit nor loss through the execution of its duties".[708]

Additionally, the operator must carry out operations in accordance not only with the rules established in the JOA, but also with any applicable regulations in the minerals law or any other legislation.[709] There is no doubt about the operator's agent status, as it must conduct the joint operations on behalf of all the parties to the JV.[710]

As mentioned previously, the operator is responsible for planning and preparing the procurement strategy, but it is not required to seek the non-operators' input in doing so. Its only obligation is to "keep the management committee informed of events and circumstances which may be of importance to the joint venture".[711] The non-operators' approval is required only where a contract exceeds the financial cap. The non-operators do not participate in the procurement of any contracts below the financial cap, which is high.

The Norwegian JOA model also provides for a body called the 'partner forum', through which the parties' views on the execution of the joint operations can be gathered.[712] However, the provision clearly states that a partner forum will be set up only "for joint venturers having the same operator". In cases where there is more than one joint venturer, this might be a useful forum through which to obtain the non-operators' input on the operator's conduct of the joint operations. However, as most JOAs do not involve this configuration, a partner forum will not be established in most cases.

Overall, the Norwegian JOA model provides for a reasonable degree of participation by non-operators. The operator must therefore ensure that its proposals are reasonable, otherwise the non-operators will reject them. The problem for non-operators is the high financial cap and the high threshold for competitive tenders. While this model adopts an interesting approach that seeks to balance the positions of the operator and non-operators, it still affords broad discretion to the operator in its performance of procurement. Finally, the extent of the non-operators' participation can be high or low, depending on the applicable financial caps.

Australian model:[713] The Australian JV model gives extensive discretion to the operator in conducting the joint operations. In particular, the operator has almost total control of procurement procedures.[714]

The only restrictions on the operator's discretion to award contracts are the

708 Norwegian JOA § 3.1.
709 Norwegian JOA § 3.1.
710 Norwegian JOA § 3.2.
711 Norwegian JOA § 3.3.
712 Norwegian JOA § 5.1, 5.4 and 5.5.
713 AMPLA JOA § 7 and 8 – The most relevant changes are the following:
- replacement of operator remuneration with operator overheads;
- reference to competitive contracts;
- reference to safety cases and health and safety requirements;
- adjustments to the cartel exception; and
- increase in the threshold for unanimous approval from US$50,000 to US$300,000.

714 AMPLA JV § 7.2.

limitations imposed by the Opcom. However, Schedule 1 of the model recommends that all parties should agree on the award of contracts above US$50,000. This constitutes valuable protection for the non-operators, as it requires the operator to obtain all participants' consent, rather than simply the usual pass mark in the Opcom. Beyond this restriction, however, there is no express reference to procurement. The non-operators thus require positive control in the Opcom in order to enforce this restriction, except where the operator will provide services using its own resources or through an affiliate. In such cases, clear restrictions are imposed on the operator.[715]

Additionally, general provisions aimed at securing higher standards of operations require the operator to act:

- in accordance with the approved work programme and budget;
- in a good, workmanlike and commercially reasonable manner;
- in good faith; and
- in accordance with the applicable laws.[716]

The operator's position under this model is somewhat complex, as a unique provision on the "remuneration of the manager" provides as follows:[717]

(a) In consideration of the performance by the Manager of its obligations under this agreement, each Joint Venturer must pay the Manager its Percentage Share of the Management Fee as part of a Called Sum.

(b) The Management Fee may be varied by the Management Committee by Unanimous Vote.

(c) As soon as reasonably practicable after the conclusion of each month the Manager must send to each Joint Venturer a statement specifying the amount payable by that Joint Venturer on account of the Management Fee as assessed in relation to that month. The amount specified in that statement is due and payable by that Joint Venturer to the Manager within 7 days from the commencement of the next month.

This remuneration provision would require to be removed from the JV in order to satisfy the basic principle that the operator shall make no profit nor suffer losses in conducting the joint operations.

It is thus evident that non-operators are placed in a relatively weak position under the Australian model, as there is limited regulation of procurement. As a consequence, the model affords extensive discretion to the operator to execute the joint operations, except where the financial cap is exceeded.

AIPN model:[718] Under this model, the operator is responsible for conducting the joint operations on behalf of all parties. The model contains detailed provisions on the operator's power to conduct the joint operations, including the award of

---

715 AMPLA JV § 7.7.
716 AMPLA JV § 7.1.
717 AMPLA JV § 6.3.
718 AIPN JOA model form 2012 § 6.6 – There is no significant change in this provision, except for references to:
- decommissioning operations;
- non-operator affiliates; and
- compliance with the budgetary and legal requirements.

contracts.[719] Procurement is thus not left entirely to the operator's discretion, as specific rules must be followed. The AIPN model allows the parties to choose between two optional procedures for procurement. The operator is afforded wider discretion under the first option, as it is not obliged to put contracts below a certain amount out to tender or to inform the Opcom of such contracts. If this amount is exceeded, however, Opcom approval is required.[720]

The operator is obliged to award the contract to the best-qualified contractor, based on cost and ability to perform the contract. In practice, it is difficult to find the best-qualified contractor if no tender is conducted, so the operator does not enjoy as much discretion as might be expected from this provision; however, the decision still remains within the operator's discretion.

The second option is a scale system, which ensures greater participation by the non-operators, as the expenditure involved increases at different stages of the JV (ie, exploration, development and production).[721]

If the parties decide on this second option, they will implement a system that involves three different procedures. Procedure A is identical to the first alternative: the operator need not tender or inform the Opcom up to a certain amount of expenditure, but must award the contract to the best-qualified contractor. Procedure B imposes more duties on the operator, including an obligation to put the contract out to tender. This procedure also allows the non-operators to participate in the tender, and their approval is required where contracts over a certain amount are awarded to affiliates of the operator. Procedure C is similar to Procedure B, but it affords more control to the non-operators by requiring Opcom approval of 'recommended bids'. This latter procedure is thus the most beneficial for non-operators, as it secures them the highest degree of participation and control.

There is little regulation of the operator's power to award contracts to affiliates, except an obligation to obtain Opcom approval where the contract exceeds a specified value.[722] The non-operators could argue that when awarding contracts to affiliates, the operator must also comply with the procedures outlined in the second option (where applicable); but the model does not answer this question expressly. On the other hand, the operator might argue that it is required to obtain Opcom approval where contracts are awarded to affiliates in the second option, with no further requirements. In other words, the precise regulations for the award of contracts to affiliates are unclear, beyond the requirement for Opcom approval if a defined amount of expenditure is exceeded.

The non-operators can control the operator's performance not only through the procurement procedures, but also by verifying whether the operator is complying with all general duties imposed on its performance of the joint operations.[723]

Under the AIPN model, non-operators will enjoy a higher degree of control over and participation in procurement if they can secure the following:

---

719 AIPN JOA § 4.2 (A).
720 AIPN JOA § 6.6.
721 AIPN JOA § 6.6.
722 AIPN JOA § 6.6 (A) and (B) (4).
723 AIPN JOA § 4.2 (B).

- a low financial cap, so that they can participate in the award of most contracts;
- implementation of the second option instead of the first option; and
- over the Opcom, so that they can block certain proposals.

A major concern for non-operators under this model form is that the alternatives must be agreed between the parties and the non-operators are usually in a weaker negotiating position than the operator. Another concern is the lack of control over the award of contracts to affiliates of the operator. However, the non-operators can always secure higher standards of operations by enforcing the general duties imposed on the operator's performance of the joint operations.

Greenlandic model: This model requires the operator to act on behalf of all the parties to the JV. The operator is responsible for conducting the joint operations "by itself, or through its affiliates, its agents or its contractors, under the overall supervision and control of the Operating Committee".[724] In addition, the operator has several duties in executing the joint operations, especially:[725]

- planning for and obtaining requisite services and materials;
- direction and control of accounting systems; and
- provision of all technical and advisory services required for the efficient performance of the JV.

However, there are special provisions to govern procurement under this model. First, the operator is subject to the NOC's determinations (if any). Second, the operator must comply with the approved work programme and budget; however, the provisions on procurement make no reference to the authorisation for expenditure provisions included in this model form. If the first and second conditions mentioned above are fully satisfied, the operator will have the right to decide on the award of contracts.[726] However, the operator is not completely 'free' to determine the procurement system, as it must follow certain procedures in this regard.[727]

Non-operators have a high degree of control over the procurement system and have opportunities to provide input during the process. However, there is no regulation of the provision of services using the operator's own resources or through affiliates. There is thus a risk that the operator might abuse its position due to this lack of regulation. However, the non-operators can rely on general terms to secure a higher standard of operations and ensure that the operator pays the fair market price for the services or goods acquired. These general terms oblige the operator to undertake procurement in accordance with the aforementioned provisions, as well as with the licence and related regulations. Most importantly, the joint operations must be carried out in a proper and workmanlike manner.[728]

The operator's obligation to pay the fair market price for goods and services is set

---

724 Greenlandic JOA § 3.2.
725 Greenlandic JOA § 3.2.
726 Greenlandic JOA § 3.5.
727 Greenlandic JOA § 3.6.1.
728 Greenlandic JOA § 3.3.2.

out in the general provision which states that the operator "shall neither gain a profit nor incur a loss as a result of the Joint Operations or the discharge of the operator's responsibilities, obligations or liabilities under this Agreement".[729]

The operator may also request, from time to time, amendments to the expenditure limits previously outlined, but only by unanimous Opcom approval.[730] This is a reasonable provision, as all parties must agree on such a significant modification.

The Greenlandic JOA model therefore provides non-operators with a high degree of control over and participation in procurement procedures. However, there is no regulation of the award of contracts to the operator itself or to its affiliates, which might prove problematic for non-operators.

Conclusion: Control over the procurement process is vital for non-operators to exert a degree of control over the operator's spending. However, the JOAs vary considerably in this regard: some give non-operators little or no control, while others give them a high degree of control.[731]

JOA model/provision	AAPL	RRMLF	CAPL	OGUK	AMPLA	Norway	AIPN	Greenland
Procurement system	Partial	No	Yes	Yes	Partial	Yes	Yes	Yes
Affiliates	Yes	–	Yes	Yes	Yes	Yes	Yes	Yes
Approval	Partial	No	Partial	Yes	Yes	Yes	Yes	Yes
Financial cap	No	No	Yes	Yes	Yes	Yes	Yes	Yes
Participation	No	No	No	Yes	Partial	Yes	Yes	Yes

Again, the North American JOAs afford extensive discretion to operators, allowing them to award contracts without any major control or participation by non-operators. The lack of procedures and regulations in the Australian model form similarly puts non-operators in a weak position (except where the financial cap is exceeded).[732] In that respect, this model form bears comparison to the North American models (though the new AMPLA model form has more to say about procurement).

The fact that operators under the North American models can award contracts at their own discretion, with no or little control by non-operators, is another indication

729 Greenlandic JOA § 3.3.1.

730 Greenlandic JOA § 3.6.5.

731 "Not all Joint Operating Agreements are so involved in so far as this issue is concerned. Others merely require the operator to obtain the approval of the Operating Committee before entering into any contract for goods, services or facilities with a third party where the operator estimates that the expenditure involved will exceed a stated value." Kenneth C Mildwaters (n 16) p538.

732 The AMPLA JOA model form improved slightly the control of operations, through requirements for competitive contracts and health and safety requirements. On the other hand, it increased the financial cap for obtaining the non-operators' approval.

that these model forms treat non-operators as akin to investors. In a business sense, investors have no operational control, but only financial control. The Australian model form, by contrast, treats non-operators sometimes as co-venturers and sometimes as mere investors. Sometimes they are given a high degree of control over operations, as a co-venturer would expect (eg, in the Opcom); but other procedures are more akin to those commonly provided for investors (eg, no participation in the award of contracts, except where the financial cap is exceeded). That said, the new AMPLA form tends is more closely aligned with other model forms, as described below.

The remaining JOA models (Norwegian, British, International and Greenlandic) not only provide non-operators with a high degree of control over and participation in the operations, but also try to secure high standards of performance by requiring competitive tenders.[733] In itself, however, a tender process is not enough: the non-operators should have access to the details of the tender and be allowed to participate in such procedures, in order to ensure the highest standard of operations.[734]

Under these models, the rights and participation of non-operators commonly increase in line with expenditure, and Opcom approval is required if the amount of expenditure exceeds a specified limit.

However, there are also certain differences between the models. The scale system in the AIPN model affords a high degree of control to non-operators, but only where this option is selected. Under the British model, a simplified scale system has mandatory application, which avoids uncertainties for non-operators. The Greenlandic model does not include a scale system, although it does provide non-operators with a good level of control and participation in the affiliate procurement route. The Norwegian JOA could have balanced the interests of the operator and non-operators by allowing the operator to prepare the procurement strategy and then providing for participation in the award of contracts by the non-operators. However, this is not the case, as the Opcom voting restriction refers to the 'manager', not the operator. In summary, it is clear that the British, international, Greenlandic and Norwegian models recognise the important role of non-operators in the procurement process, as they allow them more effectively to control the award of contracts.

From the non-operators' perspective, a common flaw in all of the JOAs is the lack of clear regulation on the provision of services either using the operator's own resources or through the affiliate route, as this might make it difficult for non-operators to secure a high standard of performance at a fair market price. Another common problem with JOAs that contain Opcom provisions is the non-operators' lack of effective control over this decision-making body. If the non-operators have no control over the Opcom, it will be a merely bureaucratic body with no benefit to them. The most difficult task for non-operators is negotiating on the financial cap beyond which approval for the award of contracts will be required: a lower cap will increase their control in this regard, while a higher cap will reduce such control.[735]

The JOAs further afford the operator broad discretion in the acquisition of goods

733 Kenneth C Mildwaters (n 16) p538.
734 *Ibid.*
735 *Ibid.*

and personnel.[736] One source of comfort for the non-operators is the fact that the operator must always secure a high standard of operations in accordance with industry best practice, and act diligently and prudently in the conduct of operations. The vast scale of many oil and gas operations, and the complexity involved, often demand highly specialised services, which are commonly provided by third parties. Control over the award of contracts to third parties is usually of more importance to non-operators than control over the allocation of personnel, but in some cases the latter might also be a concern.

Finally, non-operators are often keen to verify whether the operator is in compliance not only with the JOA procurement rules, but also with related legislation (eg, in EU member states, the EU Procurement Directive (2004/18/EC), where applicable), the petroleum laws (eg, local content regulations) and any other applicable regulations. In addition, the obligation to provide information is very important for non-operators to verify whether the operator is in compliance.

Conclusion: Ideally, any JOA should allow for full participation by all members. This is reasonable and logical, because any participant in a consortium will also share the ownership of it. It is thus natural to expect that all members of the consortium will share a common goal: the maximisation of efficiency in the exploration and exploitation of oil and gas.

However, the reality falls far short of this ideal, as the operator's strong position and broad discretion in performing and conducting the operations mean that what is termed a 'joint operating agreement' is in fact more akin to a 'joint sharing of risks and costs agreement'. Tradition has shaped these agreements, making them pro-operator. This reality is most evident in the North American JOAs, but it is also true of the remaining JOAs in cases where the non-operators cannot exert effective control over the Opcom.

If no provision is made for the non-operators to assist in managing the operations (ie, there is no Opcom), or if such a body exists but the non-operators have no effective power to control it, then the operator will not only conduct the operations, but also determine all objectives. The control of expenditure thus constitutes essential protection for the non-operators, as they do not perform the joint operations and in most cases will not participate in decisions on performance.

For non-operators, the Opcom is something of a double-edged sword. On the one hand, it is a positive mechanism, as every JOA that contains an Opcom provision also provides for a work programme and budget and a procurement system. On the other hand, it is difficult to implement an authorisation for expenditure mechanism in such cases, as the operator will regard this as a second chance for the non-operators to approve or reject operations that have already been approved in the work programme and budget. The problem lies in the fact that the work programme and budget is not a precise determination, but only an estimate, so the non-operators cannot rely on this mechanism alone.

The authorisation for expenditure mechanism affords greater control over

736 *Ibid* pp538–539.

expenditure, as the parties receive a fair amount of detail on each proposed operation. The procurement mechanisms aim to ensure the highest level of performance by the operator. In theory, non-operators can rely on the operator's duty to adhere to industry best practices. In addition, if the expenditure involved in an operation is very high, the Opcom will often have to approve it. All in all, it would appear that the most powerful mechanism through which to control expenditure is the authorisation for expenditure.

It may thus be argued that the North American JOAs afford non-operators greater control over expenditure through the authorisation for expenditure mechanism, even though they include no other mechanisms through which to control expenditure or indeed performance of the joint operations. This lack of control over the operations is in fact advantageous for North American non-operators, as it secures their position as investors – and any investor has the right to exert tight control over expenditure. In this sense, North American non-operators have more control over expenditure than those under any other JOA. That said, however, the optimal protection for non-operators would involve a combination of a fairly detailed work programme and budget and an approval-based authorisation for expenditure mechanism – albeit that this may be almost impossible to secure in practice. In addition, a system that gives non-operators full control over the award of contracts would afford a high degree of control over expenditure; such a mechanism is sometimes easier to obtain, as the operator can minimise its effect through financial caps.

Non-operators can also exert control over expenditure under the AIPN, British, Norwegian and Greenlandic models, but only if they have effective control of the Opcom. Conversely, the Australian JV is the weakest model for non-operators, as there is no authorisation for expenditure mechanism and a poor system for controlling the award of contracts. However, the new AMPLA JOA model form affords a somewhat greater degree of control through authorisations for expenditure and minor adjustments to the procurement system.

A comparison between the positions of non-operators and minority shareholders reveals that non-operators have more control over expenditure than minority shareholders. First, no authorisation for expenditure mechanism is available to minority shareholders, and this is probably the most precise and effective way to control expenditure. Second, shareholders cannot usually exert control over the award of contracts. Third, in companies, overall control of expenditure is exercised by the board of directors, which is often dominated by the strongest shareholder.[737] That said, however, minority shareholders often have some control if they have made substantial financial commitments to the company, which gives them some measure of comfort – a situation that is reflected in most JOAs.[738]

The accounting procedure, which is an attachment to the JOA, plays a crucial role in controlling expenditure, as it governs how the operator's expenditure (on behalf of the JV) will be recorded in the joint accounts and the cash calls necessary to cover all related costs. This is therefore another critical issue for negotiation when drafting the JOA. Non-operators will desire an efficient, reasonable, transparent

737 Sections 170–181 of the UK Companies Act 2006.
738 Sections 188–226 of the UK Companies Act 2006.

regime that entitles them to conduct full audits of the joint accounts.[739] The right of audit is therefore a crucial mechanism through which non-operators can control expenditure by the operator and verify the correctness of the charges incurred.[740]

In conclusion, the ability to control expenditure is crucial for non-operators, as they will have to pay their share of the costs of the operations. Ideally, the combination of a work programme and budget, an authorisation for expenditure mechanism and control over procurement would be the optimal solution. However, as is apparent from the above analysis, in practice it is unlikely that non-operators would manage to secure a high degree of control through these mechanisms. Ultimately, while the ability to control expenditure is important, the ability to participate actively in the operations through which such expenditure is incurred is an even more effective way to safeguard the non-operators' interests.

(d) Conclusion

The analysis thus far reveals that the position of non-operators can vary dramatically, depending on the JOA model form adopted. In this context, it is possible to agree with Scott Styles' argument that the role of non-operators under the North American models is akin to that of a mere investor.[741] The similarities between the two positions are outlined in the following table.[742]

Issues	**North American non-operator**	**Investor**
Conduct of operations	No	No
Overall control of operations	No	No
Control of procurement procedures	No	No
Obligation to contribute with capital	Yes	Yes
Right to receive information	Yes	Yes
Right to approve expenditure	Yes	Yes*
Right to approve work programme and budget	No	Yes*

**Limited*

739 For further information see Charlotte J Wright and Rebbeca A Gallun (n 84) pp465–543, Sandy Shaw (n 16) p21, Taylor and Tyne (n 54) pp43–45.

740 Sandy Shaw (n 16) p21.

741 See Chapter I, section 1.1(b).

742 *Ibid.*

Ernest Smith recognises the lack of control over joint operations under the North American JOA models as follows:

Is the AIPN Model Form JOA's shared responsibility conducive to efficient management of the project? Domestic JOAs give almost total operational control to the operator subject to the non-operators working interest owner's power to remove/or replace the operator. It has been suggested that the Model Form's division of authority is somewhat analogous to the division of authority that occurs between a chief executive officer of a corporation and that corporation's board of directors.[743]

While there are many similarities between the position of non-operators under North American JOAs and that of investors, one notable exception is the provision for exclusive operations. This is the most compelling difference between non-operators and shareholders, as such provisions are unique to JOAs.

Issues	OGUK non-operator	AIPN non-operator	AMPLA non-operator	Greenlandic non-operator	Norwegian non-operator
Conduction of operations	No	No	No	No*	No
Overall control of operations	Yes**	Yes**	Yes**	Yes**	Yes**
Control of procurement procedures	Yes	Yes	Yes	Yes	Yes
Obligation to contribute capital	Yes	Yes	Yes	Yes	Yes
Right to receive information	Yes	Yes	Yes	Yes	Yes
Right to approve expenditure	Yes**	Yes**	No	Yes**	Yes**

continued on next page

743 Ernest E Smith *et al* (n 16) p543.

Issues	OGUK non-operator	AIPN non-operator	AMPLA non-operator	Greenlandic non-operator	Norwegian non-operator
Right to approve work programme and budget	Yes	Yes	Yes	Yes	Yes

* *National oil company is a co-operator*
** *But only if non-operator can control the Opcom's decisions*

The remaining JOA forms adopt similar approaches, although each places non-operators in a relatively stronger position with regard to control of the joint operations.

As previously mentioned, some regions have established their own JOA model in order to address their own needs and circumstances. However, the models share similar approaches, as they all come from the same source: the historical AAPL JOA Form 610. The most distinctive JOAs analysed in this book are the International and Greenlandic models.

The international scope of the AIPN model demands extensive flexibility in its terms and provisions. Thus, whenever a JOA is being negotiated and drafted, the parties are free to choose the alternatives that best fit their specific situation. If the operator is in a much stronger position than the other parties, it will likely secure better terms under the AIPN model. However, this scenario is less common under the other models, as they are not so flexible and the overall terms are already established; they therefore afford more assurance that non-operators will benefit from some of these terms. As previously explained, the traditional scenario in which each project has a single strong operator may well change in mature provinces, where projects will more frequently be undertaken by several parties with similar financial and technical resources. In such cases the international JOA model form will secure better conditions for non-operators, because more options are available. However, the international model does have its drawbacks, since – given its international application – it must be sufficiently broad to accommodate a diverse range of issues and scenarios.[744]

744 "[Model JOAs have] evolved to reflect the particular industry standards, customs, laws and regulations in effect in the jurisdictions in which they are most commonly used. Conventional operations in Western Canada tend to involve a relatively homogeneous group of players. In contrast, international operations often involve a variety of participants from disparate political, legal and economic systems. The various participants may include state-owned oil companies whose agendas and expectations may be very different from the profit driven goals of North American exploration and production companies. International projects tend to be larger in scale than most domestic operations, and are often located in places where there may be very little infrastructure and where the cultural, political, legal and economic environments are very different from those with which we are familiar in Canada. Moreover, the petroleum rights held by the participants will usually be derived from legal sources which are quite unlike conventional Canadian petroleum and natural gas leases. A workable international joint operating agreement must address these many distinctions." Michael D Josephson (n 51) pp1, 3.

The Greenlandic model uniquely includes the NOC as a participant in the consortium. This party enjoys the status of 'co-operator', to ensure that the host government can participate actively in the consortium. However, any other non-operator would also share this desire, as the operations and liabilities are joint; it would thus be only fair and reasonable to provide for their participation. Indeed, if things go wrong (as they often will), the operator will often argue that the non-operators played a major part in the process, while the non-operators will claim the opposite (the Deep Water Horizon case is a clear example of this). These considerations are analysed in the following chapter.

Given these findings, non-operators might well ask why the North American JOAs put them in a weaker position than the other models (except in relation to the control of expenditure). Taylor and Tyne answer this question as regards the UKCS as follows:

The principal underlying reason for the adoption of this approach is probably the much greater costs and risks associated with UKCS operations as compared with a typical North American onshore operation. This has meant that most non-operators feel a need to take an active part in decision-making to protect their investment rather than simply rely either upon the expertise of the operator or a right of non-consent.[745]

Andrew Derman and James Barnes also recognise the lower costs involved in North American operations as follows:

Historically, the first model form operating agreements were drafted to address the drilling of onshore wells primarily in the United States, where individual autonomy is a prized tradition. These agreements were conceived to deal with relatively unsophisticated technology, low cost wells, high margin prices, and small lease areas held under a property ownership system that fosters unilateral initiative. Under the circumstances, it was not unreasonable for the parties to delegate broad authority to one of them to organize the drilling of an exploratory well and to develop the field.[746]

Operations in North America are commonly located onshore or in shallow waters, and thus involve lower risks and costs (not always – some shallow water operations are costly, for example, in Arctic waters off Alaska); this in turn puts the non-operators in a weaker position. In deepwater operations, where higher risks and costs are involved (eg, on the UKCS and in Norway),[747] it would correspondingly be logical to provide for greater participation and control by the other participants.[748] The AAPL recently approved Form 810, which is aimed at deepwater operations in the Gulf of Mexico. It would be reasonable to expect the adoption of a similar

745 Taylor and Tyne (n 54) p22.

746 Andrew B Derman and James Barnes, *Autonomy versus Alliance: An Examination of the Management and Control Provisions of Joint Operating Agreements* (RMMLF, 1996), § 4.03 at p10.

747 Terence Daintith, (n 16) p1143.

748 "In contrast to the broad discretion given to the operator in Canadian and US onshore JOAs, international JOAs provide for a management committee that exercises some degree of supervisory control over operations. Each participant has one representative on the committee with a vote weighted in accordance with the participant's interest in the project. The powers of the operating committee may be specifically listed or stated in general terms." Bruce M Kramer and Gary B Conine (n 83) p564.

749 "As offshore exploration and development operations in the Gulf of Mexico progress in their technical complexity, so too have the legal issues relating to the contractual risk-shifting provisions between the parties engaged in these ventures." Daniel B Shilliday *et al*, "Contractual Risk-Shifting in Offshore Energy Operations" (2006–2007) 81 *Tulane Law Review* p1579.

approach to that set out in the British model, given that this scenario involves higher risks and costs; however, this has not in fact been the case.[749]

AAPL Form 810 places non-operators in a slightly better position than its predecessors. It is also far more complex; but it still provides for little in the way of participation and control by non-operators. Once again, their position is still akin to that of mere investors.[750] But why is this, given the higher risks and costs involved? It is difficult to find a straightforward answer, but the current lack of deepwater offshore experience in the United States might be one. Once US deepwater operators have gained more experience, further adjustments may well be made to Form 810 allowing for greater participation by non-operators, as under the British model. This would be an interesting historical reversal, as the first British models were modelled on the US experience in onshore operations, using the AAPL Form 610 established in the 1950s. Today, the best model for AAPL JOA deepwater operations would be the British JOA, which reflects the country's many years of offshore experience. The British model would thus turn the tide of history by becoming a reference for the AAPL JOA offshore form.

The precise extent of the relationship between the operator and non-operators is crucial, as it may raise concerns in relation to general law (partnership, agency and fiduciary duty) which could potentially affect the rights and duties that have been carefully established in the JOA. The 2010 accident in the Gulf of Mexico starkly illustrates the importance of this issue. The operator's duties and liabilities will likely be tested in court as, faced with a massive bill for damages, the non-operators seek to escape most of their obligations due to possible failures in conduct by the operator.[751] However, this issue is by no means straightforward: there are compelling arguments for both confirming and denying liability. This notwithstanding, the parties can minimise these general law concerns by including certain provisions in the JOA (eg, on the separate disposal of production and greater control and participation by non-operators). Indeed, from the non-operators' perspective, the potential consequences will more likely be of benefit to them than to the operator, as it is the latter which is subject to the vast majority of the duties under the JOA.

In conclusion, while the role of non-operators will vary depending on the specific model form adopted,[752] all JOA model forms clearly recognise two important points:

- non-operators should receive all relevant information about the conduct of the joint operations; and
- non-operators should have a high level of participation with regard to the control of expenditure.

750 "Even domestic offshore joint operating agreements follow a format generally similar to that used in the standard on-shore forms." Ernest E Smith (n 79).

751 A non-operator, Anadarko Petroleum Corporation, makes the point as follows: "The operator of a well determines the detailed planning and execution of the well, and is responsible for the day-to-day activities of, and decisions executed by, personnel on the rig. Consistent with standard industry practice around the world, non-operating investors rely upon the operator to make the appropriate decisions on the rig." www.anadarko.com/Investor/Pages/NewsReleases/NewsReleases.aspx?release-id=1439839.

752 "Even though model operating agreements from various areas of the world deal with many similar issues, their approach in handling these issues can be quite different. For instance, there is a marked difference in various model JOAs on how the relationship between the operator and non-operator(s) is addressed." Andrew B Derman, James Barnes (n 746) § 4.03 at 10.

It is thus apparent that non-operators generally enjoy investor status at a minimum under all JOA models; but more proactive participation, akin to the role of a partner, will depend on the model form adopted. In any event, the latter is secured only to the extent that the non-operators have effective control over the Opcom; without this, they are essentially powerless. The control of operations is thus the most important concern for non-operators, as it is the main instrument through which to ensure the diligent and efficient operation of the JV. However, such a crucial issue is not effectively secured in any of the JOAs analysed in this book, except where non-operators have a high participating interest in the consortium.

The participation of non-operators in the joint operations should always be regarded as positive. Any attendant burdens are wholly justified, as this is ultimately for the benefit of the whole consortium. An inclusive procedure will ensure that the operator conducts the operations efficiently and diligently. As the non-operators are engaged in a joint enterprise together with the operator, greater cooperation between them will benefit the JV as a whole – all parties have an interest in the consortium, and everyone will benefit if the JV achieves improved standards. That said, balanced provisions are crucial, to ensure that no one party can abuse its position for its own benefit instead of the greater good of the consortium.

In practice, however, non-operators generally have little to no control over the joint operations, and are forced to rely on secondary or supplementary provisions to protect their interests. The remedies available to non-operators where the operator abuses its powers are outlined in the following sections.

3.2 Remedies and protection

It is evident from the preceding analysis that none of the existing JOAs provides for the full participation of non-operators in the performance of, or in major decisions relating to, the joint operations.

Instead, non-operators must rely on supplementary provisions that aim to secure their interests should something go wrong: the provisions on the operator's removal, default and liabilities. The provision on the operator's removal is crucial to secure a high level of performance; the provision on default is vital to preserve financial resources; and the provision on liability is the final protection against performance failures that cannot be dealt with through removal or default. Ultimately, if no other alternative is available, non-operators can exit the consortium through assignment or withdrawal. In this case, however, the effects of the provisions will serve to remove the non-operator from the consortium and the exit will be subject to horizontal and vertical regulations.[753] This is another clear similarity between the position of investors and that of non-operators, as – like investors – non-operators cannot control the project, but can decide to leave the project.

As the focus of this book is on the key terms necessary to secure a balanced and

753 Assignment and withdrawal must be according to the procedures set out in the JOA, and as prescribed in the petroleum title. The major concern about these clauses is the potential impact on the minimum work obligation and any other obligations under the petroleum title. Therefore, all parties, including the host government, will be keen to control the process. See Model Clauses 11 and 40 of the Petroleum Licensing (Production) (Seaward Areas) Regulations 2008.

enduring relationship between the JOA parties, assignment and withdrawal are not analysed further.[754] The provisions on removal of the operator and liabilities are explored in the following sections. While the provision on default is important to maintain the good standing of the petroleum title, it is not assessed further, for two reasons. First, the provision is more likely to be exercised against a non-operator than an operator, as default relates to the financial strength of the parties.[755] Second, an adequate analysis of such a complex matter under English law would be beyond the scope of this book.[756]

(a) *Removal of the operator*

The operator must perform the joint operations in accordance with various rules established in the petroleum regulations and the JOA. However, the operator must comply with more than just contractual obligations: several other principles must additionally be followed, such as the requirement to follow best practices in the industry and to conduct the operations with diligence and efficiency.

As previously mentioned, the provisions on control of operations are a vital mechanism through which to verify the high-level performance of the joint operations. However, the lengthy duration of most petroleum titles increases the risk of performance failure, so it is necessary to secure not only the non-operators' interests, but also those of the consortium, as any failure could jeopardise the whole enterprise. Consequently, JOAs should regulate the circumstances under which the operator may be removed and a successor elected.[757] Unless the operator resigns[758] or assigns its interest,[759] or is removed, it will remain as the operator of the consortium until termination of the JOA.[760]

The operator's removal is another hotly debated topic in the JOA negotiations. The operator will naturally be keen to limit the circumstances in which it might be ousted. However, should circumstances that would potentially justify its removal occur, the operator is likely to prefer that unanimous approval be required for any decision to remove it. The non-operators, by contrast, will wish to maximise the circumstances under which the operator can be removed, and will seek the right to exercise this power in such cases without interference by the operator.

---

754 For further information on assignment and withdrawal, see Adam Dann, "Asset exchanges and pre-emption" (1994) *OGLTR* 12(12), pp397–398, Rebecca Major, "A practical look at pre-emption provisions in upstream oil and gas contracts" (2005) 5 *IELTR* pp117–123, Preston R Mundt, "The Assignor Giveth and the Operator Taketh Away, Oil and Gas Working Interest Owners Beware of Continuing Liability" (2007–2008) 40 *Tex Tech L Rev* p419.

755 See Peter Roberts (n 5) p187, Hew Dundas (n 16) p12, Terence Daintith (n 16) p1147, Taylor and Tyne (n 54) pp77–78 and Richard H Bartlett, "Rights and Remedies of an operator vis-à-vis a defaulting non-operator under Joint and Unit Operating Agreements" (1972) 10 *Alberta Law Review* p291.

756 For further information, see GDM Willoughby, "Forfeiture of Interests in Joint Operating Agreements" (1985) 3 *J Energy & Nat Resources L* pp256–265, Michael Lishman, "Penalties and Relief Against Forfeiture of Joint Venture Interests" (2008) 27 *ARELJ* p223.

757 "Key provisions relating to the operator are ... (ii) the circumstances in which an operator [may] resign or be removed." John Wilkinson (n 16) p40.

758 Resignation will not be analysed as this is primarily a right of the operator (though time constraints for resignation might offer a measure of protection for non-operators).

759 Assignment will not be analysed in this book.

760 "The appointment of the party which is designated to act as the operator will be for an indeterminate period, subject to the termination of the JOA or the point at which the party-operator resigns or is removed as such." Peter Roberts (n 5) p87.

Sandy Shaw describes this situation in the following terms:

There will be provisions in the JOA for removal of the operator and this is one area in which the views of the parties during negotiations are likely to differ. The operator will want to limit removal provisions to those requiring cause, i.e. default or wilful misconduct, and will want any vote for removal to be unanimous (or as close as possible thereto) amongst the other parties. The other parties on the other hand may seek to be able to remove the operator for no reason and/or notice, thus avoiding default arguments and gaining flexibility and bargaining strength.[761]

There are several reasons why non-operators might seek to remove the operator.[762] The principle behind this provision is to protect the consortium against performance failure. In this sense, the operator's financial strength is a key factor in securing the performance of minimum work obligations and other exploration and production activities within the licensed area.[763] As a consequence, bankruptcy is the most common reason for seeking the operator's removal. This is only logical, as a bankrupt operator will face significant financial problems. However, fully executing such a provision could prove problematic, as it could conflict with creditors' rights under bankruptcy and insolvency regulations.[764] Ernest Smith describes this situation as follows:

Almost all operating agreements call for the removal of the operator if it becomes bankrupt or insolvent. In Tri-Star Resources Ltda. v J.C. International Petroleum Ltda., [1986] 48 Alta. L.R. (ed) 335; 19870 2 W.W.R. 141, the court grappled with the issue of what constitutes insolvency. The court ultimately found that the appointment of a receiver for the operator was sufficient to trigger the automatic removal provisions of the Canadian Association of Petroleum Landman's Model Form JOA which had been used by the parties.

A clause permitting the removal of the operator without cause, similar to the clause contained in typical offshore United States JOAs, may be more protective of nonoperator interests in some jurisdictions in the event of operator bankruptcy than a clause that purports to remove automatically a bankrupt operator. The reason is that the bankruptcy laws of many countries may function to prohibit removal of the bankrupt operator after the operator has filed for or has been involuntarily placed in bankruptcy.[765]

Peter Roberts also recognises the complexity involved in insolvency issues:

The exact composition of insolvency event can be defined by reference to any of the governing law of the JOA, the law which governs the country of the incorporation of the operator or the law which applies in the country when joint operations are being conducted. Given that this could lead to the application of a multiplicity of legal doctrines, the usual solution is to define the insolvency events broadly and without reference to any particular body of law, although equally a specific legislative test of insolvency might be adopted and applied across the board.[766]

While insolvency is the most common reason for non-operators to seek the

761 Sandy Shaw (n 16) p14.
762 Kenneth C Mildwaters (n 16) pp501–507.
763 Taylor and Tyne (n 54) pp20–21.
764 Ernest E Smith *et al* (n 16) p621.
765 Ernest E Smith *et al* (n 16) p621.
766 Peter Roberts (n 5) pp87–88.

operator's removal,[767] there are several other reasons that might prompt them to do so, such as a general breakdown in relations, a reduction in the operator's participating interest or general breaches.[768]

Therefore, JOAs commonly provide for the removal of the operator in case of insolvency or material breach,[769] and sometimes even in other circumstances, which might not even require a reason.[770]

From the non-operator's perspective, it is important to exclude the operator from participating in the decision on its removal, otherwise it will be difficult to implement this provision.[771] Taylor and Tyne describe the practical considerations for non-operators as follows:

One provision relating to the removal of the operator which appears in many modern JOAs is that specifying that, where the operating committee is voting upon the removal of the operator, the votes of the operator itself and of any affiliate are ignored and the matter is decided by a specific percentage vote of the remaining parties. This, again, was an important feature of the BNOC fifth and sixth round pro formas which is generally, although not universally, accepted. Sometimes, to placate the operator, unanimity, or near unanimity, on the part of non-operators is required to remove the operator.[772]

Although the JOA parties have the right to remove the operator and appoint a new operator, the appointment may be subject to governmental approval. Peter Roberts recognises this situation as follows:

Where an operator resigns or grounds arise for the removal of an operator, it will be necessary to appoint a replacement operator. This will typically be one of the other parties to the JOA and such appointment will be subject to approval at the OpCom (where the appropriate voting control, and the recusal of the party-operator and its affiliates from that voting process will apply), and also subject to governmental approval.[773]

Conversely, if the operator's status with the government authorities is affected, this loss of status might also extend to the JOA as follows:

If the operator's status as such is removed by the government in accordance with the terms of the concession, this can also trigger an automatic loss of status as the operator under the JOA (although the parties might of course take a different view under the JOA).[774]

The appointment of the operator's successor is another subject of debate,[775]

---

767 For further information about bankruptcy and insolvency involving a JOA, see John D Weidman, "Oil and Gas, operator's Liens in Bankruptcy, The Model Form Operating Agreement Versus the Trustee in Bankruptcy's Avoiding Powers" (1984) 37 *Okla L Rev* p141.

768 Peter Roberts (n 5).

769 Claude Duval *et al* (n 122) p289.

770 Taylor and Tyne (n 54) p20.

771 "The JOA will specify the level of voting control at the OpCom (by reference to number of parties voting and/or aggregate PIs) which will be needed to effect the operator's removal. The party which is the operator, and any affiliate of that party which is also party to the JOA, should be recused from the voting, given the obvious conflict of interests which they would have." Peter Roberts (n 5).

772 Taylor and Tyne (n 54) pp19–20.

773 Peter Roberts (n 5) p89.

774 *Ibid* p88.

775 "Sometimes there is fierce competition as to which party will operate. In Kashagan consortium already referred to, no fewer than five parties wanted to operate: Exxon, Shell, BP, Total and ENI. After five years of argument the prize went not to one of the giants but to a surprise outsider, ENI." Chris Thorpe (n 317) pp124–125.

particularly in relation to the passmark required.[776,777] However, the host government might approve the appointment,[778] as such a radical change will affect the performance of the operations, and ultimately the economic recovery from the reservoir.[779] On the other hand, the host government cannot unreasonably withhold its approval to the appointment, which should be based on economic and technical qualifications to perform the operations.[780]

The appointment of the new operator will become effective upon approval by the host government (where applicable). The JOA should include contractual obligations on the outgoing operator's performance in the period between its removal and the appointment of the new operator.[781]

If the petroleum regulations so allow, an interesting alternative for this interim period would be to transfer the operatorship to the party with the largest participating interest in the consortium (or the second largest, if the operator has the largest).[782] However, this might "result in the operatorship passing to an unwilling party (which may resign anyway)". There are possible solutions to this: "It might be preferable, therefore, to have any party eligible considered as the new operator. The JOA should provide that a party cannot become the new operator against its will."[783] If the operator cannot vote on its removal, is it possible to argue that the operator also cannot vote on the appointment of its successor?[784] In theory, the removal of the operator and the appointment of a new operator are two different things, so the operator should have the right to vote on the appointment of its successor. However, if the operator has a substantial participating interest, then – were it allowed to participate in the decision on its successor – it could potentially block the appointment of a new operator and remain the provisional operator for so long as it wished.

Ernest Smith describes this complexity in a case relating to a unit operating agreement, which is similar to a JOA but involves more parties and covers a larger area (ie, it results from the integration of more than one JOA). *Fasken Land and Minerals, Ltd v Occidental Permian Ltd* 225 SW 3d 577 (Tex App El Paso 2005) serves as a reminder that removal of the operator does not in itself safeguard the non-operators' position; they must also ensure that the operator cannot block the appointment of a successor, even though it has been removed from the operatorship.

It is thus necessary to restrict the operator's ability to block the appointment of

---

776 "The JOA will also contain clauses allowing the operator to resign, and which provide for the selection of a replacement. This is another area where there may be tensions over the relevant 'pass mark' for making this decision." Scott Styles (n 14) p287.

777 "The JOA will also need to include provisions to govern the election of a successor operator and the transfer of responsibilities (see clauses 5.3 and 5.4 of the Appendix). Such clauses are largely standard and it should be noted that there is normally a provision whereby the vote of an operator which has been removed (or that of its affiliates) can be ignored if, in relation to the election of a successor, it either fails to vote or votes to reappoint itself." Taylor and Tyne (n 54) p21.

778 *Ibid* p20.

779 "The choice of operator is subject to government approval." Scott Styles (n 14) p277.

780 Claude Duval *et al* (n 122) p289.

781 Taylor and Tyne (n 54) p20.

782 Kenneth C Mildwaters (n 16) p510.

783 Peter Roberts (n 5) p89.

784 Kenneth C Mildwaters (n 16) p510.

a new operator, as otherwise it will be practically impossible to remove the operator. If the parties cannot elect another operator, the ultimate solution will be surrender of the concession. Peter Roberts describes this situation as follows:

> *If it ultimately proves to be the case that a suitable replacement operator cannot be found, the parties should move towards surrender of the concession and the JOA, on the basis that their continued performance can no longer be effective. This mechanism will be broadly similar to the exercise of the withdrawal provision of the parties.*[785]

Removal of the operator is thus a key provision for non-operators, but it will be effective only if there are clear provisions on what should happen until a successor is appointed. Peter Roberts describes this situation as follows:

> *The JOA should provide for an orderly transition and handover between outgoing operator and the incoming operator. The parties may also require to audit the joint account up to the transition point, and in some JOAs audit might be automatic.*[786]

The resignation or removal of the operator will not release it from liabilities incurred through its performance of the operations, and will not affect its right to recover costs and expenses as set out in the accounting procedures.[787]

Non-operators should therefore seek to ensure that the JOA provides for the following:

- several options to remove the operator (ie, with and without good reason);
- exclusion of the operator and its affiliates from the vote on its removal; and
- a transition period between the removal of the operator and the appointment of its successor, during which the operations will be conducted by the non-operators (where permitted by the government authorities). Alternatively, if the operator must retain the operatorship until the handover to the new operator, it should not have the power to block this appointment.

AAPL model: AAPL Model Form 810 provides for the operator's removal either:

- through assignment; or
- for cause, by vote.[788]

Removal through assignment aims to encourage the operator to maintain its dominant position in the consortium: if the operator reduces its participating interest to below that of any non-operator, it may be removed by the non-operators.[789] However, the operator is not excluded from voting on the decision. As a result, unless a lower pass mark is established, this provision may be ineffective in practice.

The provision on removal for cause, by vote outlines several circumstances that might lead to the operator's removal, as follows:

785 Peter Roberts (n 5) p101.

786 *Ibid.*

787 "Cessation of the operator's position as such should be without prejudice to any accrued liability (if any – see 12.1) of the operator up to the point of cessation, and should also be subject to the operator's right to recover its costs and expenses (including any costs and expenses which are associated with effecting the change of operatorship), up to that point." *Ibid* p89.

788 AAPL JOA Model Form 810 § 4.4.

789 AAPL JOA Model Form 810 § 4.4.1.

(a) the operator is found liable by a final judicial decision or a final decision under binding arbitration for an act of gross negligence or willful misconduct regarding the Contract Area;

(b) the operator commits a substantial breach of a material provision of this Agreement and fails to cure the breach within thirty (30) days after receipt of written notice of the breach from a Non-Operating Party;

(c) the operator becomes insolvent or unable to pay its debts as they mature, makes an assignment for the benefit of its creditors, commits an act of bankruptcy, or seeks relief under laws providing for the relief of debtors;

(d) a receiver is appointed for the operator or for substantially all of its property or affairs; or

(e) the operator fails to timely commence the fabrication or acquisition of the Development System in accordance with Article 12.7.9 (Timely Operations for Development Systems).[790]

Although this list is extensive, it does not fully safeguard the non-operators' position, as the operator must breach some provision before anything can happen. In this sense, it does not protect the non-operators against poor performance that nonetheless complies with the applicable regulation. However, in this case the operator is excluded from voting on the decision, which increases the non-operators' control. The vote must be taken within 90 days of acknowledgement of the applicable cause.[791]

The voting procedure when appointing a new operator is more complex. While the operator is not clearly excluded from voting, the provision does state that the voting procedure to appoint a new operator will be the same as that to remove the operator – suggesting that the operator should indeed be excluded from voting. If there are only two parties in the consortium, the non-operator automatically has the right to become the operator; if it does not wish to assume this role, the consortium will terminate.[792]

Removal of the operator becomes effective following approval by the government authorities (where applicable). The outgoing operator must transfer all rights and obligations relating to the petroleum title to its successor.[793] However, it is not clear who should conduct the operations between the operator's removal and the appointment of its successor. Nevertheless, the appointment of a new operator will not affect any rights or liabilities incurred by the outgoing operator in conducting the operations.[794]

AAPL Form 810 thus gives non-operators a reasonable degree of control over the operatorship. However, it does not include a broad clause giving them further grounds for removal of the operator, and fails to clarify who should assume the operatorship during the transition period.

AAPL Form 610 is far more concise, as it states that the operator "may only be

790 AAPL JOA Model Form 810 § 4.4.2.
791 AAPL JOA Model Form 810 § 4.4.3.
792 AAPL JOA Model Form 810 § 4.4.5.
793 AAPL JOA Model Form 810 § 4.4.7.
794 AAPL JOA Model Form 810 § 4.4.6.

removed for good cause by the affirmative vote of the non-operators owning a majority interest ... excluding the voting interest of the operator".[795]

Good cause is defined as meaning "not only gross negligence or wilful misconduct but also the material breach of or inability to meet the standards of operation contained in Article V.A. or material failure or inability to perform its obligations under this agreement".[796] This definition is reasonably extensive, as it encompasses issues from material breach to standards of performance.

However, its application is not automatic: the non-operators must first issue notice to the operator providing details of the alleged breach. Upon receiving such notice, the operator has a specific timeframe within which to remedy the breach. Unlike under other JOAs, a change in control of the operator's structure will not lead to its removal under AAPL Form 610.[797] This is a negative provision for non-operators, as they enter into an agreement with a specific party to perform the joint operations. Any change in control clearly affects this arrangement, and the outcome might not be positive for the non-operators.

The operator will also be compelled to resign should it become insolvent or bankrupt. If its removal is not authorised under the applicable legal framework, all parties will establish an interim operating committee to serve until the new operator has been appointed. During this period all actions must be taken by at least two or more parties owning the majority of the participating interests in the consortium. If there are only two parties in the consortium, the operating committee must include a third party which is acceptable to the operator, the non-operator and the bankruptcy court, and any decisions will require the support of two participants, regardless of their participating interest.[798] This is the first reference to an Opcom in the AAPl model; it seems a fair provision, which balances the interests of the parties.

The provision on the appointment of the new operator might prove problematic, as it requires the support of two or more parties owning the majority of the participating interests. This approach expressly favours the operator, especially where there are only two parties in the consortium. On the other hand, the operator cannot vote on the appointment, which is a positive provision for the non-operators.[799]

AAPL Form 610 thus affords non-operators a reasonable degree of control over the operatorship. For example, it recognises various circumstances that might lead to the operator's removal. Provision is also made for an *ad hoc* 'Opcom', to avoid problems in the performance of operations during insolvency or bankruptcy proceedings. The operator's removal or resignation is not subject to government

795 AAPL JOA Model Form 610 Article V (B) (1). However, the updated 2015 version of AAPL Form 610 provides far more details about the removal of the operator at Article V (B). In short, it describes:
- voluntary removal of the operator;
- effect of resignation of the operator;
- effect of bankruptcy of the operator;
- removal of the operator;
- position of a non-owning operator;
- selection of successor operator; and
- effect of removal of operator.

796 AAPL JOA Model Form 610 Article V (B) (1).
797 AAPL JOA Model Form 610 Article V (B) (1).
798 AAPL JOA Model Form 610 Article V (B) (3).
799 AAPL JOA Model Form 610 Article V (B) (2).

approval, but only to procedural requirements involving timely action by the parties.[800]

To conclude, both model forms provide a reasonable degree of control over the operatorship. However, they fail to provide extensive powers to remove the operator.

RMMLF model: There is no provision for the operator's removal in the RMMLF model, except through assignment.[801] In other words, if the operator does not resign or sell its participating interest, the non-operators have no alternative mechanism available through which to remove it.

If the operator resigns or sells its participating interest, the non-operators must appoint a successor by simple majority vote. The outgoing operator will remain as the interim operator until a new operator has been appointed. However, the outgoing operator will not be required to serve as the interim operator for more than 60 days. In case of sale, if the non-operators cannot appoint a successor operator, the assignee shall become the operator. However, if no party is willing to assume the role of the operator, the consortium will terminate.[802]

The RMMLF model thus provides no mechanism through which non-operators can control the operatorship of the consortium. The operator has *de facto* control over the entire operations, as the operatorship can be modified only at its own discretion. This lack of remedies could be a major concern for non-operators in securing a high level of performance of operations.

CAPL OP model: The Canadian OP Model Form contains two provisions on the operator's removal, depending on the urgency of the situation.[803]

The first provision relates to the operator's financial strength. This is crucial to protect the consortium as a whole, as if the operator's financial strength deteriorates to the extent that it cannot perform the operations, this could jeopardise the entire enterprise. Several actions that might affect the operator's financial strength thus constitute grounds for its removal, as follows:

- the operator becomes bankrupt or insolvent;
- security is enforced against the operator's participating interest;
- the operator suffers dissolution, liquidation or winding-up;
- a court order is issued against the operator's participating interest;
- the operator is in default under the petroleum regulations; or
- the operator attempts to assign its powers under the petroleum title.[804]

The non-operators must issue the operator with notice stipulating the reason for removal. If the operator is removed, the party with the largest participating interest will act as an interim operator until a successor is appointed.[805]

---

800 AAPL JOA Model Form 610 Article V (B) (1).
801 RMMLF JOA § 4.2.
802 RMMLF JOA § 4.3.
803 CAPL OP § 2.02.
804 CAPL OP § 2.02 (A).
805 CAPL OP § 2.02 (A).

The second provision deals with issues that could affect performance of the operations, and provides as follows:

- the operator will be removed if two or more parties holding at least 60% of the participating interests so decide; however, there is no mention of whether the operator can vote on this decision;
- the operator shall be removed if it breaches its duties with regard to performance of its obligations under the petroleum title, but only if it does not remedy this breach within 30 days of receiving notice from the non-operators. In this case, the operator can be replaced by an interim operator in order to protect life, property and the environment;[806]

These rules are fairly standard in the petroleum industry. However, the CAPL form also provides a unique mechanism to remove the operator, called a 'challenge of the operator'.[807] For this mechanism to be exercised, the operator must have been performing the operations for at least two years continuously.[808] If this condition is satisfied, any non-operator can challenge the operator by issuing a notice stating that it could conduct the operations itself on more favourable terms, and stipulating what those terms and conditions would be. The notice must include sufficient detail to enable the other parties to evaluate the non-operator's proposal. The operator must state whether it can match those terms within 60 days of notice being issued. If it can, the agreement will apply *mutatis mutandis*; but if it cannot, the operator must resign within 45 days and the non-operator that issued the challenge will replace it.[809] Two years after the new operator has assumed the operations, the mechanism will once again become available.[810] Throughout this two-year period, any costs in excess of its proposal will be at the new operator's sole risk, and it cannot resign from the position.[811] No party can issue a challenge notice if it is in default or if it could be immediately removed.[812]

The challenge procedure is thus a valuable mechanism for all parties to the JOA. For the consortium, it optimises the efficiency and effectiveness of the joint operations. It is also well balanced, as the operator cannot be removed without good reason and the challenging non-operator must be able to make good on the terms of its proposal. As government approval to replace the operator is not required under the Canadian model, there is greater scope for creative solutions to remove the operator where appropriate. The challenge mechanism will be of great interest to the host government, since its take is dependent on the operator's performance (ie, the more oil or gas that is recovered, the higher its revenues will be); any challenge will thus likely receive the support of the host government. While the precise extent of any improved efficiencies may be open to debate, the challenge mechanism ultimately affords a higher degree of protection for all parties involved, as the more efficient the operations, the higher the return will be for everyone.

---

806 CAPL OP § 2.02 (B).
807 CAPL OP § 2.03.
808 CAPL OP § 2.03 (A).
809 CAPL OP § 2.03 (A).
810 CAPL OP § 2.05.
811 CAPL OP § 2.03 (B).
812 CAPL OP § 2.03 (C).

The election of the new operator is highly regulated, as follows.

- The parties must appoint a new operator as soon as practicable.[813]
- The outgoing operator or a defaulting party cannot be appointed as the new operator.[814]
- The new operator's appointment must be approved by at least two parties and by an aggregate participating interest of more than 50%.[815]
- No party can become the operator against its will.
- The party with the largest participating interest (excluding the outgoing operator) will act as an interim operator until the new operator has been appointed.[816]
- The effective date of the operator's removal will vary, depending on the nature of the removal.[817]

The outgoing operator cannot claim recourse against the other parties.[818] However, it is unclear whether it can claim expenses incurred prior to its resignation or removal. The Canadian model also regulates the transfer of property to the new operator,[819] auditing of the accounts[820] and assignment of the operatorship.[821]

The Canadian model is thus by far the most favourable JOA for non-operators in this regard. It not only provides extensive scope for the operator's removal, but also provides for optimum efficiency in the operations. While JOAs commonly provide for the operator's removal in case of breach or failure to perform the minimum work obligations, they rarely allow for its removal for ineffectiveness – so long as the operator is in compliance with the regulations, its position is safe, regardless of whether its performance is below par. The challenge mechanism under the Canadian model is thus highly advantageous.[822]

OGUK model: The British JOA model provides for the operator's removal either with at least 60 days' notice or removal at the end of the month, depending on the urgency of the situation.[823]

The first category covers situations where there is a material breach by the operator that is not resolved within 28 days or where the operator's participating interest drops below a certain percentage. Surprisingly, the British model considers these situations as non-urgent – but this is not in fact the case. A material breach in

---

813 CAPL OP § 2.06 (A).
814 CAPL OP § 2.06 (B).
815 CAPL OP § 2.06 (C).
816 CAPL OP § 2.06 (D).
817 CAPL OP § 2.06 (E).
818 CAPL OP § 2.06 (F).
819 CAPL OP § 2.07.
820 CAPL OP § 2.08.
821 CAPL OP § 2.09.
822 Al Hudec and Joni Paulus recognise the favourable conditions for an active non-operator under the CAPL OP Model form as follows: "Lastly, passive investors in oil and gas properties should be aware that, despite the many improvements to the 1990 CAPL Operating Procedure, the agreement is intended to govern the relationship between active participants in oil and gas operations and accordingly, may not be suitable, without amendment, to govern the relationship between an operator and a passive investor." Al Hudec, Joni Paulus (note 51) p194.
823 OGUK JOA § 5.3.

this case means a breach related to the operator's obligations in conducting operations, and not to its role as a party with a participating interest.

The second category covers insolvency issues in depth, as well as circumstances in which the operator loses its entire participating interest, the host government withdraws its approval of the operator, or the operator commits an act of wilful misconduct or materially fails to carry out decommissioning obligations under a decommissioning security agreement.

Both provisions are operator-friendly, as the non-operators cannot remove the operator without a specific reason. The operator cannot be removed if its performance is below par, so that efficiency can be improved.[824]

The appointment of a new operator is well regulated, as follows.

- The appointment should occur as soon as practicable.
- The Opcom must select the new operator.
- The new operator must accept the appointment.
- The host government must approve the appointment.

If the appointment fails for any reason, "the non-operator having the largest Percentage Interest and willing to assume the position of operator" (as an option) will be appointed as the operator, provided that the host government agrees. If more than one party has the same participating interest, "the non-operator having held such Percentage Interest for the longest time shall be appointed and assume the position of operator, subject to any necessary approval of the Secretary."

If none of the parties is willing to accept the appointment, they "shall be deemed to have decided to abandon the Joint Operations and to surrender the Licence in so far as it relates to the Licence Area". While the non-operators are not compelled to accept the role of operator, they are given the right to undertake the operations until a new operator has been appointed (so long as the host government agrees).

The operator is further excluded from participating in the decision on its removal and the appointment of a new operator, except where its removal is due to the dilution of its participating interest.[825] The same problem as arose in the *Fasken* case[826] is thus unlikely to occur under the British model, as the operator cannot block decisions or even remain in the transitional role of operator until its successor has been appointed. The handover to its successor is also well regulated.[827]

The British model thus affords a high degree of control to non-operators in relation to the operator's removal. However, removal of the operator is possible only for specific reasons as defined in the agreement, which reduces the non-operators' discretion in this regard.

Norwegian model: The Norwegian model provides two different procedures for the operator's removal,[828] depending on the urgency of the situation.

---

824 OGUK JOA § 5.4.
825 OGUK JOA § 5.8.
826 *Fasken Land and Minerals, Ltd v Occidental Permian Ltd* 225 SW 3d 577 (Tex App El paso 2005).
827 OGUK JOA § 5.7.
828 Norwegian JOA § 4.2.

Under the first procedure, which applies to non-urgent situations, the Opcom must issue notice at least six months in advance to the operator, outlining the reasons for its removal. While the operator can express its views on this notice, it cannot participate in the decision-making process. However, the decision to remove the operator requires the unanimous consent of all non-operators.[829]

In the second procedure, subject to the host government's approval, the Opcom may remove the operator immediately in the following circumstances:

(a) The operator's management or supervisory personnel have caused an economic loss to the Parties as the result of willful misconduct or gross negligence;

(b) The operator or any of his Affiliated companies is declared bankrupt, applies for a composition with its creditors or becomes insolvent;

(c) Any of the operator's Affiliated companies, as referred to in sub-section 14 litra a) of the definitions herein, is dissolved;

(d) The operator transfers his Participating interest or a substantial part thereof, to another entity.[830]

The Opcom must appoint a new operator, subject to the host government's approval, within 60 days. If it fails to do so, or if the host government rejects the appointment, the host government will appoint the new operator.[831]

There is no provision on the interim period between the operator's removal and the appointment of a new operator. However, the model does require that the outgoing operator and new operator cooperate "with regard to the transfer of the operatorship". Essentially, the outgoing operator will conduct the operations until its successor has been effectively appointed.[832]

The Norwegian model thus affords non-operators a high degree of control over the operatorship, as they can remove the operator for no reason or for specific reasons defined in the agreement. The operator cannot participate in the decision on its removal. However, this model does not clearly exclude the operator from participating in the decision on the appointment of its successor, although it is required to hand over certain information and documentation to the new operator.[833] The outgoing operator is also liable for the costs of removing it from its position.[834]

AMPLA model:[835] The Australian model provides limited grounds for the operator's removal.[836] The first is where the operator's participating interest is no longer the highest in the JV; in such case its removal is subject to the Opcom's determination[837] The second is where the operator "suffers Insolvency or commits a material breach or default in the performance of a material obligation under this agreement".[838]

---

829 Norwegian JOA § 4.2.
830 Norwegian JOA § 4.2.
831 Norwegian JOA § 4.4.
832 Norwegian JOA § 4.3.
833 Norwegian JOA § 4.3.
834 Norwegian JOA § 4.3.
835 AMPLA JOA §§ 6.2 and 6.4 – There is no substantial change in the new model form. The only diferences refers to style and wording of the provision.
836 AMPLA JV § 6.2.
837 AMPLA JV § 6.2 (c).
838 AMPLA JV § 6.2 (d).

However, in such case the operator can be removed only if it fails to remedy the default within 60 days. This provision does not refer to a material breach or to an insolvency situation. As a consequence, non-operators could argue that there are automatic grounds for removal in the event of insolvency or material breach, as the operator is given no opportunity to remedy these situations and there is no reference to the determination of the Opcom.

The election of a successor is reasonably well regulated.[839]

- The parties must "promptly" appoint a new operator.[840]
- The outgoing operator cannot be reappointed in case of default[841] or insolvency.[842] As a consequence, the model indirectly allows for its reappointment in the case of material breach or dilution of its participating interest.
- The party with the largest participating interest shall serve as interim operator until the appointment of a new operator.[843] The outgoing operator is not expressly restricted from serving as interim operator. However, the model does state that it "must immediately deliver to the new or interim Manager all Joint Venture Property and all documents", which would indicate that the interim operator will be a third party.[844]

The Australian model thus does not provide extensive grounds for the operator's removal. It also fails to prohibit the operator from being reappointed as the operator in case of material breach or dilution of its participating interest. However, the model does indicate that any material breach could automatically constitute grounds for the operator's removal, which is a powerful incentive to ensure that the operator performs to a high standard.

AIPN model:[845] Once again, the AIPN model contains both compulsory and optional provisions in relation to the operator's removal.[846]

The compulsory provisions apply in two sets of circumstances.[847] The first concerns insolvency and bankruptcy situations, in order to ensure that performance of the operations can continue.[848] The second relates to material breach, but it is far more complex.[849] Only non-operators representing a certain percentage of the participating interest and/or a certain number of the parties can issue a notice

839 AMPLA JV § 6.4.
840 AMPLA JV § 6.4 (a).
841 The defaulting party cannot vote in the Opcom (Section 5.8 of the AMPLA JV).
842 AMPLA JV § 6.4 (a).
843 AMPLA JV § 6.4 (b).
844 AMPLA JV § 6.4 (c).
845 AIPN JOA model form 2012 § 4.10 – This provision underwent some relevant modifications. First, it now expressly excludes any affiliated company of the operator from participating in any decision on its removal. Second, it increases the options to remove the operator by the determination of either a combined interest of the non-operators or all of the parties. The most significant change concerns an option to remove the operator if it fails to comply with anti-bribery requirements.
846 AIPN JOA § 4.10.
847 AIPN JOA § 4.10 (A) and (B).
848 AIPN JOA § 4.10 (A).
849 AIPN JOA § 4.10 (B).

requesting the remedy of a material breach. The operator then has 30 days to remedy the breach accordingly. If the operator disagrees with the content of this notice, it will remain in its position until the dispute has been resolved through final proceedings. There are thus limitations on the non-operators' power to remove the operator due to material breach, mostly due to the dispute resolution process, which favours the operator.

There are also three optional provisions on the operator's removal.[850] The first and second of these allow for the operator's removal if its participating interest drops to below a certain percentage,[851] or if it undergoes a change in control.[852] However, these provisions are not automatic: the Opcom must rather decide whether a new operator should be appointed (the operator is not excluded from this decision). The third allows the non-operators to remove the operator without any reason where a defined pass mark is reached.[853] This provision affords valuable discretion to the non-operators, as any circumstances could prompt them to seek the operator's removal. This will encourage the operator to take care to optimise its performance of the joint operations.

The appointment of the new operator is well regulated.[854]

- The Opcom "shall meet as soon as possible to appoint a successor operator".[855]
- No party can be compelled to accept appointment as the new operator.[856]
- The outgoing operator is ineligible for appointment, except in the optional cases outlined above.[857]
- The outgoing operator will be compensated (if applicable) for its reasonable expenses, except in the case of material breach.[858]
- The outgoing operator and its successor must coordinate the handover between them.[859]
- The removal of the operator and the appointment of its successor are subject to the host government's approval.[860]
- The outgoing operator remains liable until the effective date of its removal.[861]

The AIPN model thus affords a high degree of control to non-operators, as they have several options to remove the operator, including without any reason. However, such control is secured only if the third optional provision is selected; the first and second options are ineffective because the operator is not excluded from participating in the Opcom's decision on its removal. Additionally, no provision is

850 AIPN JOA § 4.10 (C), (D) and (E).
851 AIPN JOA § 4.10 (C).
852 AIPN JOA § 4.10 (D).
853 AIPN JOA § 4.10 (E).
854 AIPN JOA § 4.11.
855 AIPN JOA § 4.11 (A).
856 AIPN JOA § 4.11 (A).
857 AIPN JOA § 4.11 (B).
858 AIPN JOA § 4.11 (C).
859 AIPN JOA § 4.11 (D).
860 AIPN JOA § 4.11 (E).
861 AIPN JOA § 4.11 (F).

made for an interim operator, so there might be a gap between removal of the operator and the host government's approval.

Greenlandic model: The relevant provision of the Greenlandic model begins by making reference to the host government's approval.[862] As the NOC is a member of the JOA under this model, it is natural to expect greater concern regarding government approval.

Non-operators can seek to remove the operator on the following grounds:

(a) The operator may be removed for cause at the end of any Month by the Operating Committee giving not less than ninety (90) days' notice to it stating such cause.

(b) In addition, the operator may be removed by notice given by the Operating Committee which notice shall have immediate effect if the operator materially defaults in the performance of its obligation under this Agreement and, where such default is capable of remedy, fails to remedy or commence actions which lead to such remedy within a reasonable period specified by the Operating Committee.

(c) Furthermore the operator may be removed immediately if the circumstances described in Section 24.01 d of the Licence apply to the operator or if circumstances occur which may in the reasonable opinion of the Operating Committee materially adversely affect the ability of the operator to continue to carry out its obligations hereunder.[863]

While the first ground is fairly broad, it also gives the operator a long time to prepare for and address the situation. The second ground is fairly common, and in case of default the operator might even have to forfeit its place on the consortium. The third is probably the best alternative for non-operators, as it allows for the operator's immediate removal for broad reasons. Insolvency might fall under this provision, as it may affect the operator's ability to perform the obligations under the petroleum title.

The operator is expressly entitled to voice its views on the notice seeking its removal. While it might be difficult to enforce this 'right' in case of the operator's immediate removal, it seems possible under the first option outlined above. Moreover, it would only seem fair and balanced to afford the operator this right.[864]

Once again, the operator cannot vote on the decision concerning its removal. The decision must be approved by non-operators representing a certain percentage of the participating interest.[865]

In the case of immediate removal, the non-operator with the largest participating interest will act as the interim operator, unless the Opcom decides otherwise. In theory, this approach secures the non-operators' interest; however, if the outgoing operator has control over the Opcom, this could prove problematic.[866]

The appointment of the new operator is clearly regulated.[867]

---

862 Greenlandic JOA § 3.17.2.
863 Greenlandic JOA § 3.17.2.
864 Greenlandic JOA § 3.17.2.
865 Greenlandic JOA § 3.17.2.
866 Greenlandic JOA § 3.17.2.
867 Greenlandic JOA § 3.17.3.

- The parties must elect the new operator as soon as practicable.
- One of the non-operators will be appointed as the new operator.
- The appointment is subject to the nominee's acceptance and the host government's approval.
- The outgoing operator cannot vote on the appointment; otherwise, this will be invalid.
- The parties will specify the level of support required from the non-operators to appoint a new operator.

The handover from the outgoing operator to the new operator in terms of rights, responsibilities, materials and documents is also highly regulated.[868] However, the outgoing operator will remain liable for all the actions it performed as the operator of the consortium.[869]

The Greenlandic JOA model thus clearly reflects the government's desire to control the operatorship of the consortium. It also affords a high degree of control to non-operators, to help secure high performance standards from the operator. However, there is no clear indication that material breach constitutes grounds for the operator's removal. The non-operators might argue that this falls under the generic alternatives (a) or (c) outlined above, or that alternative (b) applies as a default.

Conclusion: Each JOA adopts a different approach to the operator's removal.[870] The similarities and differences between them are summarised in the table below. Some provide few or no grounds for removal, such as the RMMLF model; others provide extensive grounds for removal, such as the AIPN and OGUK models. The Canadian model is unique, as it allows for periodic review of the operator's performance. As any non-operator can challenge the operator should its performance fall short, the operator will have a strong incentive to maintain high standards or risk being replaced by a non-operator.

Most of the JOAs provide for the operator's removal in case of material breach of the agreement or of the petroleum regulations. This approach is reasonable, as it is necessary to ensure compliance with contractual obligations and applicable regulations. However, the situation becomes more problematic in case of recurring breaches. If the operator remedies a material breach within a certain period, it will escape any penalty. The operator can thus breach the JOA as many times as it likes and still remain in its position, so long as it remedies the breach within the applicable timeframe. All JOAs fail to deal with this situation, as there is no means to restrict or control material breaches if they are timely remedied.

Another important issue is the right of the operator to participate in the decision

868 Greenlandic JOA § 3.17.4.

869 Greenlandic JOA § 3.17.4 (b).

870 A Martin describes the different approaches regarding causes for the removal of the operator, as follows: "Given the above, one would assume that domestic model JOAs would always handle the same issues in a similar manner in contrast to how an international JOA deals with the situation. However, that is not always the case. As an example, both the CAPL model JOA and the AIPN model JOA provide for the option of the removal of an operator without cause on the affirmative vote of a number of participants holding at least a certain percentage participating interest. In contrast, the AAPL 610 only permits the removal of an operator for a good cause." A Timothy Martin (n 1) p293.

JOA/provision	AAPL	RMMLF	CAPL	OGUK	NoR	AMPLA	AIPN	Greenland
Insolvency	Yes	No	Yes	Yes	Yes	Yes	Yes	No
Material breach	Yes	No	Yes	Yes	Yes	Yes	Yes	Yes
Reduction of participating interest	Yes	No	Yes	Yes	Yes	Yes	Optional	No
Unmotivated	No	No	Yes	No	Yes	No	Optional	Yes
Voting only by non-operators	Partial	No	Yes	Yes	Partial	Partial	Yes	Yes
Interim operator	Partial	Yes	Yes	Yes	No	Partial	No	Yes
Reference to host government	Partial	No	No	Yes	Yes	No	Yes	Yes

on its removal. While the JOAs vary on this issue, they commonly exclude the operator from participating in such decisions. The operator could seek to argue that this approach is not balanced or fair. However, most such decisions require the unanimous approval of all non-operators, rather than a simple pass mark, and any change to the operatorship will further require government approval. The operator's position is thus reasonably secure, as the host government will not authorise any change to the operatorship that could harm the good standing of the petroleum title or the fulfilment of all activities and obligations. Additionally, a defaulting party normally has no right to vote or even to attend meetings, so it is thus logical to exclude a defaulting operator from the decision on its removal.

The operator might object to procedures that allow for its immediate removal, arguing that it would be arbitrary to impose such a drastic remedy without giving it any opportunity to defend its position. However, some issues require no further diligence (eg, letters from the host government outlining the failure of performance) – especially emergency issues that are improperly dealt with by the operator. However, as balanced provisions are crucial to the health of the JOA, the operator should be given time to express its views on any notice relating to its removal, insofar as this is practicable, as happens under the Norwegian and Greenlandic JOA models. The JOAs analysed in this book deal reasonably well with the transition period between the operator's removal and the appointment of its successor. However, the host government must also authorise the interim operator's activities; otherwise, such elaborate systems will be ineffective.

The provisions on the operator's removal thus constitute crucial protection for non-operators, as they encourage the operator's compliance with its contractual obligations and with the applicable petroleum regulations. However, compliance in itself is not enough: it is also essential to provide incentives to improve performance in order to optimise efficiency and maintain high standards in the joint operations. The Canadian model is the only one that gives non-operators leverage to demand improved performance. The remaining models secure only compliance with contractual obligations, except where a broad removal clause is allowed (eg, under the most recent AIPN or Greenlandic model, or the first alternative under the Norwegian model). However, a provision allowing the operator to be removed without reason is arguably somewhat imbalanced, as the operator should benefit from some certainty in performing its activities. Here again, the Canadian model represents a secure and balanced approach for all parties involved. On the one hand, non-operators can challenge the operator's performance if this is below par; on the other, the challenger will be bound by the more favourable terms it has proposed for two years, and any extra costs will be incurred at its sole risk. Thus, no party can abuse its rights without suffering severe consequences. Finally, non-operators should always take special care when drafting this provision, as the power to remove is essentially the power to influence operations.

In the vast majority of cases, however, non-operators can remove the operator on limited grounds only. The most critical problem is the failure to deal with recurring material breaches, as this leaves non-operators in a weak situation. Defining the extent of a clause to address this deficiency would be no simple task. For example, how many times would the operator be allowed to breach without penalty? Would the period between each breach (eg, two months or two years) be considered? Would the penalty vary depending on the nature of the breach? If so, how would the provision distinguish between a breach regarding the disclosure of information and a breach regarding the award of contracts, for example? While answering these provisions would doubtless be challenging, such a clause would represent valuable protection for non-operators, as the operator would take far more care to avoid breaching any provisions of the JOA. Ultimately, however, reasonable terms are required in order to prevent abuse on either side. When revising the current AIPN model, the revision committee considered whether to introduce a provision addressing repeat infractions by the operator, but this proposal was ultimately rejected.[871]

Another solution would be to introduce penalties for any breach of the agreement. This scenario is commonly adopted for service agreements, but would be far more complicated within the framework of a JOA. This is because, first, the operator assumes the role on a voluntary basis and thus receives no profit from its performance of the operations. Second, it would be difficult to attribute a value to each provision of the JOA. However, such a provision would certainly promote higher standards in the performance of the joint operations (if enforceable under the local jurisdiction).

In conclusion, the operator's removal cannot fully protect non-operators from poor performance by the operator; it is therefore necessary to strengthen the available protections in this regard. For this reason, JOAs contain two further

---

871 The proposed revisions included the following: "Consider provision for removal of operator for repeated infractions: (a) being the three of such performance failures of material or potential material impact, then if corrective measures are not properly adopted after three of such notices of failure to perform had been sent to operator under the conditions stated under this Article [ ], can ...; (b) A notice of failure to perform shall not be sent to the operator: (i) before 30 (thirty) Days after the delivery of the last notice of failure to perform; (ii) if the alleged performance failure is a mere reiteration of the same kind of performance failure already detailed in a prior notice of failure to perform; (iii) or in order to complain for lack of due implementation of corrective measures of a performance failure already detailed in a prior notice of failure to perform. [Note: consider providing for the appointment of an interim substitute operator as an alternative to this subsection (d)]."

fundamental provisions, on default and liabilities. Only the latter provision is analysed in the following section, for the reasons previously outlined.

(b) *Liability*

As discussed, non-operators have fairly limited remedies through which to secure improved performance of the joint operations. If the non-operators cannot control the joint operations, remove the operator or demand that the operator's interest be forfeited (ie, in case of default), their sole remaining option to continue in the JOA without excessive exposure is through the limitation of liability.[872]

In this regard, the distinction between the vertical and horizontal relationships in the JOA again assumes importance.[873] The former involves the host government and is thus likely to result in both joint and several liabilities for all JOA parties, as from the government's perspective, the more parties that are responsible for covering potential hazards, the stronger its protection. The latter involves the JOA parties themselves and can affect the liabilities established by the vertical relationship.

Where the JOA parties adjust their own internal liabilities, this will not affect their external liabilities to third parties. This is one of the main objectives of the JOA, as no party will wish to assume more liabilities than its position merits.[874]

Given the hazardous nature of the oil and gas industry, the parties will bargain hard on the issue of liability during the negotiations. Claude Duval recognises this situation as follows: "The question of the operator's liability is often contentious in negotiating an international JOA."[875]

With regard to internal liability, the basic rule governing the JOA is that the operator shall neither profit nor incur any additional liability from conducting the joint operations. This approach is well settled in the petroleum industry and has been observed by numerous academics and practitioners, such as Anthony Jennings,[876] Bernard Taverne,[877] Chris Thorpe,[878] Sandy Shaw,[879] Charez Golvala[880] and Hew Dundas.[881] While Claude Duval points out that the operator can recover certain costs and might even charge some sort of fee through the accounting procedure,[882] this will not affect the basic governing principle.[883]

As a consequence, the operator shall not be exclusively liable for performance of the joint operations, except under exceptional circumstances. This limitation of

872 It is not possible to cover all the issues relating to liabilities between the parties or with third parties. For further information, see Preston R Mundt (n 754) p419, Howard L Boigon, Christine L Murphy, "Liabilities of Nonoperating Mineral Interest Owners" (1979–1980) 51 *University of Colorado Law Review* p153, Michael Hardy, "Better safe than Sorry: Apologies, Liability and the Media" (2000) 19 *AMPLJ* p225.
873 See Chapter I, section 2.1(b).
874 Sandy Shaw (n 16) p16.
875 Claude Duval *et al* (n 122) p293.
876 Anthony Jennings (n 16) p24.
877 Bernard Taverne (n 90) p136.
878 Chris Thorpe (n 317) p126.
879 Sandy Shaw (n 16) p16.
880 Charez Golvala (n 6) p46.
881 Hew Dundas (n 16) p12.
882 Peter Roberts (n 5) p155.
883 Claude Duval *et al* (n 122) p294.

liability is traditionally referred as the 'exculpatory clause'[884] and provides that the operator shall be liable not as the operator of the consortium, but merely as a participant of the consortium, unless exceptional circumstances arise.[885]

The parties will provide reciprocal indemnities in order to secure the implementation of the exculpatory clause.[886] Peter Roberts recognises this as follows:

To reinforce this protection of the operator, the parties (including the party which is appointed as the operator, in its capacity as a party) will also undertake to indemnify the operator (in the proportion of their respective PIs) for any such loss or liability for which the operator might otherwise be responsible. Through this combination of disclaimed responsibility and indemnity coverage, the operator is effectively insulated from liability.[887]

However, any indemnity provided in the JOA must be "clear and unequivocal" and/or "conspicuous"; otherwise it may be struck down by courts as being ineffective.[888] JOAs do not generally address the issue of damage to the parties' own property and personnel. If the JOA is silent on this issue, such liabilities will be allocated in accordance with the applicable law. Under English law, anyone that causes damage to another person will be liable for its actions in tort or by statute.[889] If the JOA parties wish to protect themselves against the consequences of tortious liability, they can agree on a provision that is commonly adopted in service arrangements, called 'knock-for-knock' or 'mutual hold harmless'. It is beyond the scope of this book to address the complexities of such provisions, but Peter Roberts summarises as follows:

Under this model the parties each assume responsibility for any damage to or loss of their own property and personnel, even where such loss or damage is attributable to the act or omission of any other party.[890]

If such a provision is implemented, each JOA party will be responsible for damage to its own property and personnel, regardless of who may have caused the accident and the circumstances surrounding it. The rationale behind this provision is that each party is best placed to insure and secure its own property and personnel.[891]

Although exculpatory clauses are commonly accepted, the parties may disagree on the definition of the 'operator' for such purposes. The operator is likely to seek the extension of this definition to encompass affiliated companies and personnel, so

---

884 "To this end, the JOA typically provides (in what is sometimes called an 'exculpatory clause') that the operator will not be responsible for any loss or liability suffered by a party (or by a third party and claimed against the operator or any of the parties) and which results from the operator having exercised (or having failed to exercise) the obligations which it has under the JOA." Peter Roberts (n 5) p155.

885 For further information about exculpatory clauses, see Wilson Woods, "The Effect of Exculpatory Clauses in Joint Operating Agreements, What protections do operators really have in the oil patch?" (2005–2006) 38 *Texas Tech Law Review* p211, Colin Feasby, "Fiduciary Obligations and Exculpatory Clauses" (1997–1998) 36 *Alberta Law Review* p923.

886 For further information about indemnities, see Greg Gordon, "Risk Allocation" in Greg Gordon, John Paterson (eds), *Oil and Gas Law: Current Practice and Emerging Trends* (DUP, Dundee 2007) pp335–382, Ernest E Smith *et al* (n 16) pp546–579.

887 Peter Roberts (n 5) p156.

888 Ernest E Smith *et al* (n 16) p546.

889 Peter Roberts (n 5) p161.

890 Peter Roberts (n 5) p161.

891 *Ibid* p163.

that they also enjoy the limitation of liability. Conversely, non-operators will seek to ensure that this definition remains congruous with the definition in the petroleum title, in order to restrict the scope of application of the exculpatory clause.[892]

Limitation of the operator's liability will apply only to acts and operations performed under the authority expressly provided in the JOA. If the operator performs any act or operation outside this authority, it will not be covered by the exculpatory clause.[893]

The exceptions to the exculpatory clause relate to the standard of performance, as the operator must act diligently, prudently and in accordance with applicable laws, regulations and best oil and gas practice.[894] Scott Styles describes this situation as follows:

The nature of the duty is usually specified in the JOA as that of "a reasonable and prudent operator" or as the duty to perform the role of operator in "a proper and workmanlike manner" in accordance with "good and prudent oil and gas field practice". The exact nature of what counts as good and prudent oil field practice will depend upon the circumstances and will also change as technology changes.[895]

If the operator maintains a high standard of performance in conducting the joint operations, it should be held liable only to the extent of its participating interest.[896] In practice, however, even where the operator fails to maintain high standards in conducting the operations, the limitation of liability will still commonly apply,[897] except in the event of gross negligence or wilful misconduct. Claude Duval recognises this situation as follows: "A common practice in the industry is to limit the operator's liability to acts and omissions which are grossly negligent."[898]

So what are the definitions of these terms and the consequence of their implementation?[899] Claude Duval describes both terms as follows:

AIPN Model JOA defines gross negligence or wilful misconduct as conduct "in reckless disregard of or wanton indifference to, harmful consequences [that the operator] knew or should have known" the conduct would have on the safety or property of others. This gross negligence definition does not allow an operator to escape liability by proving it acted with subjective "good faith". If the operator is merely negligent, but not grossly negligent, then any liability for damages caused by the operator's conduct will be shared proportionately by all the parties rather than borne by the operator alone.[900]

A similar reference to 'wilful misconduct' is found in the 2007 UK Model JOA, but 'gross negligence' is also expressly defined to include the failure to obtain or maintain any insurance that is required by the JOA terms. This addition reflects the risks of offshore operations in the North Sea and the huge investments necessary to purchase, install and maintain the material and equipment used there. Indeed, the

892 *Ibid* p156.
893 *Ibid.*
894 Bernard Taverne (n 90) p136.
895 Scott Styles (n 14) p279.
896 Scott Styles (n 14) p279.
897 "The joint operating agreement will set the standard to which the operator should reference to what other operators would do in similar circumstances." Charez Golvala (n 6) p45.
898 Claude Duval *et al* (n 122) p293.
899 For further information see Taylor and Tyne (n 54) pp6–7.
900 Claude Duval *et al* (n 122) p294.

issue of the operator's liability is especially important in international petroleum operations because they are frequently conducted in hostile physical and geopolitical environments where problems are likely to arise. Some qualified companies will not accept the responsibility of being operator if they are exposed to any claims, including those resulting from their own gross negligence, other than their proportionate share in the JOA.

However, this exception does not include consequential losses or environmental liabilities, as these could considerably increase the operator's liability to a level which would be difficult to pre-define or justify under the 'no gain, no loss' principle.[901] Greg Gordon describes this as follows:

> *In addition to containing the indemnity provisions described above, a wide variety of oil and gas contracts will also include clauses which exclude, limit or put in place an indemnity regime in respect of liability for so-called "consequential or indirect" losses. Such provisions are commonplace in operator-to-contractor contracts and are seen in some (but by no means all) oil company-to-oil company contracts. Where such clauses are used, their purpose is to protect the parties from the full consequences of causing certain types of loss, typically delays in or loss of production, loss of use, loss of profits, and business interruption. The quantum of such losses is generally difficult to anticipate in advance, and may be hard to quantify even retrospectively. However, they have the potential to rise to exorbitant levels. As such, they are frequently either expensive or impossible to insure against, and the industry has by and large accepted that such losses should generally lie where they fall. Thus we can see that economic factors very similar to those that drive the indemnity regime underpin the exclusion of consequential loss.*[902]

JOAs commonly exclude consequential loss even where gross negligence or wilful misconduct is clearly established, in order to afford greater comfort to the operator. However, it is advisable to define[903] precisely what constitutes 'consequential loss' – just as the terms 'wilful misconduct' or 'gross negligence' should be defined – because the meaning of this term has been disputed under English law since *Hadley v Baxendale* (1854) 9 Exch 341.[904] The exclusion of consequential losses also might not be recognised in certain jurisdictions (in particular, civil law jurisdictions).[905]

It is possible to suggest that the terms 'gross negligence' and 'wilful misconduct' refer to serious mistakes by the operator, as any ordinary activities will not bring this provision into play.[906] In other words, except for consequential and environmental losses, non-operators will bear no liability for damage incurred through gross

---

901 Taylor and Tyne (n 54) pp6–7.

902 Greg Gordon (n 886) pp377–378.

903 There is debate as to whether this term is best defined by an exhaustive list or a general definition. See Greg Gordon (n 886) pp380–381.

904 Peter Roberts (n 5) p158.

905 "The issue of indemnification agreement, is, however, not one that solely arises in the United States. Whether or not indemnity agreements are enforceable in civil law jurisdictions has to be determined on a country-by-country basis. Thus, if the choice of law provision in a JOA selects a civil law jurisdiction, care will have to be taken to determine if an indemnity agreement is enforceable and if so what are the conditions precedents to creating such an enforceable agreement." Ernest E Smith *et al* (n 16) p546.

906 Taylor and Tyne (n 54) pp6–7.

negligence or wilful misconduct.[907] All other liabilities will be shared between the JOA parties in proportion to their participating interest.[908]

Hew Dundas disputes the accuracy of the term 'gross negligence':

'Gross negligence' includes the "failure to take even the slightest care" and this term was used in the UK before the BNOC pro forma was introduced. But negligence is an "on-off" switch which cannot be categorised into degrees as any adjective placed before the words makes no difference to liability.[909]

Taylor and Tyne explain the solution that some JOAs have adopted to resolve issues arising as a result of negligence:

Finally it is frequently, though not invariably, provided that "For any avoidance of doubt, the operator shall not be liable for any loss or damage resulting from the negligence of the operator, its servants, agents or employees". This specific reference to negligence is probably included because general words in an exemption clause may not be effective to exclude the liability of the party for its own negligence or that of its employees (L & N W Ry v Neilson [1992] 2 AC 363).[910]

English law does not recognise these terms, although *Porter v Magill* [2002] 2 AC 357 might give some comfort with regard to the use of the term 'wilful misconduct'.[911] Nevertheless, it is important to define carefully the precise extent of these terms; otherwise, the parties will encounter difficulties when attempting to enforce them.[912] The definitions of 'gross negligence' and 'wilful misconduct' further involve a certain degree of participation by management. Taylor and Tyne describe this as follows:

It can be contrasted with the Model Form International Operating Agreement, which suggests that liability may attach to the operator in cases of gross negligence on the part of its senior personnel but offers the draftsman various alternative quantitative limitations on such liability.[913]

The JOA parties can thus adopt either a rigid or flexible approach, depending on how these terms are defined and the level of managerial involvement that is required. Peter Roberts describes this as follows:

The existence of the operator's liability for wilful misconduct (or gross negligence) is also often weakened in the JOA by further provision that such liability will arise only where the act, or the failure to act, which is complained of was committed by a member of a defined class of persons, often referred to as 'senior supervisory personnel', in order that the operator will be so liable. This is another term which must be defined specially in the JOA and this is another area where there is some room for manoeuvring, subject to the overriding principle that the operator will wish to narrow the scope of vicarious liability for the acts of its personnel for which it might otherwise be responsible.[914]

The main objective of this requirement for senior managerial involvement is to

---

907 Sandy Shaw (n 16) p17.
908 Chris Thorpe (n 317) pp126–127.
909 Hew Dundas (n 16) p12.
910 Taylor and Tyne (n 54) pp6–7.
911 "Deliberately doing something which is wrong knowing it to be wrong or with reckless indifference as to whether it is wrong or not." Peter Roberts (n 5) pp156–157.
912 Charez Golvala (n 6) p46, Scott Styles (n 14) pp279–280.
913 Taylor and Tyne (n 54) pp6–7.
914 Peter Roberts (n 5) p158.

erect another hurdle that must be overcome before the operator will be considered liable. Peter Roberts continues:

The point to be drawn from all of this is that if the JOA provides that an act of wilful misconduct (or gross negligence) can be committed only by a person who falls within the definition of 'senior supervisory personnel' group in order to expose the operator to liability, and if the test for what constitutes a member of that group is set so high as to capture only persons who are in practical terms unconnected with the operation of the JOA, then the prospects for the commission of an act of wilful misconduct (or gross negligence) by the operator, and so for the operator to be made liable, will be greatly reduced.[915]

Some JOAs go even further and provide an extra layer of protection for the operator in the form of a cap on its liability to the other parties.[916] While this protection is already less common, it might become even more difficult to implement following the Deepwater Horizon accident in the Gulf of Mexico.[917] However, it might represent a viable solution if the parties cannot agree on implementation of the relevant indemnities.[918] Even if such a cap is implemented, it will not affect third parties and will apply only as between the JOA parties.

The JOA can further restrict what constitutes wilful misconduct or gross negligence, as it may require direct loss rather than merely a technical breach.[919] This provision might assist the operator in the event of minor breaches, but is unlikely to assist it in the event of a serious failure of performance.

The JOA parties must determine the consequences once gross negligence or wilful misconduct has been established. Several alternatives are available, which Claude Duval outlines as follows:

The parties to a JOA can choose to make the operator bear all damages caused by its negligence; bear only the actual cost of repairing or replacing joint property so damaged; or bear only a defined dollar amount of such damages and liabilities. If the first alternative is not selected, all parties will share proportionately in any liability in excess of the amounts in the last two alternatives. Under the 2002 AIPN JOA, the operator is never forced to bear more than its proportionate share of consequential losses or environmental losses.[920]

For non-operators, the first option is by far the most attractive, as there is no limitation involved. The operator will prefer any other option, as it will argue that its operatorship is 'voluntary' and thus no further liability should be involved. The parties will thus likely dispute the outcome of this provision. If the operatorship is shared or delegated to a third party, it will be much easier to control liabilities fully. Several JOAs also extend the operator's liability for issues arising from the obligation

915 *Ibid.*
916 *Ibid.*
917 For further information see H Douglas, "Gulf of Mexico Oil Spill: Likely Impact on UK Regulation and Contractual Arrangements" (2010) 8(3) *OGEL*, Jolanta Olszewska, "Operators' Offshore Responsibilities and Liabilities Increased in Australia" (2002) 21 *AMPLJ* p104, Stephen Tromans, "Deepwater Horizon and its legal ramifications" (2010) *IELR* p163, NJJ Gaskell, "The Amoco Cadiz: (I) Liability Issues" (1985) 3 *J Energy & Nat Resources L* p169.
918 Greg Gordon (n 886) p382.
919 Peter Roberts (n 5) p158.
920 Claude Duval *et al* (n 122) p294.

to obtain or maintain insurance in relation to the joint operations.[921] The JOAs commonly take a different approach to breach of this obligation.[922]

One controversial question that applies to any contractual breach by the operator is whether the limitation of liability is excluded. Claude Duval answers this question as follows:

Perhaps surprisingly it is still not clear in many JOAs whether the limits on the operator's liability to the non-operating participants (rather than to third parties) extend to its actions which are in breach of the JOA. Some operators have argued that they may not be held liable to the non-operators for breaching the JOA's provisions unless they are grossly negligent. The United States courts have ruled inconsistently on this issue when interpreting domestic JOAs.[923]

The JOA parties (in particular, the non-operators) should thus seek to extend (rather than restrict) the application of the liability section of the JOA, in order to address any contractual breach; otherwise, they will have limited grounds for remedies. Ernest Smith refers to a US case (*Stine v Marathon Oil Co* 976 F 2d 254 (5th Cir 1992)) in which Judge E Grady Jolly highlighted this danger for non-operators as follows:

It is clear to us that the protection of the exculpatory clause extends not only to "acts unique to the operator," as the district court expressed it, but also to any acts done under the authority of the JOA "as operator." This protection clearly extends to breaches of the JOA. It also reaches other acts including acts performed "as operator" under the authority of the JOA that amount to tortious interference with contracts with third parties. We, therefore, hold that the exculpatory clause protects Marathon from liability for any act taken in its capacity "as operator" under the JOA (except for gross negligence or wilful misconduct).[924]

As previously mentioned, third-party liabilities are far more complex. Generally, the provisions of the JOA will not affect them, as the petroleum title will provide for joint and several liability. If the petroleum title does not address this issue, then liability will vary depending on whether the operator is acting in its own name as an 'independent contractor' or on behalf of the consortium – in other words, whether the operator is an agent.

In this regard, it is important to remember that agency status can arise explicitly or implicitly. It is thus difficult to avoid the implications for non-operators, unless the third party has clearly consented to their exclusion.[925] However, the operator is commonly responsible for handling any litigation that arises in connection with the performance of the operations of the consortium.[926]

JOAs that provide for the participation of a NOC are also likely to limit this party's liability. Anthony Jennings describes this situation as follows:

Note that in some jurisdictions and often under a PSA regime the operator may be a

921 For further information see Scott Styles (n 14) pp279–281, Peter Roberts (n 5) pp159–160.
922 Taylor and Tyne (n 54) pp6–7.
923 Claude Duval *et al* (n 122) p294.
924 Ernest E Smith *et al* (n 16) p572.
925 Scott Styles (n 14) pp281–283.
926 Peter Roberts (n 5) p165.

company jointly incorporated by the participants and owned by them in equal shares, in which event it may well have no liability at all. We mentioned joint insurance and there will also be an obligation on the operator to obtain and maintain this and also a clause covering the operator's responsibilities in respect of litigation on behalf of or against the joint venture.[927]

Indeed, government authorities will endeavour to protect their position against liability even where an NOC is not participating in the JOA. Peter Roberts recognises this situation as follows:

The terms of the concession might also obligate the parties (in their capacity as the concession holders) to indemnify the government against any claims made by third parties against the government as the grantor of the concession, and the parties will then reallocate the indemnity liability between themselves in accordance with the terms of the JOA.[928]

Non-operators must thus exercise extreme care before 'checking the boxes' of the exculpatory clause; otherwise, they will assume far more liability than desired.

There follows an analysis of how each JOA deals with the exculpatory clause, in order to determine whether this final source of protection (from the non-operators' perspective) against failure of performance by the operator is in fact effective.

AAPL models: AAPL Form 810 demands a high standard of performance of the operator, as it provides that the operator must "timely commence and conduct all activities or operations in a good and workmanlike manner, as would a prudent operator under the same or similar circumstances".[929]

It also contains an exculpatory clause, which provides that the operator will bear no personal or exclusive liability for the joint operations, except in case of gross negligence or wilful misconduct.[930] This benefit applies only to the operator itself, as the definition of 'operator' is not extended to affiliated companies, contractors or similar. However, this model does not define 'gross negligence' or 'wilful misconduct' (the most reasonable explanation for this is that both the US courts[931] and the legislature[932] are familiar with these terms).

Consequential or indirect losses are fully excluded, without exception. As a consequence, no party will bear liability for consequential or indirect losses, even where gross negligence or wilful misconduct is fully recognised.[933] Finally, the operator must defend and protect the consortium from all claims, but must obtain the non-operators' consent if a determined amount is exceeded.[934]

Under AAPL Form 810, the operator is thus reasonably protected against most liabilities arising from performance of the joint operations. In the worst case

927 Anthony Jennings (n 16) p24.
928 Peter Roberts (n 5) p165.
929 AAPL JOA Model Form 810 § 5.2.
930 AAPL JOA Model Form 810 § 5.2.
931 For example, *Wilson v Brett* (1843) 152 Eng Rep 737 (Exch) 740; 11 M & W 113, 115–16, *Batt v State*, 901 P 2d 664 (Nev 1995), *Tracy v Wood*, 24 F Cas 117 (Story, Circuit Justice, CCDRI 1822) and *Monasmith v Cosden Oil Co*, 246 NW 623, 624 (Neb 1933).
932 Eg, Oil Pollution Act of 1990, 33 USC §§ 2701–2762 (2006) and Clean Water Act, 33 USC §§ 1251–1387 (2006 & supp 2009).
933 AAPL JOA Model Form 810 § 22.5.
934 AAPL JOA Model Form 810 § 22.5.

scenario, however, the non-operators are not, as there is no liability cap or limitation relating to managerial involvement. It is also unclear whether the operator will be liable for any contractual breaches. This model form thus affords the operator a great deal of security with regard to performance, but holds it solely liable in the event of gross negligence or wilful misconduct.

AAPL Form 610 adopts almost the same approach as Form 810.[935] The operator must conduct the operations:

- in a good and workmanlike manner;
- with due diligence;
- based on good oilfield practice; and
- in compliance with applicable law.[936]

The operator will bear no personal liability for performance of the joint operations, except in case of gross negligence or wilful misconduct (though there is controversy about whether this clause refers to physical operations or any breach of contract).[937] As a consequence, each party shall be liable in proportion to its participating interest, unless the operator is guilty of gross negligence or wilful misconduct. Once again, there is no definition of 'gross negligence' or 'wilful misconduct',[938] no reference to managerial involvement and no liability cap. Moreover, there is no direct reference to third-party liabilities, although the model does indicate that each party shall be liable in proportion to its participating interest. There is also no clear indication of whether the liabilities clause applies to any breach of the petroleum title or the JOA. The benefits of the exculpatory clause are further limited to the operator and do not extend to affiliated companies, contractors or similar. Finally, the operator will be responsible for handling any claim against the consortium until a certain amount is reached.[939]

The main difference between these models concerns consequential losses. Under Form 810, the operator is completely excluded from liability for consequential losses, regardless of the consequences. In contrast, Form 610 does not exclude liability for consequential losses in the event of gross negligence or wilful misconduct.[940] This is a clear example of the difference in the risks involved in offshore and onshore operations. It is thus evident that both US models afford reasonable protection to the operator. The historical onshore model (Form 610) provides more favourable conditions for non-operators, as consequential losses are not excluded.[941] If the parties involved in the Deepwater Horizon accident had used this agreement, then BP would most likely have been held solely liable for all damages relating to the accident if its gross negligence or wilful misconduct were fully established. However, the Deepwater Horizon operation was based on the latest AAPL version for offshore operations, which does exclude consequential losses.

935 AAPL JOA Model Form 610 Article V (A), VII (A).
936 AAPL JOA Model Form 610 Article V (A).
937 AAPL JOA Model Form 610 Article V (A).
938 AAPL JOA Model Form 610 Article V (A), VII (A).
939 AAPL JOA Model Form 610 Article X.
940 AAPL JOA Model Form 610 Article V (A), VII (A).
941 AAPL JOA Model Form 610 Article VII A.

RMMLF JOA: The RMMLF JOA does not require that the joint operations be conducted diligently and prudently. However, it does require compliance with the petroleum title and applicable laws. This JOA seems to afford more freedom to the operator.[942]

There is also an exculpatory clause, providing that the operator shall not be held personally liable for its performance of the joint operations, except in case of losses that result from bad faith.[943] The operator is unlikely to fulfil this criterion, as bad faith implies intent to cause harm. However, the RMMLF model does not exclude the operator's liability as a participant of the consortium and does not exclude consequential losses.[944]

There is also express reference to the occurrence of loss, so any merely theoretical breach will have no implications whatsoever. However, although the RMMLF does not expressly refer to breach of the petroleum title or the JOA, it does require the execution of well services only in accordance with the JOA.[945] It is thus possible to suggest that any breach of this requirement might also attract liability under the clause.

The operator thus enjoys extensive security under the RMMLF model. Its powers are extensive, as it "shall direct and have control of all operations".[946] It will be personally liable only for losses caused by actions performed in bad faith. There is no requirement to maintain a high level of performance, but only to comply with the petroleum title regulations – and these are unlikely to be breached, as wells are regulated as offshore operations. There is no consequential loss exclusion or liability cap. However, the definition of 'operator' is limited, meaning that it does not extend to affiliated companies or contractors. The imbalance inherent in this JOA would suggest that use of this agreement over an extended period would not be in the best interests of non-operators.

CAPL JOA: The Canadian model form "recommends" a high standard of performance, as operations must be carried out:

- in a good and workmanlike manner;
- in compliance with the petroleum title, regulations and good oilfield practice; and
- according to prudent reservoir management and conservation principles.[947] (However, such principles are not binding for liability purposes, as is analysed below.)

The operator's liability is clearly limited by the exculpatory clause, as the 'no gain, no loss' principle is expressly recognised.[948] In summary, the operator will bear no liability (including for any breach of the JOA), except in case of gross negligence

942 RMMLF JOA § 5.1 (C).
943 RMMLF JOA § 4.5.
944 RMMLF JOA § 16.1.
945 RMMLF JOA § 5.1 (A).
946 RMMLF JOA § 4.1.
947 CAPL OP § 3.04.
948 CAPL OP § 5.01.

or wilful misconduct.[949] The Canadian model defines the terms 'gross negligence' and 'wilful misconduct' differently from the US models. The Canadian definition requires no level of managerial involvement; but it does exclude mere negligence, or acts or omissions that have received the express consent of all parties. As a consequence, the non-operators must indemnify the operator for any losses incurred from activities that do not involve gross negligence or wilful misconduct.[950] This benefit extends not only to the operator, but also to its affiliated companies, personnel and contractors.

In addition to gross negligence or wilful misconduct,[951] there are two further situations where the operator has exclusive liability. The operator will be personally liable for:

- contractual breaches other than in relation to government payments, health, safety and environmental risk management and the proper conduct of the joint operations; and
- losses and liabilities related to breach of the insurance obligations.

Although the exclusion of liability for breaches relating to the proper conduct of the joint operations reduces non-operators' protection, the operator will be liable for other contractual breaches and for insurance breaches, which considerably strengthens their protection. There is no liability for consequential losses (extraordinary damages), except for breach of confidentiality, in accordance with the contractual definition of 'extraordinary damages'.[952] Finally, while the liability provisions primarily relate to the operator, they also relate to non-operators insofar as the non-operators conduct any of the joint operations.[953]

The Canadian model thus affords strong protection to non-operators, as it expands on the exceptions to the exculpatory clause, even though consequential losses are excluded. However, the operator still enjoys protection from liability in case of negligence. Finally, as is common, the operator is responsible for dealing with any claims against the consortium.[954]

British model: The British model promotes high standards of performance, as it requires not only compliance with the relevant agreements and regulations, but also diligent conduct and observance of good oilfield practices.[955]

This model also recognises the 'no gain, no loss' principle, but in the accounting procedures rather than within the body of the JOA itself.[956] As a result, the operator bears no personal liability for the performance of its activities, except in case of wilful misconduct.[957]

---

949 CAPL OP § 3.04.
950 CAPL OP § 4.01.
951 CAPL OP § 4.02.
952 CAPL OP § 4.03.
953 CAPL OP § 4.04. The new version also refers to the operators' affiliated companies (CAPL OP §§ 4.01 and 4.02).
954 CAPL OP § 20.01.
955 OGUK JOA § 6.2.2.
956 OGUK JOA – Accounting Procedures § 1.2.
957 OGUK JOA § 6.2.4.

The definition of 'wilful misconduct'[958] makes specific reference to managerial involvement, but there is no reference to gross negligence.[959] While the definition of 'managerial involvement' is reciprocal – that is, it applies to both the operator and non-operators – it relates only to staff with a high level of authority, which increases the operator's protection.

Importantly, no party bears exclusive liability for consequential losses,[960] even in case of wilful misconduct – a provision that benefits the operator.[961]

The exceptions to the limitation of liability include insurance breaches.[962] Thus, the operator will not bear exclusive liability for the conduct of the joint operations, except in case of wilful misconduct or an insurance breach. It further will not bear exclusive liability for consequential losses resulting from its performance of the joint operations. The non-operators must indemnify the operator for any damages or costs arising from its performance in proportion to their participating interest.[963]

Another disadvantage for non-operators is the broad scope of the exculpatory clause under the British model. It affects all obligations of the JOA, as it refers to damages, claims or liabilities that arise –

> *directly or indirectly, out of the performance, non-performance or misperformance by the operator of any of its duties or obligations as operator hereunder [or acting on behalf of the Participants under any Associated Agreement], irrespective of negligence and/or breach of duty (whether statutory or otherwise) on the part of the operator.*[964]

This give the operator greater security, as simple errors or negligence will not incur exclusive liability. Conversely, non-operators must rely on the operator's good faith, as the limitation of liability is far too extensive.

Significantly, the British model is the only standard form to recognise expressly the agency relationship between the parties.[965] It contains several provisions that protect non-operators against liability to third-party contractors.[966] The operator is the sole party with responsibility to contractors and must insert such limitations in the relevant contracts, as well as the right to enforce any obligation on behalf of the non-operators. As previously mentioned, however, it might prove difficult to enforce these provisions under the UK Unfair Contract Terms Act 1977. While this provision might initially seem to strengthen the non-operators' position, the extensive scope of the exculpatory provision is ultimately likely to encompass third-party claims.

The operator is thus well protected under the British model, as it bears very limited liability for the conduct of the joint operations. The operator is responsible for handling any claims against the consortium up to a certain amount; beyond this, Opcom approval is required and any non-operator also has the right to participate in

---

958 OGUK JOA § 1.1.
959 OGUK JOA § 1.1.
960 OGUK JOA § 1.1.
961 OGUK JOA § 6.2.4 (b).
962 OGUK JOA § 6.2. (a) ii, 6.2.4 (b).
963 OGUK JOA § 6.2.4 (a).
964 OGUK JOA § 6.2.4 (a).
965 OGUK JOA § 6.5.8.
966 OGUK JOA §§ 6.5.7 and 6.5.8.

the claim.[967] The main reason for this approach is likely the higher risks involved in offshore operations and the 'no gain, no loss' principle. Once again, however, the Deepwater Horizon accident might prompt a reconsideration of this approach.

Norwegian model: The Norwegian model requires compliance with regulations and the petroleum title, but makes no reference to international principles such as best oilfield practices.[968] This is disadvantageous for non-operators, as regulatory compliance does not necessarily guarantee a high level of performance.

The operator's liability is limited by the exculpatory clause as the 'no gain, no loss' principle is clearly recognised.[969] The operator thus bears no personal liability for its conduct of the joint operations, except in case of gross negligence or wilful misconduct. Liabilities are therefore shared between the parties in proportion to their participating interests. However, the operator will have exclusive liability in case of gross negligence or wilful misconduct,[970] although these terms are not defined in the agreement. The benefits of the exculpatory clause extend to affiliated companies.[971]

Moreover, the operator will not be personally liable for consequential losses (including to third parties), irrespective of their cause (ie, even in case of gross negligence or wilful misconduct).

The operator thus enjoys a strong position under the Norwegian model. First, there is no effective obligation to achieve a high standard of performance. Second, there are only minor restrictions to the exculpatory clause. Third, no party will be held responsible for consequential losses. On the other hand, however, a certain level of managerial involvement is not required in order to establish gross negligence or wilful misconduct. In this regard, a financial cap could help non-operators to avoid excessive risks in relation to consequential losses; but this would also affect the direct damages.

Finally, a higher duty of care in relation to decommissioning obligations applies under the Norwegian model, as the parties must jointly prepare an abandonment plan.[972] The reasons for this are twofold. First, as a mature province, Norway is likely to experience issues with decommissioning in the near future. Second, the host government has the right to join the consortium at any stage.[973]

Australian model:[974] The Australian model approaches liability in much the same way as the other JOAs. The operator is required to achieve a high standard of

---

967 OGUK JOA § 8.3.
968 Norwegian JOA § 3.1.
969 Norwegian JOA § 3.5.
970 Norwegian JOA § 7.1.
971 Norwegian JOA § 3.5.
972 Norwegian JOA articles 30, 31 and 32.
973 See note 61.
974 AMPLA JOA §§ 1.1, 3.5, 6.3, 6.5, 6.6 and 7.2 – This model retains a similar structure to the JV for mining. Changes are mostly to style and adaptation to a JOA format relevant to oil and gas. However, there are two significant changes:
- it follows the recent trend of including additional obligations regarding bribery.
- it removes any reference to the remuneration of the operator for overhead costs.

performance in conducting the joint operations, as it is bound by several duties, such as adhering to "good Australian mining practice" (ie, acting with diligence and prudence), and complying with applicable laws.[975]

The applicable exculpatory clause excludes the operator's personal liability for performance of the joint operations (including acts of third parties), except in case of gross negligence or wilful misconduct, where the operator will be exclusively liable.[976] This benefit extends not only to the operator, but also to any affiliated company, personnel, agents and contractors – a positive provision for the operator.

Significantly, the Australian model defines 'wilful misconduct' differently from 'gross negligence'.[977] While the former definition concerns the application of the concept, the latter concerns the meaning behind the concept. Moreover, there is no requirement for managerial involvement: any of the operator's personnel can trigger this provision. The operator will not be held exclusively liable for mere negligence, but only for serious mistakes. This limitation is fairly standard in the oil industry. However, the advantage for non-operators is the extension of its application to any breach of law, the petroleum title, the JOA and the work programme and budget (except in emergencies).

Each party will also be liable for consequential losses, as these are not included in the reciprocal indemnities given to each other to secure implementation of the exculpatory clause.[978] This is a positive provision for non-operators, as consequential losses could be extremely high, as in the case of the Deepwater Horizon accident.

The most distinctive feature of the Australian model is its express provision for remuneration fees, as follows:

Remuneration of the Manager

(d) In consideration of the performance by the Manager of its obligations under this agreement, each Joint Venturer must pay the Manager its Percentage Share of the Management Fee as part of a Called Sum.

(e) The Management Fee may be varied by the Management Committee by Unanimous Vote.

(f) As soon as reasonably practicable after the conclusion of each month the Manager must send to each Joint Venturer a statement specifying the amount payable by that Joint Venturer on account of the Management Fee as assessed in relation to that month. The amount specified in that statement is due and payable by that Joint Venturer to the Manager within 7 days from the commencement of the next month.[979]

This provision contravenes the 'no gain, no loss' principle (although the overhead provisions in other JOAs are arguably similar). Interestingly, the relevant accounting procedures nonetheless recognise the 'no gain, no loss' principle as follows:

It is the intent of this Accounting Procedure that, except as otherwise expressly provided by this agreement, no party (including the Manager) will gain or lose by reason of carrying out its duties and responsibilities pursuant to this agreement.[980]

975 AMPLA JV § 1.1, 3.5, 6.5 and 7.2.
976 AMPLA JV § 6.6 and 6.7.
977 AMPLA JV § 1.1.
978 AMPLA JV, § 3.4.
979 AMPLA JV § 6.3.
980 AMPLA JV – Accounting Procedures § 1 (b).

Non-operators could argue that the exculpatory clause should be revised, as otherwise the 'no loss, no gain' principle will be compromised. For its part, the operator could argue that the fee outlined in Clause 6.3 concerns overheads and does not affect the application of this principle.

The Australian model thus adopts a similar approach to liability as most other standard JOAs. However, the express reference to remuneration fees could prove problematic when negotiating on the exculpatory clause, as non-operators will argue that there should be fewer limitations of liability. The exclusion of consequential losses might be a counterargument in the operator's favour, as its exposure is likely to increase. Finally, the operator is responsible for defending the consortium against any claims.[981]

AIPN model:[982] The AIPN model contains several requirements that aim to secure a high standard of performance.[983] The operator must conduct the operations diligently, safely and efficiently, in accordance with international practices. It is further obliged to comply with all applicable regulations, the petroleum title and the terms of the JOA.

The AIPN model also recognises the 'no gain, no loss' principle.[984] As a result, it contains an exculpatory clause that limits the operator's liability in its conduct of the operations. However, the construction of this clause is fairly unusual. As the AIPN is aimed at global operations, greater flexibility is again provided in this regard. An optional provision[985] excludes the limitation of the operator's liability for gross negligence or wilful misconduct.[986] This provision requires the participation of an appointed senior supervisor, as determined by the parties.[987] The AIPN offers alternatives in this regard, from lower-level to higher-level personnel.[988]

The parties can also decide which liabilities the operator will exclusively bear for gross negligence or wilful misconduct. There are three options. The first includes everything: the operator thus bears all costs and liabilities related to such acts or omissions. The second obliges the operator to replace, repair or remove any joint property that is damaged. The third involves a financial restriction, as it provides for a financial cap. No party can be held personally responsible for consequential[989] or environmental losses.[990] The first option is by far the best for non-operators, even though consequential and environmental liabilities are excluded. The second option

981 AMPLA JV § 7.8.
982 AIPN JOA model form 2012 § 4.6 – The new AIPN model does not modify the limitation of operator's liability or the definitions of gross negligence, environmental loss or consequential loss. However, it does include other changes which could ultimately affect the liability of the parties, especially the operator: There are extensive regulations against bribery.
There are additional options as to the definition of 'senior supervisor' which could increase or decrease the likehood of establishing a link between damage and the trigger for liability.
983 AIPN JOA § 4.2.
984 AIPN JOA § 4.2 (B) (4).
985 AIPN JOA § 4.6 (C).
986 AIPN JOA § 1.36.
987 AIPN JOA § 4.6 (C).
988 AIPN JOA § 1.54.
989 AIPN JOA § 1.13.
990 AIPN JOA § 1.26.

is limited to property damage only, and the last will depend on the cap that is negotiated between the parties.

If none of these options is selected, the operator will have no personal liabilities to the non-operators – even if these arise due to its poor performance.[991] The operator will share in the liabilities as a participant of the consortium, and the non-operators will indemnify it for any costs or liabilities relating to performance of the joint operations beyond this exposure.[992]

The exculpatory clause further applies to the operator's personnel and to the personnel of its affiliated companies; however, it does not ordinarily extend to contractors. In addition, it is unclear whether the clause applies to breaches of the petroleum title and the JOA, or to third-party liabilities. The operator again has the authority to manage any claims against the consortium up to a specified amount, although the non-operators' right to participate in such claims is also recognised.[993]

The operator thus enjoys a strong position under the AIPN model, as there are several opportunities to limit its personal liability. If the optional clauses are not selected, the JOA parties will share liability for all damage in proportion to their participating interests, regardless of the cause. Even if the non-operators secure the inclusion of one of these optional clauses, they will also have a fight on their hands in relation to the definition of a 'senior supervisor', which could determine whether an act constitutes gross negligence or wilful misconduct. Helpfully, however, the AIPN clearly defines all key terms in relation to liability.

Greenlandic model: The Greenlandic JOA model requires a high level of performance from the operator.[994] An exculpatory clause based on the 'no gain, no loss' principle is also included,[995] which provides that the operator will bear no personal liability for its performance of the joint operations, except in case of gross negligence or wilful misconduct.[996] These terms are not defined under the agreement.

The scope of the exclusion for gross negligence or wilful misconduct is extremely limited, as it must involve the managerial or supervisory personnel of the operator or its affiliates.[997] On the other hand, the operator's personal liability also extends to insurance obligations.[998] No party will be personally liable for consequential loss.[999] These benefits are extended to the NOC, as co-operator.[1000]

The Greenlandic JOA model is thus something of a mixed bag. Some provisions benefit the operator, such as the requirement for managerial involvement and the consequential loss exclusion. Others benefit non-operators – for example, the operator bears liability for insurance obligations and the exculpatory clause does not extend to contractors. The Greenlandic JOA model thus attempts to strike a balance

991 AIPN JOA § 4.6 (A).
992 AIPN JOA § 4.6 (B) (D).
993 AIPN JOA § 4.5.
994 Greenlandic JOA § 3.3.2.
995 Greenlandic JOA § 3.2.
996 Greenlandic JOA § 3.3.3.
997 Greenlandic JOA § 13.1 (v).
998 Greenlandic JOA § 3.3.3 (C) (b).
999 Greenlandic JOA § 3.3.3.
1000 Greenlandic JOA § 3.3.3

between the parties' interests, although ultimately it tends to favour the operator. Once again, the NOC is afforded a strong level of protection, as it enjoys the same protections as the operator.

Conclusion: The liability provisions of the JOAs typically focus on a "consideration of the prospective liability which the operator might have to the parties for any loss or liability which the operator causes in the exercise of its responsibilities, and how that liability might be limited in the operator's favour".[1001]

In essence, the liability clauses are nothing more than a reflection of the 'no gain, no loss' principle – either express (eg, AIPN, CAPL, Norway) or implicit (eg, the US models). In reality, it is highly unlikely that an operator would fulfil the criteria to incur exclusive liability, so long as all 'boxes' have been ticked. Peter Roberts recognises this as follows:

> *The combination of a relatively high threshold for determining what constitutes wilful misconduct (or gross negligence), with the addition of exceptions for special circumstances and good-faith acts or omissions and the senior supervisory personnel qualification, together with the possibilities of a test of materiality and an overall cap on liability, and also a disclaimer of liability for consequential losses, means that the reality is that under the JOA it can be very unlikely that any meaningful degree of liability will be imposed on the operator.*[1002]

The Deepwater Horizon accident starkly illustrated the enormous risks and liabilities involved in offshore operations.[1003] So post-Macondo, are the JOA parties still willing to observe the 'no gain, no loss' principle?[1004] Are they willing to share the bill whatever the outcome of the operations (eg, severe consequential losses)? The answer is not as straightforward as it would seem, because the operator will not agree to bear further risk without receiving something in exchange.[1005] However, the risks presented by the exculpatory clause represent a massive burden for non-operators. There are, therefore, two solutions from the non-operators' perspective. The first is to appoint a third-party operator, as service agreements are not founded on the 'no gain, no loss' principle. Alternatively, the operator could retain its position, but with less extensive limitations to its liability.

Non-operators are therefore in a difficult position. As the exculpatory clause will protect the operator against almost any failure in performance, the main remedies available to them concern control of operations, removal of the operator and default.[1006] However, none of the JOAs analysed in this book gives non-operators

---

1001 Peter Roberts (n 5) p155.

1002 *Ibid* p159.

1003 See note 917.

1004 See Daniel B Shilliday *et al* (n 749) p1579, Wayne G Holt, "Problems Relating to Artic Farmout and Joint Operating Agreements" (1972) 10 *Alberta Law Review* p450.

1005 "As this book is going to press, the AIPN is re-thinking its Model Form IOA insofar as it deals with the issue of the appropriate standard of performance owed by the operator to the non-operating working interest owners. Included within the areas to be discussed are the definitions of gross negligence and willful misconduct and an attempt to define what a reasonable and prudent operator is in terms of specifying the duties owed to the non-operators. The AIPN Committee is also considering whether to differentiate the scope of the exculpatory clause as it might affect third parties or parties to the JOA." Ernest E Smith *et al* (n 16) p545.

1006 Peter Roberts (n 5) p160.

strong control over operations; nor are non-operators afforded wide discretion to remove the operator, unless they control the Opcom. Terence Daintith describes this situation as follows:

If a JOA contains all these restrictions on the liability of the operator for wilful misconduct it would be very difficult, first, to prove wilful misconduct and then to recover any significant damages. (...) This leaves the non-operators with only one real remedy if the operator fails to perform its duties adequately, namely to remove the operator. This is, however, clumsy and rarely, if ever, used.[1007]

In other words, in most cases non-operators can only hope for the best, as the JOA will not fully protect them against failures in performance of the joint operations. They could also try to rely upon the fiduciary duties that arise under their relationship with the operator in order somehow to secure a higher standard of performance.[1008]

There is an important distinction between the position of non-operators and that of minority shareholders with regard to liability. A director under the UK Companies Act 2006 enjoys no special limitation of liabilities in performing his activities, as directors' liability is clearly regulated by common law.[1009] One practical example can be found in section 578(3): "A director is not so liable if he proves that the default in the repayment of the money was not due to any misconduct or negligence on his part." This is no exculpatory clause: the director must prove the diligence and prudence of his activities, rather than certain types of mistake being excluded from liability. Minority shareholders are thus in a far stronger position than non-operators.

Most of the JOAs examined in this book do not directly address the issue of third-party liability, but espouse the general principle that each party will be liable in proportion to its participating interest. The British model is the only JOA to address agency liabilities, as it is the only model that recognises this relationship (though other models recognise it by implication, as they empower the operator to represent the consortium).[1010]

Further, the JOAs do not commonly cap liability, but rather focus on the types of damage to be shared between all parties and the types of damage that trigger exclusive liability. However, these provisions ultimately aim to protect the operator, rather than anything else. It is important to remember that the courts may not enforce exculpatory clauses in the way that the parties anticipated, as the decision in *Farstad Supply AS v Enviroco Ltd* [2010] 2 Lloyd's Rep 387 bears out.[1011] Finally, the imbalance between the JOA parties leaves non-operators with no protection against the operator's failure of performance, except for potential court review – which is by no means easy or certain in outcome. A new, balanced JOA is thus required to provide fair and reasonable protection for all parties involved.

1007 Terence Daintith (n 16) p1141.

1008 See Chapter 2, section 2.2(c).

1009 Companies Act 2006, section 178.

1010 See section 2.2(b).

1011 For further information, see Greg Gordon, "Case Comment Contribution, indemnification and exclusion: Farstad in the Supreme Court" (2011) *Edinburgh Law Review* p259. Further examples of cases dealing with exclusions and indemnities clauses offshore between operator and non-operators are: *Caledonia North Sea Ltd v London Bridge Engineering Ltd* [2002] 1 Lloyd's Rep 562, 563, HL; and *EE Caledonia Ltd v Orbit Valve Co* [1995] 1 All ER 174; [1994] 1 WLR 1515, CA (both cases arising out of the Piper Alpha disaster).

(c) Conclusion[1012]

The above analysis of the control of operations clearly reveals the operator's dominance under the existing JOAs. In this situation, non-operators have no option but to rely on secondary sources to protect their interests.

First, the provisions on the operator's removal were analysed. Ideally, these would constitute effective means to prevent poor performance by the operator, under threat of it losing its position in the consortium. In practice, however, the circumstances in which non-operators can remove the operator are at best extremely limited, at worst non-existent.

The parties' liabilities were then examined. If non-operators can neither control the operations nor remove the operator nor demand that it forfeit its interest, then their last resort is to impose liability on the operator. Non-operators might expect the operator to attract all or most of the liability for failure of performance, as in most cases it enjoys a great deal of freedom when performing the joint operations. Once again, however, the reality is very different. The exculpatory clause severely restricts the operator's exclusive liabilities; and even in those few cases where the operator can be held personally liable, there are so many hurdles to overcome that it is unlikely that an operator would ever bear exclusive liability for mistakes and errors in conducting the joint operations.

Essentially, the liability provision is drafted in such a way that the sole remedy available for non-operators lies in control of the operations. Claude Duval and Charez Golvala recognise this as follows:

> *The non-operators can guard against negligent operators by supervising the joint operations through the operating committee. The parties may also elect a provision allowing the removal of the operator without cause, a provision which seldom appears in onshore JOAs. Nonetheless, the model form JOAs in use generally grant the operator expansive authority with rather little liability for its errors.*[1013]

Given this limited liability, many pages are devoted to the control of the operator and of expenditure.[1014]

However, such control is not in fact available under current JOAs.[1015] The most effective way to protect the non-operators' position in the JOA is thus to ensure that a JOA actually means what it says and provides for joint participation in the performance of operations.

1012 The new AIPN JOA model form 2012 and the new AMPLA JOA model form provide no substantial changes to the provisions analysed in this section. Non-operators cannot participate actively in the joint operations or control them effectively. The operator still holds the ultimate power in the JOA; the only option for non-operators is to seek to secure a higher pass mark, so that they have the power of veto. However, the operator generally has increased obligations to promote transparency of operations and greater responsibilities towards the consortium members (eg, regarding anti-bribery requirements, decommissioning regulations, supply of information).

1013 Claude Duval (n 122) p295.

1014 Charez Golvala (n 6) p46.

1015 "Given the infrequency of the operating committee meetings, the standard of performance by the operator is critical." DAW Maloney, "Managing the Multi-Participant Joint Venture" (1988) 7(2) *Australian Mining and Petroleum Law Bulletin* p116.

Chapter 4: Conclusion

In order to maximise the effectiveness of the joint operations, the parties to a JOA will appoint one party to conduct the operations on behalf of the whole consortium.[1016] The remaining parties are the non-operators.

However, the title of the agreement would suggest a reasonable collaboration between all parties to the consortium – not only in relation to the consequences of the operations (eg, costs and liabilities), but also in relation to their preparation, planning and performance. The US models completely ignore this premise. The Canadian model is the only one that clearly reflects the reality, as its title does not include the word 'joint'. The remaining models attempt to adopt a middle ground by providing for an Opcom. The operator might claim that as non-operators can provide input through the Opcom, everything is decided jointly. However, the operator undeniably sets the pace: it chairs not only the Opcom, but also any sub-committees that are established, and prepares most of the proposals to be analysed by the Opcom. As a consequence, the operator has far more control over the joint operations than the non-operators.[1017]

As discussed, non-operators will seek a greater level of participation in the decision-making process, while the operator will seek more discretion so that it can dictate the pace of the operations. Above and between these different positions is a host government that will seek to optimise efficiency and maximise production.

So how can these different views be addressed in a balanced manner? Is it possible for all of these interests and views to co-exist equally within the same agreement?

It would seem that the key is to allow for greater cooperation by all participating parties. The development of fields that lie close to the borders of two different countries provides an interesting analogy. As a sovereign state, each country would prefer to maintain close control over its own resources and operations.[1018] However, this would not be in their best interests: efficient exploration of the field instead requires cooperation between them. The countries involved might thus sign an

1016 "It would be impractical for all participants in a jointly owned contract to undertake the actual operations. Thus, the JOA provides for the designation of one of the participants as the operator who is in exclusive charge of conducting all joint operations on behalf of all participants." Claude Duval (n 122) p289.

1017 See Chapter I, section 1.1(b).

1018 "The parties wanted a strong powerful JC. In view of this, they needed a kind of check on those powers." Chidinma Bernadine Okafor, "Model Agreements for Joint Development, a Case Study" (2007) 25 *J Energy Nat Resources L* p98.

agreement establishing a joint development zone (JDZ) in order to maximise recovery of the natural resources.[1019]

The JDZ is commonly controlled by both countries, because neither would accept a partial abdication of its sovereignty. Peter Reid describes the practical application of the JDZ between Australia and Indonesia (now between Australia and independent East Timor) as follows:

> *It is proposed that there will be established a Joint Authority to administer the JDZ comprising the Indonesian and Australian Ministers for Resources and Energy. The Joint Authority will be serviced by the following four support groups: secretariat; technical; legal and fiscal, which will be located in Darwin, the capital of Australia's Northern Territory.*[1020]

The same principle would apply to a JOA, as the nature of the operation is the same – albeit that it involves private parties rather than sovereign states. The similarity is even more pronounced with regard to the sharing of costs.[1021] All JOA parties and the host government are keen to maximise production as efficiently as possible; they all share the same end goal. However, while some operators will argue that an efficient operation will devolve more power to the operator, a higher degree of efficiency can be achieved only if a balanced agreement is established between the parties, so that everyone can participate equally in the conduct and performance of the joint operations, through a real and effective combined effort.[1022]

While a JOA is predicated on a context in which one party has a dominant position, the parties to a JDZ will likely be in an equal relationship, as each has its own sovereignty. The JDZ is thus a good example of a balanced agreement for the joint exploration and exploitation of hydrocarbons.[1023]

Some parties might attempt to redress the balance by establishing another entity to conduct the joint operations (ie, an incorporated operator), comprising all parties to the consortium.[1024] In simple terms, this approach would create another Opcom to perform the day-to-day activities in a way that mirrors the approach adopted under many JDZs (eg, Australia/Indonesia and Nigeria/Sao Tomé e Principe). This might allow for a greater contribution by non-operators; but the operator would still likely control this entity if the participating interest were the decisive factor in this regard. Rajendra Ramlogan describes the practical application of this solution as follows:

> *There have been two situations in Trinidad and Tobago of the use of joint operating companies formed by parties to a joint venture to conduct development activities. These joint operating companies are Trinmar Limited which comprises Texaco Trinidad Inc., and the State oil companies and the wholly-owned local joint operating company, Trintomar, comprising the State oil companies and the National Gas Company of Trinidad and Tobago. Today joint operating agreements are more frequently prescribing that*

1019 Peter C Reid, "Joint Development Zones Between Countries" (1987) 6(1) *AMPLA Bulletin* pp4–13.

1020 *Ibid.* Such joint authority was implemented by the Timor Gap Treaty, signed in 1989. For further information see: www.austlii.edu.au/au/other/dfat/treaties/1991/9.html.

1021 Chidinma B Okafor (n 1039) p73.

1022 Peter C Reid (n 1040) pp4–13.

1023 Chidinma B Okafor (n 1018) p58.

1024 "In exceptional instances, a separate entity may be formed to serve as operator and that entity may be staffed by the various participants." Claude Duval (n 122) p289.

developmental activities will be conducted by a joint operating company to be designated as the operator and to be staffed by personnel nominated by the parties participating in the joint ventures. The use of the joint operating company mechanism results in greater involvement by the State oil companies' personnel in the development operations.[1025]

Peter Roberts also recognises this possibility:

Another situation which can emerge, somewhere between the existence of an incorporated joint venture and the appointment of a contracted operator (see above), is represented by decision of the parties to incorporate a company in which the parties will be the shareholders (with their interests corresponding to their PIs unless they agree otherwise), to act as the operator for the purposes of the JOA:[1026]

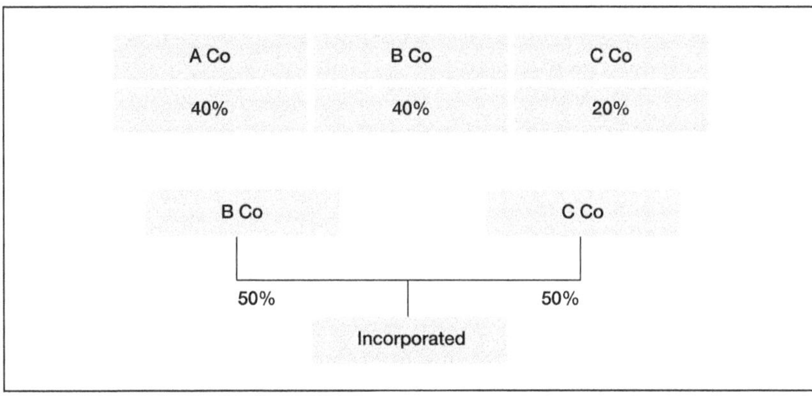

Thus, in the UKCS the Britannia field is operated on behalf of the parties by a company called Britannia Operator Limited, which is owned jointly by two of the parties that hold the relevant licence. The resultant incorporated operator could be appointed directly as the operator by the parties, or there might be a further contract for services entered into between an appointed party-operator and the incorporated operator. In this latter scenario the position outlined above in respect of the contracted operator would effectively be repeated.[1027]

Another alternative to avoid conflicts in the conduct of the joint operations is to delegate day-to-day operations to a third-party contractor. Scott Styles describes this situation as follows:

In recent years there has been a tendency towards delegating operating functions to professional contractors who are not actually members of the JOA. Such contractor-operators are not generally dealt with the JOA. Rather, the tendency is for the JOA operator to delegate in turn much of his day-to-day management role to the contractor-operator. Such delegation would generally require the consent of the other members.[1028]

This approach might prove problematic in some jurisdictions where government approval is required. However, the host government might be keen to approve such

1025 Rajendra Ramlogan (n 105) p284.
1026 Peter Roberts (n 5) p92.
1027 Peter Roberts (n 5) p92.
1028 Scott Styles (n 14) p278.

a move where the third-party contractor has a strong reputation in the market (eg, Schlumberger) and will act without prejudice towards the JOA parties' joint and several liabilities.[1029]

Under this arrangement, conflicts between the JOA parties would be avoided, as a neutral third party would perform the work in accordance with Opcom decisions. Sandy Shaw points out that this alternative is increasingly used to address concerns about overheads, as follows:

There is a growing trend in delegating major operating functions to contractors in an effort to reduce operating costs and overheads. At present, JOAs do not tend to deal in any detail with contractor-operator situations. In cases where contractors' services are used for day to day operations, the parties will expect to be fully consulted and consent to such arrangements and any JOA amendments that may be required.[1030]

Peter Roberts describes the implementation of this third-party alternative as follows:

As an alternative to the conventional route of a party-operator being appointed for the duration of the JOA, consideration might be given to the introduction of some form of hybrid operator arrangement. This could take the form of the appointment of a contracted operator, an incorporated operator or a split operator (…).

An independent third-party contractor may be appointed to perform the necessary operational services on behalf of the parties, in accordance with the terms of a specific contract to do so. Under this 'contracted operator' arrangement, either a party-operator will be appointed in the customary manner and then the third party will be retained under a contract for services, entered into between the party-operator (on behalf of all the parties) and that third party, or the third party might step straight into the role of the operator and there will be no party-operator. This latter formulation is less common in practice, so the following analysis assumes that there will be a party-operator in the JOA. The JOA might provide that if there is a contractor which is appointed by a party-operator for the discharge of certain of the operational responsibilities, then the party-operator shall nevertheless remain fully responsible for the performance of those responsibilities as if it were continuing to perform them itself; this principle could apply equally in respect of a contracted operator.[1031]

Delegation to a third-party operator would prevent most potential conflicts between the JOA parties from arising; and none of the JOA parties would have any difficulty in demanding improved control or performance under such a service agreement.

The challenge for this new form of contractual arrangement lies in its implementation. Peter Roberts explains this issue by analysing the main distinctions between the relevant provisions of the various JOAs, from the perspectives of a party-operator and a contracted operator respectively, as follows:[1032]

Several other aspects of the contracted operator's appointment will differ from the customary party-operation situation:

1029 Peter Roberts (n 5) p90.
1030 Sandy Shaw (n 16) p14.
1031 Peter Roberts (n 5) pp89–90.
1032 *Ibid* pp90–92.

Provision	Party-operator	Contracted operator
Duration of appointment	For the life of the JOA, subject to earlier resignation or removal	Fixed-term period with a possible option to renew
Appointing person	Parties	Party-operator
Duty holder responsibility	Party-operator	Contracted operator
Performance standards	As per law and the JOA	As per law and the contract
Authorising person	Opcom	Party-operator
Compensation for performance	None beyond the recovery costs incurred	Commercially based compensation structure
Provision for personnel	Party-operator's staff and possibly also secondees	Contracted operator's staff
Approval of operational expenses incurred	Opcom	Party-operator
Approval of retained contractors	Opcom	Party-operator
Freedom to undertake competitive activities	Possible unless excluded, subject to fiduciary duties	Possible unless restricted by the contract
Liability for loss of/damage to joint property	None unless caused by wilful misconduct (or gross negligence)	Liable, subject to limitations
Liability for consequential losses	None	Liable, subject to limitations
Liability for defective service performance	None, subject to risk or removal	Re-performance at the contracted operator's expense, loss of compensation, obligation to compensate (subject to limitations), risk of removal
Suspension of engagement	Not applicable	Suspension by the party-operator as per the contract
Termination of engagement	Subject to Opcom approval, defined circumstances	Termination by the party-operator as per the contract
Transfer of engagement	Subject to Opcom approval and governmental approval	Subject to party-operator approval
Relationship management	Through the Opcom	Through the party-Operator and contracted operator management committee

Another solution through which to establish more balanced participation of the JOA parties is to split the operatorship. Peter Roberts describes this as follows:

It could be that the role of the operator is divided between more than one person over the lifetime of the JOA. The presumption is that the party which is appointed as the operator will remain as the operator through every phase of the JOA, but the JOA might be structured so that the mantle of operatorship is rotated between more than one party according to the needs of the joint operations. It may be, for example, that one of the parties has a particular pedigree which suits it to be the operator for the exploration and appraisal phase, but with another party assuming responsibility for the production phase. Similar considerations might apply in respect of decommissioning phase. Alternatively, if the prevailing mineral law grants a concession by reference to a series of distinct operational phases, then different operators for each of the phases might be feasible. Where the existence of a split operatorship is a possibility, the role of operator might be formally transferred between the relevant parties for defined periods; alternatively, one of the parties might be appointed as a sub-operator ... another of the parties as the principal operator, with that sub-operator having absolute responsibility for the operation of the JOA in respect of a defined part of the joint operations in accordance with a form of worksharing agreement. The appointment of a separate operator for the performance of a defined exclusive operation is also effectively a form of split operatorship.[1033]

In conclusion, while a third-party operator is an interesting option to balance the positions of the JOA parties, this might alter the format of the JOA. First, the third party is not a member of the JOA, so the JOA will need to be revised accordingly. Second, the JOA parties will need to sign a separate contract with the third party. In this case the limitations of liability may be reduced, as the third-party operator will profit from its activities. Third, the third-party operator will likely require government approval. The practicalities of implementing this solution are thus complex. However, the main obstacle is the difficulty of executing two agreements simultaneously and transferring the operator's powers to a third party. This is why this option is not commonly utilised in exploration and production – although it is often used for lifting agreements, where a third party is appointed to manage the parties' lifting entitlement and accounting.

Split operatorship and incorporated operators are far more common in the exploration and production industry. The practicality of these options is reflected in agreements not only between countries (eg, establishing JDZs), but also between private parties – such as the unit operating agreement (UOA),[1034] which establishes a similar concept to the JDZ (unitisation) within the same jurisdiction, even though the contexts are different. If JDZs, UOAs and lifting agreements address similar situations to a JOA,[1035] then why is it not possible to provide for similar terms in a JOA? Some practical examples of JDZs (eg, Australia/Indonesia and Nigeria/Sao Tomé

1033 Peter Roberts (n 5) pp92–93.

1034 Kenneth Barnhill explains the similarity between a JOA and a UOA as follows: "'Joint operations' is the term generally used to refer to the procedure whereby co-owners of mineral properties agree upon the development and operations of such properties by one or more of the co-owners for the benefit of the other co-owners. 'Unitized operations' denote a similar arrangement, but generally on a larger scale, such as for the exploration, development, and operation of an entire pool, structure or field, or a substantial portion thereof." Kenneth E Barnhill Jr (n 176) p133.

1035 For further information see David Edward Pierce, "Coordinated Reservoir Development, An Alternative to the Rule of Capture for the Ownership and Development of Oil and Gas" (1983) 4 *J Energy Law & Policy* p129, David M Ong, "The 1979 and 1990 Malaysia–Thailand Joint Development Agreements: A Model for International Legal Co-operations in Common Offshore Petroleum Deposits?" (1999) 14 *International J Marine & Coastal L* p207.

e Principe) might serve as an indication of whether they could work in practice; but it is clear that each mechanism represents a valid alternative that would balance the differing wishes and views of the parties. One key reason why these mechanisms are not widely used in relation to JOAs is that they would require far more complex management structures than a single party-operator. However, the main stumbling power is resistance to any reduction in the power that is currently vested in the operator.

Although more complex arrangements and greater cooperation may be required to implement them, these alternatives could achieve a reasonable balance between the parties' interests. Without exception, however, not one of the JOA model forms recognises any such alternatives to balance the positions of the operator and non-operators. This is probably the most blatant evidence of the operator's sheer dominance, and of non-operators' acceptance of their diminished position both as parties to the consortium and (perhaps more importantly) as investors.

Clearly, many companies and even governments will be hesitant to allow more than one party to act as operator at the same time, on the basis that it might generate more confusion and less efficiency in the conduct of operations. As the saying goes, two captains will sink the ship; many companies would argue that the same principle should apply to a JOA.

A distinction might be made between a technical operator and an administrative operator. The technical operator is likely to be the IOC, and the administrative operator the NOC. Arguably, this would not amount to a truly dual operatorship, but rather one company dealing with the main business of the consortium and another with the formalities of implementation.

The Greenlandic JOA provides for a fairly unique co-operative agreement as an attachment to the main body of the JOA, as follows:[1036]

APPENDIX B

CO-OPERATION AGREEMENT

This Co-operation Agreement is made the [date] [year] between: [Full name of licensee company] as Operator

and NUNAOIL A/S as Co-operator regarding Exclusive Licence no. [yyyy]/[xx].

Whereas it is stipulated in Section 12.06 of the Licence and Appendix 4 to the Licence that the licensee shall co-operate with NUNAOIL in order to develop the know-how and expertise of NUNAOIL;

Whereas according to Appendix 4 to the Licence regarding the development and exploitation periods this co-operation will take place in the form of a co-operatorship for NUNAOIL, which will be further specified in a separate Co-operation Agreement to be annexed to the Joint Operating Agreement for the Licence (the JOA) as Appendix B; and

Whereas this Co-operation Agreement is accepted by all the Parties by their signing of the JOA.

Now therefore [Full name of licensee company] and NUNAOIL agree as follows:

1036 www.govmin.gl/images/stories/petroleum/udbud/udbud_2018_2018/Davis_Strait_2018/Model%20Joint%20Operating%20Agreement_App%20B_Davis%20Strait%202018.pdf.

1. *Purpose of Co-operation Agreement*
   1.1 *The purpose of this Co-operation Agreement is to establish a co-operation between NUNAOIL as the Co-operator and [Full name of licensee company] as the Operator in relation to the activities under an exploitation Licence in which NUNAOIL participates and to define the principles governing such co-operation. The objective of the co-operation is to actively involve the Co-operator with regard to the performance of the operatorship under the first exploitation Licence in order to transfer know-how and experience of operatorship with respect to the development and production phases to the Co-operator, and to contribute to enable the Co-operator to perform operator functions in the production phase and with a view to Co-operator, at a reasonable early date, to perform one or more significant parts of the total activities under an exploitation Licence such as the operation of an offshore production system and/or an onshore natural gas liquefaction plant, but under the overall responsibility of the Operator.*

   This Co-operation Agreement will specifically define the organisations to be established for the development and production phase and the respective role and responsibilities of NUNAOIL and [Full name of licensee company] in these organisations.

2. *Scope of Co-operation Agreement*
   2.1 *The activities under this Co-operation Agreement are carried out as matters ancillary to and therefore subject to the provisions of the JOA to which this Co-operation Agreement is attached as Appendix B.*
   2.2 *Terms used in this Co-operation Agreement that have a defined meaning in the JOA shall have the same defined meaning in this Co-operation Agreement unless otherwise stated. If any conflict between the provisions of this Co-operation Agreement and the provisions of the JOA, the latter provisions shall prevail.*
   2.3 *The Operator and the Co-operator shall at all times be subject to the provisions of the JOA and the Accounting Procedure, attached as Appendix A to the JOA, and in particular nothing in this Co-operation Agreement shall authorize the Operator or the Co-operator to take any action which is not within the powers of the Operator under the JOA.*
   2.4 *Activities under this Co-operation Agreement shall at all times be compatible with activities being carried out under the JOA and its appendices. No activity under this Co-operation Agreement shall take place if it would in any way prejudice any Joint Operation.*
   2.5 *Unless a joint operating Company is created, Operator and Co-operator shall establish a co-operation structure including a Co-operation Committee (referred to as the Committee) and a Team organization (referred to as the Team). To this co-operation structure shall be assigned the activities under an exploitation Licence. The Committee shall exercise a senior management review and supervisory role in order to secure a safe and efficient operation at all times.*

2.6 *The Committee and the Team shall be established by the Operator and the Co-operator not later than 1 month after the submittal of a satisfactory request for extension of the Licence for exploitation under Section 8.02 of the Licence.*

2.7 *Following the commencement of an appraisal programme and up to the establishment of the Committee and the Team under Section 2.6. Co-operator is entitled to participate with a reasonable number of qualified employees in Operator's work regarding an appraisal programme under Section 6.06(b) of the Licence and the Operator's preparation of the material indicated in Sections 8.02 and 8.07 of the Licence.*

2.8 *The Committee and the Team shall at all times be subject to the same direction and control of the Operating Committee as the Operator and in particular to any guidelines consistent with this Co-operation Agreement which may be issued by the Operating Committee from time to time regarding activities under this Co-operation Agreement.*

2.9 *The Team shall manage the day-to-day activities and shall be manned with competent and qualified personnel and shall use all appropriate management systems and procedures. The Operator and the Co-operator shall each endeavour to minimize expenses in the administration and operation of this Co-operation Agreement and in particular they shall each ensure that there is no unnecessary duplication of activity.*

2.10 *The Team shall be situated in the Operator's, its Affiliate's and/or the Co-operator's offices in Greenland unless otherwise agreed between the Operator and the Co-operator.*

2.11 *The Operator and the Co-operator shall within the framework of this Co-operation Agreement each use its reasonable endeavours to ensure that the Co-operator's personnel on the Committee and the Team are given opportunities to participate in the Operator's internal courses and to receive on-the-job-training regarding relevant parts of the Joint Operations in order to acquire the necessary skills to carry out operator functions.*

2.12 *Pertinent technology and operating systems shall be made available and utilized for the activities regarding the Licence Area.*

3. *Co-operation Committee*

3.1 *The Committee shall consist of two management representatives, one from the Operator and one from the Co-operator. Each may designate an alternate. The chairman shall be from the Operator and the vice-chairman shall be from the Co-operator. Each representative may bring advisors to all Committee meetings.*

3.2 *The Committee shall always make every effort to reach agreement and consensus on all matters handled by it. The Committee shall keep minutes showing the position of the companies as represented by the chairman and the vice-chairman. In the event of a disagreement between the Operator and the Co-operator, the Operator shall pursuant to Section 5.2 put these matters before the Operating Committee for its decision.*

3.3 *The Committee shall normally meet monthly and in advance of the*

Operating Committee meetings, or as required and requested by either party. Matters for discussion shall, to the extent possible, be established at a reasonable time in advance of the Committee meetings.

3.4 *The Committee shall have a reviewing and supervisory role for senior management matters pertaining to all activities under an exploitation Licence and its duties shall further include:*

1. *endorsement of a Team manager from the Operator and an assistant Team manager from the Co-operator based on qualifications;*
2. *review of the Team's organization and manpower needs, with the aim at all times to involve to the extent reasonably possible personnel from the Co-operator's organization;*
3. *review of other important matters such as key operating systems as indicated in Section 8.1, financial and other audits carried out on the Team's activities;*
4. *review of all matters which will require review, approval or decision by the Operating Committee;*
5. *review of any other matter relating to the co-operation that either the Operator or the Co-operator wishes to place before the Operating Committee.*
6. *review, supervise, direct and advise the Team.*

4. *Team Organization*

4.1 *The Team shall, on a day-to-day basis carry out planning, organizing and performance of all activities associated with the operatorship.*

4.2 *It shall throughout be the responsibility of the Operator that the Team has the required personnel with the appropriate skill level.*

4.3 *The Team shall be headed by the Team manager and the Assistant Team manager. The manager and the assistant manager shall have management responsibility for the day-to-day activities of the Team and shall be responsible for staffing of the Team with qualified personnel and for its organizational structure.*

4.4 *The Team manager and the Assistant Team manager shall agree on the selection of the management members of the Team's key organizational units (technical, operational and staff).*

4.5 *Periodic reviews of the Team's organization, manpower needs and performance of its personnel shall be prepared and agreed by the manager and the assistant manager. The results will be reviewed and endorsed by the Committee and appropriate actions shall be taken.*

4.6 *The Team shall report to the Operator, who shall also have the responsibility for directing matters to the Committee and for calling Committee meetings to deal with such matters.*

4.7 *When a new position is established and/or existing positions are to be filled the Co-operator shall be entitled to nominate personnel to the Team at all levels except the Team manager. The Operator will in fulfilment of the purpose of this Co-operation Agreement to a reasonable extent agree to accept such nominated personnel provided that the person in question meets the necessary skill level and that a reasonable balance of Operator and Co-operator personnel is maintained.*

5. Relationship of the Parties and Relationship with the Operating Committee

5.1 Nothing herein shall prejudice individual voting rights of the Parties or affect the Operator's responsibilities as stated in the JOA.

5.2 It shall be the responsibility of the Operator (without prejudice to the rights of any other party) to submit to the Operating Committee or to any sub-committees any matter requiring determination by the Operating Committee or sub-committees. The Operator and the Co-operator will make a bona fide effort to resolve all major differences between the Operator and the Co-operator prior to such submissions.

6. Technical Information, Licences and Ownership

6.1 All drawings, reports or other documents prepared by the Team or by the Operator or the Co-operator, their contractors, consultants or Affiliates for the Joint Account and as part of support rendered by the Operator, the Co-operator, their contractors, consultants or Affiliates shall be the Joint Property of the Parties.

6.2 For the duration of this Co-operation Agreement the Operator shall to the extent reasonably requested and confidentiality restrictions permit provide the Co-operator and the Team with relevant proprietary information owned by the Operator or its affiliates. Such proprietary information may include, but is not limited to, systems, computer programmes and specifications and will be clearly marked as proprietary to the Operator when provided in written form. Such disclosures shall be subject to the agreement of reasonable confidentially provisions.

6.3 Likewise the Co-operator shall provide the Team with relevant proprietary information owned by the Co-operator. Such proprietary information provided by the Co-operator will be subject to similar provisions as stipulated for proprietary information owned by the Operator.

6.4 Proprietary information shall generally be provided on a non-exclusive, confidential basis, for operations related to the Licence only, against payment to be charged to the Joint Account to be negotiated each time. However, the Operator and the Co-operator may agree that the Co-operator shall have the right to use any such proprietary information in its operations within the Greenland territory.

6.5 When an invention results from activities under the Licence and is charged to the Joint Account, patents based on such inventions shall be jointly owned by the Parties, and the Parties shall have all rights of joint ownership including access to such inventions on a royalty-free basis.

6.6 The Operator and the Co-operator each warrants, that it or its Affiliates will have title to any information provided to the Team hereunder, and that it has the authority to grant the rights specified herein or shall otherwise advise of the limitations applicable to its title or the grant.

6.7 Neither the Operator nor the Co-operator warrants the utility or accuracy of technical information provided hereunder by it or its Affiliates.

7. Confidentiality

7.1 Each party shall at all times keep confidential all data and information acquired or received by any party under the Co-operation Agreement according to the confidentiality provisions of the JOA.

8. *Procedures/Operation System*
   8.1 *The Team shall establish systems and procedures appropriate to the agreed level of present and future activities under the Licence.*

9. *Cost and Payment*
   9.1 *The Operator shall prepare the Programme and Budgets pursuant to the provision of Section 5 of the JOA and the Accounting Procedure. Such Programmes and Budgets shall be reviewed and endorsed by the Co-operation Committee before the Operator presents them to the Operating Committee.*
   9.2 *Without prejudice to the provisions of the JOA, neither the Co-operator nor the Operator shall gain profit nor suffer loss as a result of approved activities carried out under this Co-operation Agreement. The principles laid down in the Accounting Procedure shall apply. The activities of the Committee and the Team will be charged to the Joint Account and appropriate amounts will be included in cash calls by the Operator to be made in accordance with the JOA and the Accounting Procedure.*
   9.3 *The administrative costs for tasks for which NUNAOIL is responsible shall be charged to the Operator at the fixed rate on expenditures, defined in Section 3.1.8 of Appendix A, Accounting Procedure.*
   9.4 *Cost of personnel provided by the Operator, the Co-operator or one of the other Parties and services specifically authorized by the Committee shall be charged to the Joint Account according to the provisions set forth in the Accounting Procedure, attached as Appendix A to the JOA. This also applies to Co-operator's personnel under Section 2.7.*
   9.5 *NUNAOIL's manpower costs, travel cost, inspection costs, etc. will be charged monthly direct to the Operator for approval and payment within thirty (30) days after receipt of the invoice.*
   9.6 *NUNAOIL's overhead regarding third party charges will be calculated monthly and charged directly to the Operator based upon the billing for approval and payment within thirty (30) days after receipt of the invoice.*
   9.7 *Books and records will remain at NUNAOIL's offices as part of the Joint Account and be subject to the same control procedures.*

10. *Liability*
   10.1 *As between the Operator and the Co-operator, the Co-operator shall not in its role as Co-operator be liable for and the Operator shall indemnify and hold the Co-operator harmless from and against:*
      1. *any physical loss or damage to the property of the Operator,*
      2. *personal injury or death of the Operator's employees or persons otherwise working under the direction of the Operator or its authorized representative, and*
      3. *equipment being in Operator's custody, care and control,*

arising out of this Co-operation Agreement, unless caused by the gross negligence, wilful misconduct or wilful failure to act of the Managerial or Supervisory Personnel of the Co-operator or any of its Affiliates. Under no circumstances shall the Co-operator be liable for any consequential damage suffered by the Operator arising out of this Co-operation Agreement. For the purpose of this Section consequential loss shall include but not be limited to inability to produce Hydrocarbons, environmental damage caused by discharge of Hydrocarbons, lost production or loss of profits.

10.2 *As between the Operator and the Co-operator, the Operator shall not in its role as Operator be liable for and the Co-operator shall indemnify and hold the Operator harmless from and against:*

1. *any physical loss or damage to the property of the Co-operator,*
2. *personal injury or death of the Co-operator's employees or persons otherwise working under the direction of the Co-operator or its authorized representative, and*
3. *equipment being in the Co-operator's custody, care and control,*

arising out of this Co-operation Agreement, unless caused by the gross negligence, wilful misconduct or wilful failure to act of the Managerial or Supervisory Personnel of the Operator or any of its affiliates. Under no circumstances shall the Operator be liable for any consequential damage suffered by the Co-operator arising out of this Co-operation Agreement.

10.3 *For the purpose of this Section consequential loss shall include but not be limited to inability to produce Hydrocarbons, environmental damage caused by discharge of Hydrocarbons, lost production or loss of profits.*

10.4 *With respect to Co-operators liability for loss or damage to third parties Section 3.3.3 of the JOA shall apply mutatis mutandis to the Co-operator and to the extent that the Co-operator is not liable according to Section 3.3.3 of the JOA the Operator on behalf of the Parties in the JOA except The Government Owned Company shall indemnify and hold the Co-operator harmless from and against any claim from third parties even if such loss or damage arise from or is contributed to by the fault, negligence or strict liability of the Co-operator.*

10.5 *Any party other than the Operator and the Co-operator shall in respect to this Section be regarded as a third party.*

10.6 *The provision of Articles 8, 10 and 12 shall survive the expiry, repudiation or any termination of the Co-operation Agreement.*

10.7 *The parties shall arrange waivers of subrogation from their respective insurers in respect of insurances covering their respective liabilities hereunder. All liability provisions in this Co-operation Agreement shall apply whether there is insurance or not.*

11. *Changes, Termination and Assignment*

11.1 *This Co-operation Agreement shall remain in force and effect for the duration of the Licence or may be terminated by mutual consent of the parties.*

11.2 *In case of an assignment by the Operator or the Co-operator or their respective operatorship or co-operatorship under the JOA the non-assigning party may require also the assignment of rights and obligations under this Co-operation Agreement to the relevant assignee. If in such case no assignment is required by the non-assigning party, this Co-operation Agreement shall terminate on the earliest possible date to be agreed by the Operator and the Co-operator.*

11.3 *Any change, termination or assignment of this Co-operation Agreement shall require prior agreement by the Parties in the JOA and approval by the MRA.*

12. *Governing Law and Arbitration*

12.1 *Subject to Articles 3.3 and 5.2 of this Co-operation Agreement, the provisions of the JOA on Arbitration, see section 12.6 of the JOA, and on Applicable Law, see section 12.7 of the JOA, shall also apply to this Co-operation Agreement.*

IN WITNESS WHEREOF the Operator and Co-operator have caused this Co-operation Agreement to be executed by their duly authorised representatives as of the day and year first above written.

Signed for and on behalf of [full name of licensee company]

Signed for and on behalf of NUNAOIL A/S.

This agreement demonstrates in the wider sense how an NOC – not necessarily with extensive knowledge or expertise – might become an operator in an oil and gas exploration project. However, the scenario is easier to envisage in Greenland, as Nunaoil is the NOC and the agreement is provided as an attachment to the relevant operating licence. Any IOC interested in exploration and production projects in Greenland might face difficulties in negotiating similar terms without the legislative backing enjoyed by the NOC.

The final question is whether non-operators are still willing to accept this imbalance while continuing to share all risks and costs of the operations. The Deepwater Horizon accident and the dispute over liability between the JOA parties (BP, Anadarko and Mitsui) revealed that non-operators may seek to challenge agreements on any available grounds in order to avoid the draconian consequences of a failure of performance.[1037] However, the difficulty of succeeding in such challenges was illustrated by Anadarko's recent decision to drop its case and agree to pay $4 billion to BP, together with its acreage in the Macondo.[1038]

Indeed, prudent operators should be more committed to securing the non-operators' participation, as this could obviate the risk of future litigation against it based on their lack of input in the conduct of the operations.[1039]

In conclusion, all JOAs should include balanced and equitable provisions in order to minimise uncertainty[1040] and maximise efficiency.[1041] D Maloney describes this as follows:

1037 "As the liabilities associated with Deepwater Horizon mount, Anadarko and BP will surely square off in court to determine whether or not Anadarko has to kick in 25%. Anadarko will litigate how culpable BP was for the spill, an effort that directly aligns its interest with the plaintiffs' in all the other pending litigation. Indeed, BP is currently considering initiating that war." For further information see www.dailyfinance.com/2010/06/21/bp-oil-spill-update-anadarko-turns-on-bp-is-20-billion-enough.

Given the likelihood that the members of a multi-participant joint venture will have disparate financial resources, joint venture agreements ordinarily include provisions which are designed to ensure that:

(a) the weaker participants are not forced out of a joint venture by reason of being unable to 'keep up' with the rate of expenditure of the stronger participants; and

(b) exploration, appraisal and development progress at a reasonable rate, rather than that at which the weaker participant's financial resources permit.[1042]

Moreover, for mature operations, where the parties are likely to be of equal calibre,[1043] none of the current JOAs provides adequate terms, so these agreements will ultimately lose their functionality.[1044] If all standard forms provide more favourable terms for the operator, non-operators will be increasingly unlikely to accept them in situations where they can match the operator's financial and technical capabilities. They will therefore seek to propose new terms for their contractual arrangements, rather than adopting any of the available models.

Finally, for current and – most of all – future operations, balanced terms providing for full participation by all JOA parties will be necessary, to promote greater collaboration between the parties with the aim of enhancing the efficiency and effectiveness of the joint operations. The current imbalanced JOAs seek to achieve this aim by establishing a unilateral mechanism for performance of the joint operations;[1045] this model has proved wanting. Even under a more balanced model, however, management of the joint operations will likely be equally as challenging as under the current imbalanced scenario.[1046]

1038 www.ft.com/cms/s/0/8a2ceb6c-0405-11e1-98bc-00144feabdc0.html#axzz1fnjK1m1A.

1039 See Chapter I, section 1.1(b).

1040 "In most alliance agreements there will inevitably be some issues that are left open, but this is the nature of the agreement." James Lacey, "Partnering and Alliancing, Back to the Future?" (2007) 26 *ARELJ* p82.

1041 Thomas C Marvin, "Above the Law? Dealing with the abuse of Joint Operating Agreements under the Newspaper Preservation Act" (1995–1996) p42 *Wayne L Rev* p1719, Michael Moy, "Beware! The Unfair Contracts Jurisdiction" (2005) 24 *ARELJ* p227, John Tarrant (note 101) p281, James D Dinnage, "Joint Activities Among Gas Producers, the Competition Man Cometh" (1998) 16 *J Energy & Nat Resources L* p249.

1042 DAW Maloney (n 1015).

1043 Rachel A Hird, "Thomas W Walde and Fair and Equitable Treatment" (2009) 27 *J Energy & Nat Resources L* p377, Roscoe L Barrow, "The Fairness Doctrine: A Double Standard For Electronic and Print Media" (1974–1975) 26 *Hastings LJ* p659, Dominic E Markwordt, "More Folly than Fairness, The Fairness Doctrine, The First Amendment, and the Internet Age" (2009–2010) 22 *Regent U L Rev* p405.

1044 See John R Meyer, William B Tye, "Toward Achieving Workable Competition in Industries Undergoing a Transition to Deregulation, A Contractual Equilibrium Approach" (1988) 5 *Yale J on Reg* p273.

1045 "Multi-participant joint ventures are difficult and expensive to manage. At technical committee meetings, the number of geologists, geophysicists and engineers present makes it difficult to reach consensus on technical strategies. The same is true of operating committee meetings, at which the programs and budgets to give effect to the technical committee's recommendations must be considered and adopted. As the number of participants increase, so do the costs of duplication of reports, maps, minutes and general communications. Field inspections become expensive and difficult to manage. Joint venture managers become pre-occupied with co-venturer's queries and suggestions, rather than with the implementation of approved programs." DAW Maloney (n 1015).

1046 "Managing a multi-participant joint venture is a difficult task. The task is made easier if the co-venturers selected have similar financial capacity, corporate objectives and exploration strategies. In the troubled times ahead, the importance of selecting compatible co-venturers will be amplified." *Ibid* p125.

About the author

Eduardo G Pereira
Professor of Energy Law
Founding partner, International Energy Law Advisory Group
egp.portugal@gmail.com
egp@ielag.com

Eduardo G Pereira is a professor of energy law and partner at the International Energy Law Advisory Group. He has been active in the oil and gas industry for more than 10 years and is an international expert on joint operating agreements. His experience in this area – both academic and practical – is extensive. He has practical experience in over 40 jurisdictions covering America, Europe, Africa and Asia. Dr Pereira concluded his doctoral thesis on oil and gas joint ventures at the University of Aberdeen. He is a professor of natural resources and energy law at the Externado University of Colombia; adjunct professor of energy law at the University of Eastern Finland; visiting professor of energy law at the University of Reykjavik; visiting professor at the Centro de Estudos de Ciências Jurídico-Econômicas e Socias – Agostinho Neto University (Angola); visiting professor at the Umaru Shinkafi Centre for Africa Extractive Policy Research (Nigeria); research fellow at the Scandinavian Institute for Maritime Law – University of Oslo; research fellow at Centro de Estudos em Regulação e Infraestrutura – FGV (Brazil); and International Program Manager of Extractive Resources Governance at the Strathmore Extractives Industry Centre – Strathmore University (Kenya). He is the managing editor of *UEF Energy Law Review* and associate editor of *Oil, Gas and Energy Law*. He is also the author and editor of several leading oil and gas textbooks. Further information about his publications can be found at: www.jus.uio.no/nifs/english/people/aca/eduardog/list-of-publications_egpereira.pdf.

Index

New journal – Modern Legal Practice

Globe Law and Business

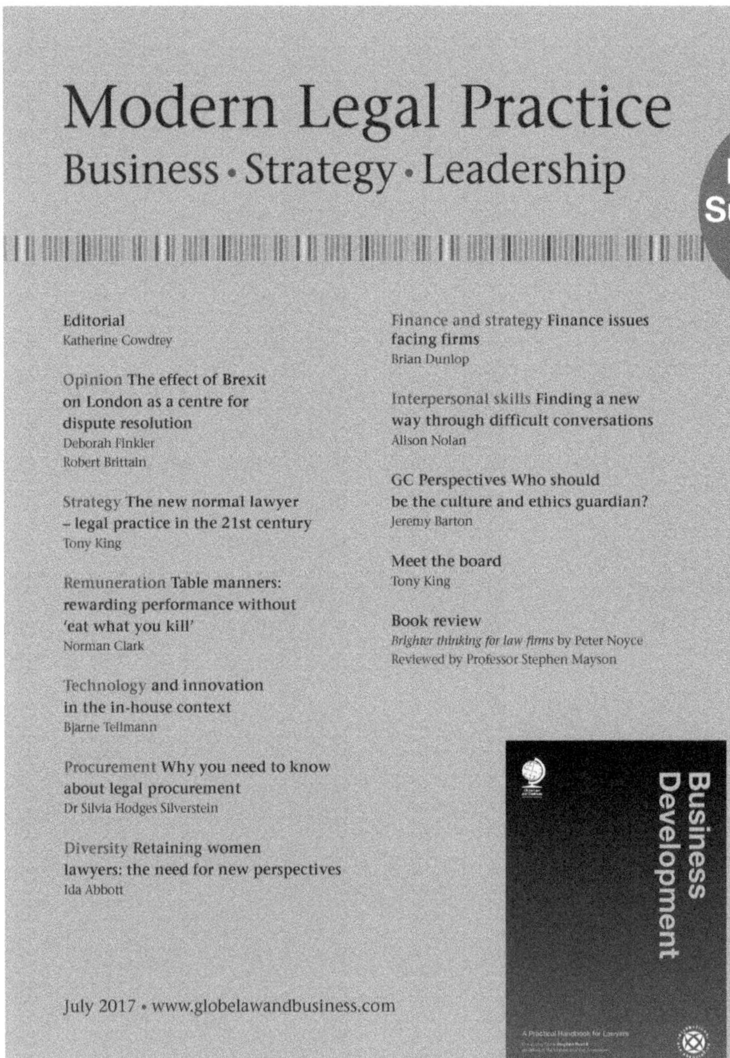

Modern Legal Practice

Business • Strategy • Leadership

Editorial
Katherine Cowdrey

Opinion **The effect of Brexit on London as a centre for dispute resolution**
Deborah Finkler
Robert Brittain

Strategy **The new normal lawyer – legal practice in the 21st century**
Tony King

Remuneration **Table manners: rewarding performance without 'eat what you kill'**
Norman Clark

Technology **and innovation in the in-house context**
Bjarne Tellmann

Procurement **Why you need to know about legal procurement**
Dr Silvia Hodges Silverstein

Diversity **Retaining women lawyers: the need for new perspectives**
Ida Abbott

Finance and strategy **Finance issues facing firms**
Brian Dunlop

Interpersonal skills **Finding a new way through difficult conversations**
Alison Nolan

GC Perspectives **Who should be the culture and ethics guardian?**
Jeremy Barton

Meet the board
Tony King

Book review
Brighter thinking for law firms by Peter Noyce
Reviewed by Professor Stephen Mayson

July 2017 • www.globelawandbusiness.com

Business Development
A Practical Handbook for Lawyers

Founder Subscriber Offer

Subscribe today as a founder subscriber, and receive:

- Your first issue free of charge
- Over 20% discount on your first year's subscription
- A free ebook copy of our best-selling, 240 page book, *Business Development: A Practical Handbook for Lawyers* (usual retail price £130/$220)

Publication dates: Quarterly
Hard copy ISSN: 2398 - 5410
Hardcopy only: £295 per annum
Discounted price: £236 per annum

Go to **http://modernlegalpracticeoffer.globelawandbusiness.com** for full details and subscription offer.

About Globe Law and Business

Globe Law and Business was established in 2005 as an imprint of Globe Business Media Group. We set out to create law books which are sufficiently high level to be of real use to the experienced professional, yet still accessible and easy to navigate. Most of our authors are drawn from Magic Circle and other top commercial firms, both in the UK and internationally.

In autumn 2015, we had an exciting turn in our history when Globe Law and Business was bought by a management team which includes my colleague Jim Smith and me, Sian O'Neill.

We love books, and our hardback titles are carefully produced, with the utmost attention paid to the editorial, design and production processes. We hope this results in high-quality titles which are easy to read, and a pleasure to own.

Our customers and authors are of paramount importance – we are committed to devoting time and attention to each book as well as everyone involved in the publishing process.

We'd very much like to hear from you with your thoughts on our titles or ideas for improving what we offer. Please do feel free to email me at sian@globelawandbusiness.com with your views.

Sian O'Neill
Managing director
Globe Law and Business

www.globelawandbusiness.com